SATHER CLASSICAL LECTURES

VOLUME NINE

CATULLUS

and

THE TRADITIONS OF ANCIENT POETRY

CATULLUS

and

THE TRADITIONS OF ANCIENT POETRY

by

Arthur Leslie Wheeler

UNIVERSITY OF CALIFORNIA PRESS

BERKELEY AND LOS ANGELES

1964

UNIVERSITY OF CALIFORNIA PRESS
BERKELEY AND LOS ANGELES, CALIFORNIA

CAMBRIDGE UNIVERSITY PRESS
LONDON, ENGLAND

Second Printing, 1964
(First Paper-bound Edition)

MANUFACTURED IN THE UNITED STATES OF AMERICA

FOREWORD

The present volume had just been put into type when the author was fatally stricken. It was not his to add the *summa manus* to this work to which he had already given so much careful attention. The task of final revision was undertaken by colleagues at Princeton, who thus gladly pay a heartfelt tribute of respect and regard.

Never in such a case can the purposes of an author be fully realized; but the friends who have cooperated in carrying this work through the press have rendered a valuable service in bringing to completion one of the substantial fruits of Professor Wheeler's sound and thorough scholarship. For the help thus given grateful acknowledgment is here made.

H. C. NUTTING.

PREFACE

This volume contains the lectures which were delivered on the Sather Foundation at the University of California in Berkeley, in 1928. It was my hope that they would appear in printed form within a year from the time of their delivery, but for reasons which need not be set forth here publication has been delayed. The delay has not been an unalloyed disadvantage, however, for it has permitted me to make certain supplements based on material and discussions which appeared too late to be properly considered, or in some cases to be considered at all, when the lectures were being delivered. Prominent among these are the new papyrus fragments of Callimachus' *Coma Berenices* published by Vitelli (1929) and my friend Professor Frank's book, *Catullus and Horace* (1928), although I was already familiar with most of Professor Frank's views from his previously published articles. It seems to me fitting, however, that published lectures should fairly represent their original oral form and so I have confined these recent supplements—except the few based on new original material—to the notes.

The point of view and the method of these lectures are in the main those of the philologist. In all the topics which I have discussed I have kept steadily in mind one special purpose: to improve if possible our understanding of the relation of Catullus to Graeco-Roman poetry and thus to define his own position more clearly by investigating one of the most important influences to which he was subjected. Catullus possessed both genius and originality, but at the same time he was an excellent illustration of the principle so well stated by Pierre de Nolhac: *Aucune originalité littéraire, si puissante quelle soit, n'est sans emprunter des éléments à ce qui la précède.* He owed a large debt to the past and for the most part he was a willing debtor. These lectures deal with the nature of his debt and with the light it throws on his work. It is one of many similar problems in literary history, which though never completely solved are, nevertheless, as our knowledge increases, ever approaching nearer and nearer to a solution. In the case of Catullus, whose importance in the history of both ancient and modern poetry is admitted, the subject is especially attractive. The labors of many scholars have had a bearing upon it, and with the purpose of serving those readers who may wish to follow various details beyond the confines of these lectures I have given, chiefly in the notes, many bibliographical references. It has not been possible, however, to state in every case how far my own views agree or disagree with the views of others. The interested reader will make his own comparisons.

The problem with all its implications is a large one—too large for complete treatment in a few brief lectures—especially since it has been my aim to include enough material to support the argument and to show how the results have been obtained. At the expense of a good deal of cursory treatment I have deliberately chosen this method in the hope that the central problem and the topics connected with it, all of which are interesting in themselves, would prove to be still more interesting if they were presented with a considerable amount of the evidence from which the scholar seeks to win results. Thus the lectures are in the nature of popularized philology, but they reveal more of the machinery of scholarship than is the case with the ordinary *oeuvre de vulgarisation*. The specialist, I am sure, will make due allowances for the shortcomings of this somewhat hybrid work, and the more general reader—the reader who though not a specialist yet has an interest in classical poetry—will find, I hope, that at all events the manner in which the subject is presented will yield a fairly well defined impression of the aims and methods of Catullus as a poet.

In conclusion I wish to express my gratitude to the many friends of the Classics in Berkeley for the patience with which they heard these lectures and the kind encouragement which they gave to the lecturer.

A. L. W.

St. Huberts, New York
July 27, 1931

CONTENTS

CHAPTER I

THE HISTORY OF THE POEMS

It would be possible to approach the central problem of these lectures in many ways, but *not* every single one of them is right, and my own approach, which is somewhat roundabout, demands a word of justification. The time-honored method of dealing with the work of a poet suggests first of all a lecture on the life of Catullus and in his case such an opening would have special advantages since a large part of his poetry is closely connected with the events of his life. But for one who has a special interest in the relations of Catullus to the traditions of poetry a less direct approach is preferable, and I have chosen to begin with a few topics—the history, the publication, and the grouping of the poems —in which I hope to find answers to certain questions which underlie many parts of the general problem. The first two lectures are preparatory; they are designed to clear away some rubbish and to establish a basis for the work that is to come later. Incidentally the topics with which I shall begin, quite apart from their bearing on my special purpose, are interesting in themselves and provide a general introduction to the detailed study of Catullus.

First of all, let me call attention to certain aspects of the collection of poems that has come down to us. The entire extant work of Catullus comprises less than twenty-three hundred lines and can easily be read through at a single sitting. And yet this slender volume, even less in bulk than the first three books of the *Aeneid*,[1] is characterized by a remarkable variety. Within these narrow limits we distinguish at a glance specimens of no less than five kinds of poetry: lyric, epithalamium, epic, elegy, and epigram. All these *genres* had been in existence for hundreds of years before the time of Catullus and it is obvious that, whatever the ways in which his originality may have been manifested, he was at the same time following along many of the lines laid down by his predecessors, both Greek and Roman. It is clear at first sight that much of his work was not isolated but was connected with some of the main currents of ancient poetry. So far as these *genres* at least are concerned his work was well rooted in tradition. I mention these well-known facts in order to emphasize at the outset that among the various influences which combined to produce the work of Catullus, tradition played a very important part, and on this point I shall dwell for a moment.

Catullus was not merely a genius. He knew books and he reflected deeply about his art. He was both student and critic. At the same time he knew life, in the ordinary sense of the term, and he lived his life to the full. Nevertheless the poems which spring most directly from his own experience and observation are always more or less connected, especially in matters of form, with the traditions of literature. There is an intellectual Catullus side by side with an emotional Catullus, although we are prone to forget the former because of our greater interest in the latter. Both these aspects of the man are abundantly reflected in the poems, and they are often inextricably interwoven. It is nevertheless possible to form a fairly adequate conception of the intellectual Catullus in distinction from the Catullus who gave himself recklessly to the enjoyment of life. Anything that throws light on the man is of importance for the comprehension of his work, but if our main object is a better comprehension of his position in the development of poetry, this intellectual side of the poet is of special importance. We shall be engaged presently in studying the poems kind by kind, group by group, type by type. In that work it will be highly important to bear in mind ancient points of view and especially, wherever we can be sure of them, the views of Catullus himself. At the same time we shall need, if only for practical purposes, to group the poems as far as possible in accordance with the poet's views.

For Catullus held views about poetry. By his time most of the major kinds of poetry and prose had long been established, the Greek poets and critics had long been theorizing about them, principles and "rules" had been set up and hotly debated. This literary war was well understood in the cultured circles of Rome. Indeed it continued to be waged on Roman ground and Catullus himself was a partisan who took a prominent part in the fight. This subject must be considered in due course and here at the outset it would be very helpful to know as precisely as possible what distinctions Catullus himself recognized amid the almost bewildering variety of his own poems. Any information that we can gather on this point will clear the way for the work that is to come.

As I have already noted, there are in the collection obvious specimens of several *genres:* the sixty-fourth poem is epic, the sixty-first and sixty-second are epithalamia,[2] the sixty-sixth and sixty-eighth are elegies, and so on. Here and in many other cases we have reliable bases of classification. But differentiation is not everywhere so easy. Is the seventy-sixth poem, for example, the beautiful *Si qua recordanti*, an elegy or an epigram? And in the mass of short poems many questions arise, the most important of which is this: Did Catullus regard a short poem in "lyric" meter as something essentially different from a short poem in elegiac couplets which we usually call an epigram? This question involves the major part of the poet's best work. If we can answer it even partly, we shall have advanced a long way toward a solution or a reasonable explanation of the poet's aims and we shall have secured a basis for determining the extent or at least the character of his success.

All these questions merely illustrate the importance of knowing the poet's attitude toward his work. It is quite possible that Catullus did not carry distinctions to an extreme; but wherever he made clear distinctions, and especially wherever he recognized kinds, or groups, or types of poetry, it is important for the student of his art to know the fact, for such knowledge may help to explain differences of technique. It is clear to any careful reader, for example, that to Catullus as to other ancient poets the technique of elegy was a very different thing from that of epic. How far did he carry such differentiations? We wish to interpret his work as far as possible from his own point of view.

It is here that I turn to the history of the text. Presumably Catullus arranged and published a large number of his poems. If we could ascertain precisely how he arranged them and in what groups he published them, we should know what poems from his point of view belonged together and we should be able to make valuable inferences concerning the distinctions which he recognized. The history of the text may give at least a partial answer to this question. To what extent have the manuscripts preserved the grouping and order which Catullus himself established?

In the widest sense, the history of the text comprises the history of the poems from the time when each or any of them left the hand of their author to the present day, a period of some two thousand years. Fortunately, however, we can limit our examination to those parts of this long history which throw light on our problem; our survey need not be extended beyond the early years of the fourteenth century.

Any conservative edition of the poet's text represents fairly well the form in which the poems have been transmitted in the most complete manuscripts. If we neglect for the present the lacunae and dislocations which are due to mere errors of transmission, we have a collection which falls into three parts: first, about sixty poems (I–LX), all short and all in various lyric meters;[3] second, four poems (LXI–LXIV), all long and in three different meters; third, about fifty poems (LXV–CXVI), long and short, all in the elegiac meter.

If we could accept the view of Vahlen, Wilamowitz, and many others[4] that Catullus himself arranged and published this collection, we could at once proceed with our inferences, allowing of course for the injuries which the collection has suffered during its transmission through the centuries. But unfortunately we cannot lightly reject the arguments of those who in opposition to Vahlen and his adherents have believed that our collection was not made and published by Catullus, but was put together after his death; that in fact its arrangement has greatly obscured the poet's own purposes and methods.

At the outset then we are precipitated into a controversy. The question is one, however, which it is worth while to examine. Can our collection, the collection traditional in the manuscripts, be traced back with probability to Catullus himself, or are there traces of other collections or other forms in which all or any part of the poems circulated? Is it possible to make any reliable inferences about the poet's own procedure? These are some of the questions we shall try to answer in our effort to infer the poet's attitude towards his work.

For the present purpose it is sufficient to recognize three periods in the long history of the poems. The first begins with the literary activity of Catullus, *ca.* 70–54 B.C., and closes with the death of Martial, *ca.* 102–104 A.D. It is not probable that any poems of Catullus were known to a considerable audience before 70 B.C., although he began to write when he was very young, and in fact the poems to which definite or probable dates can be assigned belong to the years 61–54 B.C.[5] In round numbers then the first period comprises somewhat more than one hundred and fifty years. The second period extends from Martial's time, *ca.* 102–104 A.D., to Isidore of Seville, who is the latest author in antiquity whose references to Catullus can be approximately dated. Isidore died *ca.* 636 A.D. The third and last period extends from Isidore to the rediscovery of the full text late in the thirteenth century or early in the fourteenth, not long before or after 1300 A.D.

The most illuminating evidence concerning the problem of publication and arrangement—the form or forms

in which the text was known—is found chiefly in the
first period. We should approach this period however
by way of the later centuries for these also have a
bearing on the problem.

In all the twelve hundred years from Martial to the
fourteenth century the history of the text is a fairly
simple one. The extant collection of poems survived
the dark ages in a single manuscript which was discovered at or near Verona about the year 1300.[6] This
manuscript is known to scholars as the Verona Manuscript (*Codex Veronensis*) and it is now lost. But it
was copied at least twice, and we possess three fairly
good representatives of it dating *ca.* 1350–1400: O,
the *Codex Oxoniensis*, G, the *Codex Sangermanensis*
(now in Paris), and R, the *Codex Romanus* in the
Vatican—the manuscript rediscovered by William
Gardner Hale in 1896. In addition there are more than
a hundred later manuscripts all descended from copies
of the *Veronensis*, although their exact relations to
it and to one another have not yet been fully worked
out.[7]

Apart from the *Veronensis* and its descendants there
is in Paris a part of an old *florilegium* or collection of
elegant extracts, containing only the second wedding
poem (LXII), which is also included in the fuller
manuscripts. This manuscript was written in the ninth
century and is by far the oldest direct source of any
part of the text.[8] It is known as T (*Codex Thuaneus*).

Thus our so-called "complete" manuscripts (they
have a number of omissions due to accidents) contain
all that has survived from Catullus' poetry except four
or five very brief fragments which are assigned to him
by grammarians and scholiasts. By comparing T and
the descendants of V we see that all the manuscripts

are derived ultimately from the same archetype—a manuscript which was written earlier than T, i.e., at latest in the ninth century and possibly a century or two earlier.

The manuscripts then, the direct sources of the text, enable us to follow the poems far back into our third period but hardly as far as its beginning in the seventh century. They reveal but a single line of tradition. The evidence of the very meager indirect sources—the references made to Catullus by those who read any part of his work within this period—point to the same conclusion. The most interesting of these references occurs in one of the sermons of Bishop Rather of Verona in 965 who says that he had never before read Catullus.[9] Since the good bishop, at the time when he made this reference, had been in Verona for four years, it is very probable that he found there the same manuscript, the Verona Codex, which appeared in that neighborhood about three hundred and thirty-five years later. Our poet was all but unknown for more than six centuries. His fate hung by a single thread, for if the Verona Codex had not been drawn from beneath that "bushel" (*sub modio*)[10] where some Veronese discovered it about 1300, we should know only the sixty-second poem (in T) and the meager citations which happen to exist in other writers.[11]

Now the interest of all this for the present purpose is that in all the long period from Isidore to the discovery of the Verona manuscript there is no good evidence that there was any other full form of the text than that represented by our complete manuscripts. If the poems entered the dark ages in any other form, that form has left no positive trace. We conclude, therefore, that the archetype of our collection was probably derived from an ancient edition which contained the same poems—of course in less damaged condition—in essentially the same arrangement as they appear in our manuscripts. This assumed edition or corpus of the text is called the *Liber Catullianus*, the Book or the Collection of Catullus. The date when this Book of Catullus was put together is the question at issue. Did Catullus himself make it? Or was it made after his death by others? Let us glance now at our second period, the period between Martial and Isidore, and see whether we have any evidence on the point.

Martial died *ca.* 102–104 A.D., Isidore *ca.* 636. The period covers therefore somewhat more than five hundred years. During this period Catullus is quoted or referred to sixty or seventy times by more than twenty writers. Exact figures cannot be given because the dates of some of the references, especially certain scholia and glosses, are very uncertain. My statement is conservative, perhaps too conservative. However, even if we include all the references which are collected in Schwabe's list (1886), we shall obtain the same result: that there is no positive proof that the Book of Catullus existed or did not exist as a unit in this period. The manner in which the citations are made is noncommittal. The authors quote or refer to a large number (approximately one-third) of the poems included in our collection and the quotations extend over the major part of the poems (from I to XCVII), but they are never so explicit that we can infer the form of the text from which they were made. Generally a quotation is preceded merely by the poet's name: *Catullus* (or *Catullus Veronensis*). Sometimes there is an addition indicating the meter, e.g., *Catullus in hendecasyllabis* (Charisius). Sometimes the content is indi-

cated: *Catu[llus in coloniam]* (Festus on XVII. 19)—
the poem beginning *O colonia.*

Only twice the word *liber*, "book," is used. In the
second century Aulus Gellius (VI.20.6) discusses the
text of XXVII. 4,

> ebria acina ebriosioris

and makes the interesting remark that those who read
ebriosa or *ebrioso* in this passage have "books" (*libri*)
copied from corrupt models. But what does he mean
by "books?" Does he mean a fairly complete Catullus
like that which our manuscripts contain? Or does he
mean a smaller collection which contained XXVII?
It is impossible to say. Similarly Terentianus Maurus
(2899), a writer of the same century, citing LXIII, 1,
for certain principles of prosody, says "the book itself"
(*ipse . . . . liber*) proves that Catullus observed these
points. Again the word "book" (*liber*) tells us nothing
explicit concerning the form in which Terentianus read
Catullus.

But although the existence of a collected edition of
the Book of Catullus in this period cannot be positively
proved, it is nevertheless probable. The archetype of
our manuscripts must have been derived from such an
edition as we are seeking. Within the period under
discussion, in the third and fourth centuries, began
the general transfer of classical texts from the roll form
to the *codex* form. It is very probable that the text of
Catullus was no exception to the rule and there is one
good reason at least for assuming that the process
which fixed his text in the form known to us occurred
at a relatively early period—before the fifth or sixth
century at latest—and this reason is the absence of
spurious poems. The book which has come down to

us under the name of Tibullus contains many poems not written by Tibullus; it was probably compiled at a late period when reliable tradition had grown weak. The opposite is true of Catullus; his poems were put together while there was a reliable tradition concerning them, and this fact argues for an earlier rather than a later date—a date possibly as early as the first or second century, although not, I shall try to show, as early as the lifetime of the poet.

So far our efforts to define positively the form or forms of the text during the five hundred years from Martial to Isidore have been inconclusive. There is one fact, however, that is certain: the readers of this period knew poems which do not appear in our collection and they quote six lines from them. These bits are known as the fragments. Two of them are quoted from a Priapean poem, or perhaps from two such poems, the first of which appears in part as early as the first century A.D. In addition there are statements (without actual quotations) which imply the existence of other poems now lost to us. Servius, in the fourth century (commenting on Vergil's *Georgics* II. 95) says that "Catullus criticizes Rhaetian grapes"—which were grown not far from his native town of Verona[12]— "asserting that they are good for nothing and wondering why Cato praised them?" The Elder Pliny (*N. H.* XXVIII.19)—this takes us to the first century of our era—refers to a poem of Catullus which he describes as *incantamentorum amatoria imitatio*, perhaps a lover's incantation to soften the heart of some obdurate fair.[13] Many scholars have doubted the authenticity of these fragments (with the exception of the *Priapea*). The suspicion seems unjustified. Both Servius and Pliny are good authorities, and the latter at least, as we see

from other references, was well acquainted with the
poetry of Catullus whom he calls in the preface to his
Natural History his "fellow countryman" (*conterraneus*)
because both were natives of the region beyond the Po.
We may be certain therefore that from the first century
of our era to the seventh, and probably still later,
poems of Catullus were known which are not included
in our collection. Were they, or were any of them,
ever in our collection? The question cannot be definitely
answered. Our collection has suffered losses, but the
efforts to insert the fragments into it here and there
have not been convincing and are now discredited.
The Priapean verses at least were probably never included in this or any other exclusively Catullian book.
Such poems were composed by many Romans for the
amusement of their friends. The authors had no
interest in them as literary property; they correspond
very closely with a certain type of limerick of which
thousands circulate *sub rosa* and for the most part
anonymously today. It was the practice to make
collections of these squibs quite separate from other
work by the same authors. One of these collections
has come down to modern times and there were certainly others. In all probability Catullus' experiments
in this type of verse were read in such a collection,
not in any book composed exclusively of his own
poems.[14]

Hitherto, in an effort to outline the history of the
text, I have been receding, crab fashion, through the
centuries from the date of our earliest complete manuscripts in the fourteenth century to Martial's time about
100 A.D. Let me summarize very briefly. In the
period of about seven hundred years from Isidore to
the fourteenth century (the discovery of the *Codex*

Veronensis) there are no reliable traces of any other form of the text than that which is represented by our collection. In the preceding period of about five hundred years, from Martial to Isidore, the situation is different. In those centuries one ancestor at least of our collection, the Book of Catullus, must have existed—quite possibly came into existence; but—and this is for my purpose the important point—there were other poems of Catullus circulating apart from this collection. It is impossible to determine in what form these poems were known, but for the present purpose it is not necessary. It is sufficient to state the situation in a fashion so conservative that nobody, I think, will object, namely: the evidence, meager though it is, indicates that our collection did not include all the work of Catullus that was known from *ca.* 100 to *ca.* 600 A.D.

We are now ready to consider the earliest period, somewhat more than one hundred and fifty years from Martial's time back to the years in which Catullus was writing—especially the last six or seven years of his life, *ca.* 61–*ca.* 54 B.C. We are in general still receding, for the later years of this period throw a bright light on earlier events, but we shall wander freely backward and forward over the whole period seeking the form or forms in which the poems circulated. In sharp contrast with the two later periods the evidence with which we shall have to deal here is definite, although it is sometimes difficult to interpret. This evidence may be classified roughly under three heads: (1) the external characteristics of our Book of Catullus and other ancient books of poetry, (2) certain testimony of ancient writers, notably Martial, concerning the poems of Catullus, (3) internal evidence, i.e., the words of Catullus himself and the character of some of his poems.

The Book of Catullus must have existed, as we have seen, in the period after Martial. Did it exist in Martial's time or before? Were there other smaller units of Catullus' poetry? What light is thrown on these questions by a comparison between the Book of Catullus and other ancient books of poetry? This last question has been before the world of scholarship since Brunér's interesting discussion in 1861.[15] The most striking facts which emerge from the comparison are these: the Book of Catullus is very abnormal, not to say unique, among all known Greek or Roman books of poetry in length, and in the heterogeneousness and grouping of its contents.

If Catullus himself published this Book as a unit, on one single roll, he violated normal ancient practice. It is just possible that other books of the same character once existed which are now lost to us—myriads of ancient books are lost—and yet an abundance of material from which to infer ancient practice still survives. The sands of Egypt may sometime yield a roll of Greek or Roman poetry as long and as varied in content and in meter as the one which many scholars assume to have been the original form of our Book of Catullus, but such a discovery is extremely improbable. At any rate we cannot deal with the unknown; we must deal with the known. We are bound to formulate a theory which takes into account every consideration pertinent to the Book of Catullus. Let us consider first the question of length.

To modern readers, accustomed to see all the work of a poet collected in a single volume, the slender book of seventy-five or eighty pages containing the work of

Catullus seems inordinately short—a book to be compared with the first volume of some budding young poet, not with the total production of a Shelley or a Tennyson. But we must judge by ancient standards for books of poetry, and by ancient standards this little book is abnormally long. Theodor Birt examined one hundred and forty-eight books of Greek and Roman poetry and found the extreme length, in books containing relatively short poems like those of Catullus, to be about eleven hundred lines, the favorite length being between seven hundred and eight hundred lines.[16] In the single books of long poems such as Virgil's *Aeneid* the extreme length is somewhat greater; Apollonius' *Argonautica* IV, for example, has 1779 lines, Lucretius V has 1457 lines. Such inferences as can be made from the more or less fragmentary papyrus books discovered since Birt's time (1882) confirm in general these results. The Book of Catullus has 2284 lines, not allowing for possible titles or spaces at the head of each poem. Moreover it is not complete since there are a number of certain lacunae (9, Birt), even if we take no account of the fragments and possible lost poems. It must once have had, on a very conservative estimate, over twenty-three hundred lines.[17] This book is therefore more than twice the length of the longest of other similar books, i.e., books containing many relatively short poems, and more than five hundred lines longer than any other extant book of Greek or Roman poetry.

Even more abnormal than its length is the heterogeneous content of this book. Again we must employ ancient standards. A complete volume of Tennyson, for example, contains not only shorter and longer lyrics, satires, etc., but also long narrative poems (the *Idylls of the King*, etc.) and even dramas (*Becket*, etc.). The

Book of Catullus is much less varied, and yet by ancient standards the content far transcends mere variety; it is a sort of hodgepodge: short lyrics of many different types and in many meters, two wedding poems in two different meters, elegiac poems, long and short, the *Attis* in galliambic meter, and even a long narrative poem of more than four hundred lines. No other extant ancient book of poetry written by one and the same poet approximates this extreme variety. Even among anthologies or books of verse by various hands as, for example, the Theocritus collection (if it ever was a unit) or the Tibullus Book, there is no good analogy.

Let us try for a moment to visualize the Book of Catullus in roll form. Suppose the twenty-three hundred and more verses to be written in columns of twenty-five verses, each column requiring a space of about eight by five inches, the size of a rather large octavo page. We should then have about ninety-two columns—not allowing for spaces or ornament—written side by side on pieces of papyrus attached to each other so as to form a continuous strip. This strip of papyrus, which could be unrolled by one hand and rolled up on its rod (if it had one!) by the other as it was read, would be our ancient book or roll (*volumen*) and it would be no less than thirty-eight feet long, an inconvenient and unwieldy thing; and I am sure that my estimate of its size in the form of an ancient roll is conservative.

You have here the chief reason why ancient books of poetry, which were intended for frequent reading by persons who were often careless,[18] were short: for convenient handling and a reasonable chance of preservation such rolls could not be very long. Indeed Isidore (*Et.* VI.12) says that books of poetry (and prose letters, too) were written in shorter form (*breviori forma*). When in the third and fourth centuries these ancient rolls were for the most part transferred to books with leaves and pages (the *codex* form), each book division normally represented the beginning of a roll. Each of the twelve books of the *Aeneid*, for example, in Vergil's time had its own separate roll; at this period they could all be combined in one *codex*.

The Alexandrians standardized the size of the rolls which were used for literary purposes and this had a strong effect on all later literature including the Roman. Authors often composed with due regard to the size of the rolls on which their work was to be published. If the amount was too great for one roll of convenient size, then two or more were used, and they made the divisions of their work correspond. Evidence derived from extant papyrus rolls the size of which can be accurately estimated,[19] indicates that while there are many short rolls of six or seven feet, the extreme upper limit is about thirty feet. Sir F. G. Kenyon, one of the foremost authorities, says that this limit was "rarely, if ever, exceeded."[20]

From the purely mechanical points of view, then, it is clear that the entire contents of the Book of Catullus were probably never included in one roll. The unexampled variety of the poems strongly supports this conclusion. The poems must have circulated for a long time in several rolls and it is probable that they were not assembled as a unit until they were published in the form of a *codex*, not earlier, to judge by the general history of ancient books, than the second or third century of the Empire when the jurists, for example Ulpian (*Digest* XXXII.52), were beginning to be puzzled by the question, "When is a book not a book?" The term "book" (*liber*) had normally meant a roll (*volumen*), but at the time, the book was often in the form of a *codex*. Was a *codex* also a *liber*? If a man bequeathed his books (*libri*) to a friend, were his *codices* included or not? The question was decided both ways, for the term *liber* was applied at the time to the two different forms.

Our Book of Catullus was probably formed from a number of smaller elements long after the lifetime of the poet. The history of the poems and certain characteristics of the Book itself substantiate this general statement and throw considerable light on details. In the first place the Book is arranged in a form which may easily be due to compilation. It consists of three clearly marked parts: (1) I–LX, poems all short and in various meters (842 lines); (2) LXI–LXIV, all long and still in various meters (797 lines); (3) LXV–CXVI, long and short but all in the same meter (645 lines). The basis of this grouping seems clearly to have been partly the length, partly the meter of the single poems. The first poem is a dedication of all or of a part of the poems to Cornelius Nepos—this point will be discussed later—and some critics discover in LXI a similar dedication of Part II to Manlius Torquatus, and in LXV a dedication of Part III to Hortensius Hortalus. I am convinced that the last two poems are not dedications, though LXV is introductory to LXVI.

There is some difference of opinion as to the exact poems with which the second and third parts begin, but at least it is clear that each of these three parts is short enough and, excepting the long sixty-fourth poem, homogeneous enough to have filled a separate roll. Is it possible that Catullus published these poems in three or four rolls and that later some editor combined them in the same order into our Book? This is the simplest form of the compilation theory. I cannot accept it because it does not account for a number of facts which we must now consider.

Martial, who was a great admirer of Catullus and refers to him twenty times or more, mentions a work of Catullus which he calls *Passer, The Sparrow*. It was a common custom among the Romans to refer to a literary work by quoting the words with which it began. Thus Cicero calls his *Essay on Old Age* the *O, Tite* from the opening phrase of the quotation from Ennius with which it begins. So the great poem of Lucretius was called the *Aeneadum genetrix*[21] and the *Aeneid* the *Arma virumque*. Clearly Martial knew some collection of Catullus which began not with the dedication to Nepos which begins our collection but with *Passer, deliciae meae puellae* (II), and he was referring not, as some scholars have contended, to this one poem (or the two sparrow poems) only, but to a book (*libellus* or *liber*)[22] beginning with the first sparrow poem, since his clearest reference occurs in a poem (IV.14) which he composed to accompany a copy (or several copies) of his own books (*libellos*) sent to Silius, the epic poet. "So," he says, "perhaps Catullus ventured to send his *Sparrow* (*Passerem*) to mighty Vergil." The whole run of Martial's poem, the comparison of himself to Catullus, of his epic friend Silius to Vergil, of his own book or books to the *Sparrow* of Catullus, render the conclusion unavoidable that the *Sparrow* was a book of poems of the same general type as the poems of Martial—chiefly short poems in various meters. There are probable echoes of this *Sparrow* in Pliny the Younger,[23] another great admirer of Catullus, and in a scholium on Juvenal (VI. 8) we discern a tradition that Catullus dedicated such a book to his sweetheart Lesbia.

The *Sparrow* was a collection, as Martial implies, of lighter verse. It was possibly the same as the collection which Catullus dedicates in the first poem to Cornelius Nepos. In this case, as was suggested long ago,[24] the sparrow poem (II) was first in the body of the text; the dedication, now I, was written in connection with the title and did not count as the first poem. At any rate the book dedicated to Cornelius—if it was a different book—resembled the *Sparrow* in character, for Catullus implies (I.4) that it contained only poems which he calls *nugae*, "trifles." A long controversy has raged over this word *nugae*. Those who hold that Catullus published our collection as a unit are forced to the view that Catullus includes under the term all the poems in the collection. Catullus is modest, they say, and contrasting his work with the serious and laborious history of Nepos he calls all his poems, light and serious alike, "trifles," just as Goethe, for example, refers to his poems, including *Faust* and *Egmont*, as trifles (*Sächelchen*). But Goethe made his remark in a prose letter, not in one of the poems to which he referred as *Sächelchen*.[25] Catullus is modest, to be sure, but this is a question of usage to which we must apply ancient standards. If he included under the word *nugae* all his poems—the long elaborate pieces, especially LXIV which is epic, one of the most elevated kinds of ancient poetry, as well as the short pieces of various types—then he used the term in a sense without parallel elsewhere in Roman literature. *Nugae* is a fairly common term[26] and in its proper use it means light or short pieces such as the sparrow poems, the kisses, the anecdotes, the epigrams—all the pieces which Catullus calls elsewhere *ineptiae*, "nonsense," "foolishnesses," or *versiculi*, "versicles," or what you will. Why for the sake of adapting the dedicatory poem to the whole collection should we here assume a unique meaning for this term? And why should we cast aside the normal meaning of *libellus* (which the poet applies to the Cornelius Book)? Why should we discard the evidence which is derived from our knowledge of the ancient book and the history of Catullus' poems and assume that he was fortunate enough to collect and publish in one roll all these poems just before an untimely death cut short his career?

The probable view is that the first poem was originally the dedication of one small book to Nepos, and that when our collection was formed, this poem, as the most appropriate dedication for the whole, was placed or was left at the beginning.[27]

Catullus himself published at least one book of poems, the *libellus* dedicated to Cornelius Nepos containing "trifles" (*nugae*). Martial knew a book of similar character which he calls the *Sparrow*. It is possible though not probable that these two books were one and the same. But both together, if there were two, did not contain all the poems of our present collection. Did Catullus himself publish all the rest of his poems? I think it improbable. The fact that we have today more than a hundred of his poems proves that in some way during or after his lifetime they were made public. But this does not prove that he himself published all of them, as he published the Cornelius Book, by giving them over to some book dealer for multiplication and sale in the form of rolls.

In antiquity literary works often became publicly known before they were "published" in the stricter sense.[28] We can prove this in the case of Catullus, not to mention Cicero, Horace, Ovid, and others. In XVI

Catullus attacks Furius and Aurelius, "Do you think me effeminate," he says, "because you have read of many thousands of kisses (*milia multa basiorum*)?" This is a reference to V, where Catullus speaks of *milia multa* of kisses, and perhaps to VII, where the same topic is continued.[29] Clearly the fifth poem was known to the poet's readers or to some of them (and that means ultimately all of them) before he wrote the sixteenth. The fifth poem was, therefore, either in a different book from the sixteenth or it had been separately read (or sent) to friends. The latter assumption is the more probable, for the practice of reading compositions to smaller or larger circles (Horace preferred smaller ones!) or sending them to friends was common. As soon as a poem was thus read or sent nothing but the discretion of the auditors or the recipient could prevent it from becoming public property. There was no copyright law.

Poems LXV, LXVI, and LXVIII were certainly sent to Hortensius and Manlius respectively in response to their requests for something written by Catullus, and XXXV, the little letter to Caecilius, is similar. Such poems had at first a separate existence. Besides there are poems written for special occasions: LXI, for example, was written for the wedding of Manlius Torquatus and Vinia Aurunculeia, just as Ovid wrote a special poem for the wedding of his friend Fabius Maximus and a lament for Messalla, but both poems are lost to us because nobody attached them to the collections which have survived. Fortunately Horace's *Carmen Saeculare*, composed for a more important occasion, was attached to the other works of its author.

It is certain therefore that many poems were made public before they were collected and published in rolls.

I have given some illustrations and many other poems must have had the same history. The attacks on Caesar and his henchmen, for example, are pamphlet literature and were probably issued at first separately. And how could Catullus hold back very long such gems as *The Gentleman with the Eternal Grin* (XXXIX) and *The Egregious Cockney* (LXXXIV)?

The case of LXIV, *The Wedding of Peleus and Thetis*, is somewhat different. This poem was very probably published in a separate roll—a *monobiblos*, to use the ancient term. In Catullus there is no positive proof of this, but the argument from analogy is convincing. The poem, more than twice the length of any other in Catullus, is an epyllion or short epic, a type which was all the rage in the circle to which Catullus belonged, and a study of the evidence concerning these poems from the *Hecale* of Callimachus to the *Ciris* (attributed to Vergil) shows that it was the custom to publish them as single books, *monobibloi*.[30] There is every reason to think that Catullus' poem was published in the same way.

The foregoing facts indicate that when Catullus wished to publish a book (*libellus*) he collected, as Ovid did in later times,[31] the poems which had already acquired a certain publicity. Probably he excluded some pieces, for example the *Priapea*, perhaps he added others which for some reason he had not sent forth separately. Naturally scholars have attempted to assign all the extant poems to definite rolls, but in this they have gone too far. Let us try to state the results conservatively. Catullus himself certainly published one book of *nugae*, chiefly lighter types of verse—the book dedicated to Cornelius Nepos. Probably he published the epyllion (LXIV) as a single book. Beyond this point we enter the realm of conjecture, for we do not know what poems, apart from the dedication to Cornelius, the book of *nugae* contained, and we must allow for the possibility that the *Sparrow* was a second, a different book of *nugae*. It is easier to conjecture what was not included in books of this character than what was included. It is difficult to believe that the carefully studied sixty-third poem, the *Attis*, the very long and elaborate sixty-eighth poem, and perhaps the two wedding poems (LXI, LXII), were, from the point of view of Catullus, *nugae*, "trifles." And finally the fact that the third part of our collection is made up exclusively of poems in elegiac verse suggests that Catullus himself may have published at least a part of these in a separate book. There are analogies for such a book both before the time of Catullus in the Theognis Book and in the *elegi* of Callimachus, for example, and soon after his time in the works of the Augustan elegists.[32] Perhaps we shall be able later to throw some light on these problems. Meanwhile it is clear that at the time of Catullus' death there were in existence at least two published rolls of his work and, whether there were other published rolls or not, there must have been scattered poems known to be his which in the strict sense he had never published.

Probably this condition did not long persist for there was no question about the authenticity of the poems; the tradition was well guarded. Most of the scattered pieces—not all, as we have seen,—must have been gathered in rolls under the name of Catullus, either expanding the rolls already existing or forming new ones. Martial knew at least one roll, probably one of those originally published by the poet. Some scholars have believed that he knew also an edition of all the poems in one roll.[33] He mentions among the books which were given away as souvenirs at dinner parties a *Catullus* (XIV.195), but who knows what this *Catullus* contained? Among such souvenirs there were also books on parchment in the form of our books (*codices*). Martial mentions a complete Vergil with the author's portrait on parchment. But these were curios and it is not probable that Catullus was among them.

The process, which may have been a slow one, of gathering the scattered pieces into rolls and later transferring the contents of these rolls to the manuscript or *codex* form, naturally exposed the text to various changes and dislocations which tended to obscure the work of the poet's own hand. I am speaking here not of the ordinary corruptions caused by the ignorance of medieval scribes but of changes which occurred during the period of two hundred and fifty years or more from the date of the poet's death to the formation of the Book of Catullus. There are indications of such changes in our manuscripts.

It is a curious fact that the latest datable poems are scattered pretty well over the whole collection. The certain dates fall very late in the poet's life. Poems XI, XXIX, XLV, LV, CXIII refer clearly to events in the years 55–54 B.C., for example the first invasion of Britain by Caesar and the second consulship of Pompey. Perhaps Catullus was able to include these poems in books which he himself published just before he died, but it is certainly more probable that some of them at least were among the scattered pieces which were included in his work by others after his death.

There are also certain poems which were composed for a very special audience—an audience which was in possession of the facts by which to interpret them, an

audience which, in plain English, knew what Catullus
was talking about. So much of his poetry springs from
the circumstances of his life that there are many
allusions which are quite obscure to modern readers.
This is to be expected. But I am at present referring
to those poems which not even a contemporary Roman
or Italian could have understood unless he was familiar
with the affairs of Verona and the region beyond the Po.
They are provincial poems, intensely local in character.
Poems XVII and LXVII, for example, are concerned
with bits of provincial scandal full of obscure allusions
and innuendo. Perhaps these pieces are examples of
those youthful trifles to which Catullus alludes in the
first and in the sixty-eighth poems. He may have
published them before Rome became, as he tells us,
his real home.[34] It seems improbable, however, that
he would have included them in a collected edition
made just before his death. They must have been
added at a later period.[35]

A much stronger argument may be derived from the
order of the poems. If our collection is the result of
combining several rolls just as they were published by
the poet, then the order of the poems, apart from a few
dislocations caused by accidents during the transmission
of the text, ought to be the order which Catullus himself
determined. Many scholars have believed that such
is the case. Wilamowitz, for example, has said that
Catullus himself deliberately arranged and published
the poems, whether in one roll or several, in the order
in which we have them today in our collection.[36] I
have not time to consider Wilamowitz's argument in
detail. It is in many ways interesting and suggestive,
but it is not convincing. His reasoning is and must be
by analogy. He argues that Catullus followed Greek

practice and in this he is certainly correct, but when he tries to show that our collection as a whole conforms with Greek practice, we are confronted with the same old difficulty that there is no good analogy. Some of its parts, such as the group of long and short pieces in elegiac meter or the group of wedding poems, conform with Greek practice, but not the whole.[37]

Wilamowitz deals with the larger groups of the poems. He hardly touches the real center of the problem, the arrangement of the single pieces within the group, and in this he is wise. All the numerous efforts to demonstrate that Catullus arranged the poems in detail as they stand in our collection have almost utterly broken down. The exceptions to the many "principles" of arrangement which have been suggested are, as Ellis says, "sufficiently serious to throw doubt on the whole theory."[38] The subject is at best a difficult one for when scholars attempt to account for the position of this poem or that, they are investigating a question of ancient taste and there is constant danger of assuming that the taste of Catullus was the same as our own. But there is a more serious difficulty. As a basis for inferences concerning ancient taste in a matter of this kind we need a text, such as that of Horace, which retains the author's arrangement and with which we can compare similar texts of contemporaries—for tastes change from generation to generation. In the case of Catullus both these prerequisites are lacking. We have no contemporary work of the same kind with which to compare him, and the history of his own text has shown that in details of this character it cannot be trusted to give us much reliable information about its author's intentions. Clearly we must be extremely conservative in assigning the arrangement of any part of the poems to Catullus himself. And yet I am not absolutely skeptical. In a few instances, some twelve or fifteen at most scattered through the first and third parts of our collection, I believe that we can discern the poet's intention.[39] These arrangements are of two kinds: (1) the grouping of two or more poems which are related in content, and (2) the separation of two such related poems by a third on a different theme—an arrangement called *variatio* by which all three poems are brought into greater relief.[40] To illustrate, XV and XVI both deal with Aurelius, LXXXVIII–XCI all deal with Gellius, whereas V and VII, the kisses, are separated by VI, quite a different type.[41] It is possible that some of these groupings were made by the compiler of our collection or are due to pure accident, but it is more reasonable to assign most if not all of them to Catullus. In many matters of technique Catullus served as an intermediary between the Greek poets of the Alexandrian period and the Roman poets of the Augustan Age. Much attention was paid in the Augustan Age to the artistic arrangement of poems within a book, and the beginnings of this tendency, although it was then not nearly so strong, occur in the collection of Theocritus (made by Artemidorus), the only Alexandrian whose work can be adequately studied from this point of view. It is probable that Catullus and his school followed along the same lines and the assumption certainly agrees with what we know of their literary tendencies. If this assumption is correct, we may attribute these rather simple devices of arrangement to Catullus himself.[42]

Of artistic arrangement based on meter, which Horace often practiced in the *Odes*, there is practically no trace in Catullus.[43] The third part of the collection, where the meter is the same throughout, offers no opportunity, and the second part offers little more. The conditions in the first part (I–LX) are much better but far from ideal. With the poems which now fill this section no greatly varied metrical arrangement could be made, since no less than forty-three poems[44] are in the same meter—the hendecasyllable—so that sequences of poems in this meter are unavoidable. It is noteworthy, however, that no thoroughgoing effort has been made to relieve the metrical monotony by placing to the best advantage the seventeen poems in other meters. Three times they occur in sequence, namely, XXIX–XXXI (iambic, Asclepiad, choliambic), LI–LII (Sapphic, iambic), and LIX–LX (two choliambics). This was a waste of good ammunition if there ever was a purpose to vary the meters. It is probably for the most part the result of the compiler's work. If we possessed unaltered the books of short poems which Catullus himself arranged, we should probably find a more artistic metrical arrangement, perhaps helped out by a considerable number of the forty-eight little elegiac poems which now stand in the third part of the book.[45]

But the traces of purposed arrangement, if indeed they are due to the poet, are far too few to establish anything like pervasive principles, and if we are to assign the arrangement of the poems to Catullus, we need to demonstrate something like pervasive principles. The apparently purposed sequences are the exception, not the rule. The rule in the detailed order of our collection is planlessness.[46] Poems which might have been grouped side by side or set off against each other by *variatio* of content or of meter are scattered not only within the first part (I–LX) but in some

cases in both the first and the third parts. I need
mention by way of illustration only the Lesbia and the
Juventius cycles, some elements of which seem to be
purposely arranged, others scattered. If we bear in
mind the process by which our collection was formed,
the situation is about what we might expect it to be.
Catullus published two or three rolls consisting mostly,
perhaps wholly, of short poems, a roll containing LXIV,
and another containing exclusively elegiac verse. This
last assumption is strengthened by the fact that the
cases of purposed arrangement are slightly more
numerous in the third part of the collection, where the
meter does not vary; Catullus may himself have
arranged a small collection of elegiac verse which was
later enlarged by the addition of all his known elegiac
work. After his death these rolls were expanded (or
others were formed) by the addition of scattered pieces
such as LX, LXI, LXVIII, and others.[47] In Martial's
time the work of Catullus was known in a number
of rolls, and it is probable that this condition was not
materially altered until the collected edition was made
in the form of a codex.[48] During all these years the
text was exposed to arbitrary treatment, and since
Catullus unlike Horace and Vergil was not a school
author,[49] there was no widespread demand at an early
period for a fairly complete collection of his poems.
He was interesting to all who loved poetry, and, on
the technical side, especially interesting to the metri-
cians. We can trace the first of these interests back to
his own lifetime and the second to the first century of
the Empire.[50] It was partly the metrical interest which
caused the collected edition to be arranged somewhat
more systematically than before on the basis of meter,
for all the poems in elegiac verse were grouped at the

end.[51] All this activity, covering a period of two hundred years or more from the poet's death to the time when the collected edition was made, greatly confused such evidences of the poet's arrangement as originally existed. That the result was not utter confusion lies in the nature of the collection. Those who transmitted the text had to deal with more than a hundred short poems—not to mention the longer pieces—and whatever dislocations of order they caused, some poems must have remained in the order which Catullus had given to them. On purely mechanical grounds, therefore, we expect to find here and there certain sequences which reveal the poet's intention, and this is in fact the condition which still exists.

We have traced the history of the poems from the beginning of the fourteenth century back into the lifetime of the poet—a space of almost fourteen hundred years. It is a very imperfect history, full of gaps. It resembles the course of a stream in a limestone country which runs for longer or shorter distances underground: only where the stream comes to the surface is it possible to study its character. As we have followed the text farther and farther back, we have found, as we should be likely to find in the case of the stream, that it did not spring into full tide at its birth, but was formed by smaller affluents.

The theory that Catullus himself arranged and published as a unit all the poems essentially as we have them in our collection accounts for the few facts at our disposal during the seven hundred years from the fourteenth century back to Isidore, but in the five hundred years preceding Isidore it becomes dubious, and it grows more and more improbable the more closely we approach the ultimate sources in the lifetime of the poet. The richer the evidence—and it is richest in the earliest period—the less probable this theory becomes. The compilation theory, on the other hand, accounts for all the facts. Our collection is best explained as derived from an edition of Catullus which was put together not earlier than the second or third century. This text has suffered many injuries in the course of its transmission, but the more serious distortions of the poet's intention occurred during its formation (or before it was formed) in the parts of which it was composed. Catullus himself is not responsible for the three main groups of poems as they stand in our collection. The arrangement of the poems in detail is, with few exceptions, probably not his. He did not compose the first poem as a dedication for the whole miscellany which constitutes the collection.

My chief purpose in reviewing the history of the text has been to determine whether the traditional arrangement of the poems can be attributed to the poet himself. The conclusion is almost completely negative. But negative results are sometimes useful. The survey has had the advantage of clearing away certain assumptions which would have hindered an attempt to know more of Catullus' attitude toward his work, and it has suggested various interesting possibilities which will be considered in the next lecture. If one method has proved barren, others may prove more fruitful.

CHAPTER II

KINDS AND TYPES OF POETRY

In the first chapter emphasis was laid upon the importance of ascertaining as exactly as possible what kinds and types of poetry Catullus himself recognized. But the effort to learn something of his attitude from the history of the poems and especially from their detailed arrangement as they have come down to us in the manuscripts had little positive result. Other hands have so obscured the poet's own arrangement that few reliable traces of it have survived. But the probability that Catullus himself did not arrange and publish as a unit this heterogeneous collection has at least one advantage; it frees us from troublesome restraints in the use of other evidence which may help to solve our problems. This evidence is to be found partly in the words and poetic practice of Catullus, partly in other ancient writers and in the history of ancient poetry.

We must constantly bear in mind that almost all kinds of poetry were already old before Catullus tried his hand at them. The wedding poem, for example, was developed from popular into literary forms at least as early as the time of Sappho; it had had a history of approximately five centuries and a half before Catullus attempted it. There had been ample time for *genres* to develop and decay. In literature definite distinctions do not persist forever. But some give way sooner than others, and new distinctions arise. At any given period there are always confusions, nebulous regions. In Catullus some *genres* are clearly distinguishable.

Others are centrally clear but marginally vague; there is overlapping or merging, for example, between elegy and the epigram in distichs. Some poems resist classification within a definite *genre*, and it is the part of wisdom not to coerce them. It is better to recognize that they are a symptom of the relatively late period of Graeco-Roman poetry in which Catullus was writing.

In Catullus we recognize at first sight clear examples of well-known kinds of poetry: the epithalamium (I use the term in the general sense of wedding poem), LXI and LXII; the short epic or epyllion (LXIV); and the elegy (LXV–LXVIII, LXXVI). Without at present attempting to define the terms, we recognize also epigrams and lyrics of various sorts.

But at this point difficulties arise. Can we draw an equally sharp line between an epigram and an elegy (both in distichs) on the one hand or between an epigram in elegiac meter and a little poem in lyric meter on the other? Did Catullus and his contemporaries recognize distinctions here? Or (better) were such distinctions as they recognized, especially in meter, important enough to influence the technique and grouping of such poems? Much confusion still exists concerning the ancient attitude on these points. Most scholars have been in the habit of calling the short poems in elegiac meter "epigrams." Many of them certainly are epigrams in our sense of the word; indeed Quintilian one hundred years after Catullus calls LXXXIV—about the gentleman who misplaced his aspirates—a famous epigram (*nobile epigramma*). But what are we to do with LXXVI, which is as true and unrestrained an expression of the poet's own feeling as we find in any of the so-called lyrics? Shall we call it an epigram because it is written in elegiac distichs, and is comparatively short (26 lines), or as one scholar argues, are we to infer, because it stands among epigrams, that Catullus regarded it as an epigram?[1] This last argument at least must be rejected since we are pretty sure that neither Catullus nor anybody of approximately Catullus' period placed the poem where we find it. Or again shall we call it an elegy, relying on its length and other characteristics which certainly tend to align it with the work of the great elegists of the following generation? Or lastly, since all poems in elegiac couplets could be called in ancient times *elegi*, was Catullus satisfied with this term? There were collections of long and short *elegi* both before and after his time. But this problem can properly be postponed to the lecture on elegy. I have mentioned it here merely to illustrate the difficulties of classification.

Meanwhile a larger question requires an answer. It will be admitted that almost all the short elegiac pieces could properly have been called epigrams in the time of Catullus. Even a cursory examination of the little poems in other meters shows that many of these also might easily have been grouped under this term, for many have parallels both in the *Greek Anthology* and in Martial. Could all the little poems have been called epigrams or should we distinguish at least those in elegiac meter from the rest?

Let us consider some points in the history of the epigram—a history which had already covered centuries before Catullus was born.[2] The term means, as we all know, an inscription and originally the thing itself was an inscription. Thousands of these little verse inscriptions, Greek and Latin, have been preserved from antiquity and the archaeologists are constantly discovering new ones.

But very early the epigram passed into literature. Sometimes these literary epigrams were written as if they were to be inscribed whereas in reality they had nothing to do with this purpose; they were merely short poems simulating the inscriptional type. There are hundreds of these little poems among the 4500 in the *Greek Anthology*.[3] As time went on, however, the literary epigram became quite dissevered, so far as purpose and (very often) its content are concerned, from the inscription whether real or simulated, although it still retained the favorite metrical form, the elegiac couplet. It was Martial more than any other writer who gave to this literary epigram the character which we still regard as most significant: a brief, pointed utterance in verse, a definition well phrased by Coleridge:

> What is an epigram? A dwarfish whole,
> Its body brevity, and wit its soul.

And yet even for the epigram of modern times many critics have objected to such definitions as this, pointing out that many epigrams do not have a point, witty or otherwise, or even (within very narrow limits) brevity.

This statement applies with greater force to the ancient epigram. Indeed many of Martial's epigrams possess nothing of the darting wit for which he is famous. In him even brevity and the more or less traditional metrical forms were not absolute essentials. A critic objects to a long epigram of thirty-two verses in hexameters (VI.64) but Martial answers that both the length and the meter are customary and permissible (*solet . . . . licetque*), and he maintains his right to compose such pieces (VI.65) in spite of the fact, abundantly proved by his own practice, that they are exceptional. He was in a more normal mood when he wrote X.9 in which he says that his fame is due to witty poems in elegiac and hendecasyllabic meters.

In fact the epigram includes poems of such bewildering variety that a satisfactory definition of the *genre* as a whole is quite impossible. One may recognize types and define a given type fairly well. Coleridge's definition fits a certain type. One may sometimes define the dominant characteristics of the epigram at a given period, but such definitions are not often satisfactory. Reitzenstein, who has written the best history of the ancient epigram, says that to Meleager, who was writing about a generation earlier than Catullus (*ca.* 100–95 B.C.), the epigram meant a short poem in elegiac couplets on love. The collection for which Meleager was responsible contains hardly anything else.[4] But this only means that he was especially interested in this one type of epigram. For the first century B.C.—including, that is, the period of Catullus —Reitzenstein ventures only the statement that the epigram was a short poem. He does not venture to define its purpose or to restrict its content; even its metrical form displays wide variation, although the elegiac couplet remained the favorite. Speaking of Catullus, who holds a very important place in the history of the epigram, Reitzenstein asserts that meter is of no importance.

In the first and third parts of our collection there are over one hundred little poems on a great variety of themes clothed in more than a dozen meters of which the elegiac couplet, employed in over forty per cent, is far the commonest. If we were to take Reitzenstein's statement about meter quite literally, we might believe that Catullus regarded all these poems as epigrams. But a closer examination shows that we cannot construe his phrase so exactly. His general characterization of the epigram admits such a conclusion, but his detailed comment forbids it. He points out many interesting parallels between Catullus' little poems in lyric meters, e.g., II–III (on *sparrows*) and epigrams of the *Greek Anthology* in elegiac meter, but he is careful not to call these little poems of Catullus epigrams.

The history of Meleager's *Garland* throws an interesting light upon our problem. The scholiast calls this collection *A Garland of Epigrams* (ἐπιγραμμάτων στέφανος) and the extant poems are almost exclusively in elegiac meter. But in its original form, before parts of it were incorporated in the *Anthology*, it presented quite a different aspect. Meleager's prefatory poem survives[5] and from this we know that he included poems in lyric meters. Forty-eight writers ranging from Archilochus and Sappho to Meleager himself are mentioned, and the terminology is significant. Generally Meleager characterizes the work of each poet by using the name of a flower; Sappho's poems, for example, are "all roses." But he also uses a number of terms which clearly imply lyric forms: "hymn" (ὕμνος), "song" (ἀοιδή), "melic" (μέλισμα). From Anacreon he took both melic and elegiac pieces. Probably he included his own spring song in hexameters, which now stands in the ninth book (363) of the *Anthology*, and certainly his introductory poem of fifty-eight elegiac verses. Meleager's *Garland*, before it was broken up and parts of it lost, must have contained a considerable number of pieces in various lyric meters.[6]

Such was the collection which became the chief nucleus of the *Greek Anthology*. Meleager called it a

Garland—the *Proem* makes this certain—and it is not improbable that he added the word *"epigrams"* which is found in the *scholium*. At any rate his *Garland*, with its mass of elegiac pieces interspersed with a considerable number of poems in lyric meters, fore-shadowed metrical conditions in the *Anthology*[7] as a whole in which the proportion of elegiacs to non-elegiacs is about ten to one.[8]

There was, then, about a generation before Catullus, at least one collection of little poems predominantly elegiac, but including also so-called lyric forms. Recall-ing the probable history of the first and third parts of Catullus we see that here, as in the case of Meleager's *Garland*, one at least of the constituent parts may have been a book of elegiac and lyric forms, although it is impossible to say in what proportions the two were combined. Among the small poems which have sur-vived the elegiac pieces are in the minority. In the *Garland* one may hazard the conjecture that from the first the reverse was true: the elegiac poems were considerably more numerous than all others together. In view of the strong tendency to write epigrams in elegiac meter[9] it would have been easier for Meleager to call his *Garland* "epigrams" than it would have been for Catullus to apply this term to any group of small poems in which lyric meters predominated. But the important point is not the terminology, but the ten-dency, proved in the case of Meleager, to group small poems of varying meter with others in elegiac meter. Meleager had done this and I think it probable that Catullus followed this Greek precedent as he followed so many others.

The history of Meleager's *Garland* supplies another interesting parallel to what I conceive to have been the history of Catullus' poems: somebody took the elegiac pieces out of the *Garland* and rearranged them in the *Anthology* just as somebody took the elegiac pieces from Catullus' original *libelli* and rearranged them at the end of the collected edition.[10]

The tendency, which we have noted in Meleager, to group together little poems of various metrical forms was the natural result of an important change in aims of poetry. Most poetry was no longer written to be sung or chanted to a musical accompaniment, but for recitation and reading. It is impossible to define the phases of this change and there was never a period of Greek or Roman antiquity in which the delivery of poetry with some kind of musical accompaniment was entirely abandoned. Nevertheless there was a marked difference in this matter between the Alexandrian Age and the preceding centuries, and it affected most powerfully the so-called lyric meters and lyric forms of poetry.[11] In the fourth and later centuries poets had much greater freedom to use a given meter for a variety of purposes—to widen the scope of meters and to work up a given theme in a variety of metrical forms. Unfortunately it is impossible to trace the details of this change in the Alexandrian period because so little of the work of that period survives in the lyric forms. They practiced these forms to a certain extent, but they seem greatly to have preferred the elegiac couplet for the small poem, and like Catullus they applied the term παίγνιον, "plaything," a close parallel to the Latin poet's *nugae*, to little poems in both elegiac[12] and lyric meters. The condition of affairs in Catullus may reflect conditions in the Alexandrian Age more closely than we can prove with our defective evidence.[13] It is certainly true that in his time the composition of poetry for recitation and reading was the rule. It is doubtful whether he himself composed any piece for song.[14]

In Greek literature, therefore, just before the time of Catullus, collections of epigrams were very hospitable to little poems of lyrical form. The force of metrical distinctions was weakening and the Alexandrian epigrammatists, retaining the elegiac couplet as their favorite meter, nevertheless made use of other meters also, notably the hendecasyllable. If a poet preferred lyric meters, did he make similar concessions and include a certain proportion of elegiac poems among his lyrics? Turn about is fair play, but there is no reliable means of answering the question. At least a poet would hardly have called such a collection "epigrams." We hear from Suidas that Callimachus wrote lyrics ($\mu \acute{\epsilon} \lambda \eta$) and though we know hardly anything about them, his epigrams and probably his iambics seem to have been separate collections.[15] Stobaeus quotes two short bits (6 lines) from Philetas' $\pi a \acute{\iota} \gamma \nu \iota a$, but they are elegiac couplets and we can see no difference between them and the two fragments (also elegiac) which he quotes from the same poet's epigrams.

In Latin literature just before the time of Catullus—in fact at just about the time Meleager was writing, *ca.* 90 B.C.—Laevius composed a series of poems in lyric meters which are called by Porphyrio[16] "lyrics" and are cited no less than eight times by Gellius and others as *erotopaegnia*, "erotic playthings."[17] The number of fragments is considerable, but no elegiac verse occurs among them. The term paegnion ($\pi a \acute{\iota} \gamma \nu \iota o \nu$) was of course applied to lighter poetry of many different types, including the elegiac epigram, but the interesting thing here is that neither Callimachus nor Laevius seem to have called their small lyrics "epigrams,"

although the two groups were showing a strong
tendency to overlap.

From the fourth to the first century B.C.—the
significant period for a comprehension of Catullus—
the history of the epigram is well understood. The
history of the little lyric, on the other hand, is very
imperfectly known. There are hints that these two
varieties of poetry were encroaching upon each other.
Differences, especially metrical differences, were being
levelled, but the extent of this tendency cannot be
defined because the evidence is too scanty. May the
sands of Egypt yield us some of the lyrics of Callimachus, for example, or more of the hendecasyllables
of Phalaecus!

With Catullus, however, the material becomes abundant—nearly sixty small poems in various lyric meters,
nearly fifty in elegiac meter. In the work of this one
poet at least, it is possible to learn much about the relations of the two groups. Did he regard them as distinct
or as in most respects alike? By comparing the similar
poems of both groups we shall arrive at some interesting
results.

The phrase "similar poems" implies some kind of
classification for purposes of study. Since the extent
to which Catullus was restricted by metrical form is
one of the points at issue, I suggest a rough grouping
not by metrical criteria, but by the content, the
purpose, the tone of the individual poems. Distinctions
of meter must be constantly borne in mind. A metrical
classification is clean cut and is properly the basis for a
study of the poems from the point of view of the
development and scope of the meters; it is useful up to
a certain point. But it is too narrow for the present
purpose; it overemphasizes the metrical element—a

distortion of which Lafaye's book, *Catulle et ses modèles*, is a good illustration.

At present I am seeking to discover the poet's attitude and I wish to approach each poem in a way which will reflect as truly as possible his own procedure. Catullus' interest in meter is obvious. He employs ten meters, not counting subspecies, and in the fiftieth poem he tells how on a certain evening he and his friend Calvus "played now with this meter, now with that." Occasionally the metrical interest seems to be foremost, as in the sixty-third poem, in which he adapts the difficult and complicated galliambics to the Latin tongue. But in general, and particularly in the short poems, I am convinced that his approach was the opposite—the normal approach. When he had an idea, an experience, which he wished to put into verse, he clothed it in any one of a number of meters which to his taste seemed adapted to it. As Wilamowitz well remarks, he did not ask whether the "rules" permitted this meter or that.[18]

No system of classifying such a varied mass of poems is satisfactory. It is impossible to force every poem into a category and I shall not attempt it. Some poems partake of the characteristics of more than one group. The sparrow poems, for example, belong from one point of view among the erotic poems, from another among the numerous ancient poems on animals, birds, insects, etc., and one of them (III) is at the same time a miniature epicede; cf. Ovid's lament on the parrot (*Am.* II.6). In such cases one must seek the dominant note, the dominant characteristic. There is considerable debatable ground, and yet if we allow each poem to align itself with others having obvious identities and similarities, a number of well marked types will emerge. I must limit myself to a few illustrations.

Catullus is the poet of hate and love, and his own words, *odi et amo*, might serve as captions for the two largest groups of his poems, the invective and the erotic. There are groups of anecdotes (X, LIII), poems of invitation and greeting (IX, XIII, XXVIII, XXXV), of reproach (XXX, XXXVIII, LX), of consolation (XCVI), a hymn or cult song (XXXIV), a drinking song (XXVII), and many others.[19]

By far the largest group consists of the invective or satiric poems,[20] a total of about forty or nearly forty per cent of all the short poems. Let us study parts of this group for a moment, keeping in mind the purpose of determining the relation of content to meter between those members of the group which are written in elegiacs and those which are written in other meters. The tone of these poems ranges in intensity from the absolutely unbridled and foul-mouthed utterances which too often disfigure the poet's pages to those jesting, simulated attacks which are often the strongest proofs of friendship. "When you call me that, *smile!*" as the Virginian said.

None of these poems are more violent, though some are even coarser, than those whose purpose, superficially at least, is political. There are nine of these. The most famous is XXIX, the bitter attack upon Caesar and his henchman Mamurra with a lash at Pompey. Mamurra is a grafter, an adulterer, a rake, a spendthrift, and yet he is a pet of the triumvirs, and they, especially Caesar, are responsible for supplying him with the means of satisfying his inclinations. This is the poem which penetrated the usually impervious skin of Caesar, and no wonder. He admitted, says Suetonius, that an everlasting stigma had been laid upon him by Catullus' verses about Mamurra.[21]   Yet, so far as

Caesar himself is concerned, LVII is even more abusive.
There is no need to paraphrase the remaining members
of the group. Catullus keeps hammering at the bosses
and various minor members of their ring. The tone
and the details vary, but the type remains the same—
political and personal attack.

The interesting thing is the meter. Two of the
group are written in pure iambics, two in hendecasyllables, and five in elegiac couplets. But there is no
reason why all should not have been written in the same
meter, and any one of the three was at that period
well suited to poems of this character. But Catullus
chose three different meters! He felt entirely free to
select any one of several meters which seemed to him
suitable vehicles for such a content and such a purpose.
The iambics and the elegiacs had been thus employed
for centuries, but it was not primarily the force of
tradition which influenced Catullus; in the iambics,
for example, he was not a mere imitator of the great
Archilochus. Tradition undoubtedly played a part,
but the chief influence was just as undoubtedly the in-
stinctive feeling of a great poet for the right verse form.

Let us take a few more illustrations from the group of
invectives. The attacks upon Furius and Aurelius
(XVI, XXIII), couched in the foulest language, are
written in hendecasyllables. Of the same sort are
XXVIII (against Memmius), XXXIII (against Viben-
nius), XL (against Ravidus), XLI and XLIII (against
Ameana), XLVII (against Porcius, Socration, and
Piso). Some of these poems have other elements.
From the point of view of abuse, however, nothing
more revolting could be imagined. And yet we can
match them in this respect by the choliambics of
XXXVII and XXXIX (against Egnatius) and LIX

(against Rufa and Rufus), and again by the elegiacs of
LXIX (against Rufus), LXXX, LXXXVII–XCI (all
against Gellius), LXXVIII (against Gallus), and several
others (LXXIX, XCVII, XCVIII).

Considering for a moment the lighter and sometimes
merely simulated invectives, we find the same tendency
to vary the meter. There are hendecasyllables (XII,
XLII), iambic septenarii (XXV), choliambics (XXII,
XLIV), and elegiacs (LXXXIV). Three of these poems
are directed against individuals who had filched some
small article of personal property from the poet. In
one case certainly the theft was regarded by the thief
as a good joke (XII). But the purloined article, a
handkerchief or napkin of Spanish linen, was highly
valued by Catullus because it was the gift of two dear
friends and he feels, as we say, sore:

O Marrucine Asinius, I'd have you understand
'Tis not a pretty way you have of using your left hand.
When jest and wine are going round, it sneaks up like a thief,
While some poor guest is off his guard, and gets his hand-
          kerchief.
You think this clever, do you? Nay, 'tis crude as it can be.
Just ask your brother Pollio, if you will not trust me.
He'd gladly pay a talent down, your thieving to undo,
For he's a lad of polished speech, and wit and humor too.
So send me back my handkerchief, whose loss I now deplore,
Or else expect lampoons like this—a full three hundred more.
'Tis not intrinsic worth alone that makes the thing so dear,
But it is doubly precious as my comrades' souvenir.
Fabullus and Veranius sent it to me from Spain,
And I must love it like my friends till they come back again.[22]

In the large erotic group the situation is the same.
The thirty poems (more or less) dealing with Lesbia
are written in Sapphics, choliambics, hendecasyllables,

and especially—over half of them—in elegiacs. The metrical variety persists even when the theme is essentially the same. The poet pays tribute to his lady's beauty in Sapphics and in elegiacs (LI, LXXXVI), he jests with her in choliambics (VIII),[23] hendecasyllables (XXXVI), and elegiacs (LXX), and he deals with her degradation in hendecasyllables (LVIII), elegiacs (LXXII, LXXIX, etc.), and Sapphics (XL).

In the smaller groups the same tendency appears. Here it is even more significant because there are only a few poems in each group. There are but six poems, for example, whose dominant note is reproach (XXX, XXXVIII, LX, LXXIII, LXXVII, XCI) and yet four different meters are employed.

But enough of examples. Evidently Catullus often clothed identical or approximately identical themes in two or more metrical forms. And we may apply this evidence drawn from his practice to the solution of our problem. To him the metrical form was not of first importance. But this conclusion must not be made too sweeping. The evidence does not extend to all the poems of both groups; there are types in lyric meter which have no counterpart among the elegiac poems, e.g., XXXIV, the hymn to Diana. We must then recognize carefully the limits of the evidence. But fortunately these limits are rather wide. Let us attempt a conservative summary.

The commonest meters are the elegiac, the hendecasyllable, and the choliambic. It is safe to say that Catullus regarded his little elegiac poems as not essentially different from the little poems in hendecasyllables and choliambics. It is safe to say that any of the themes which appear in hendecasyllabic or choliambic form might have appeared in elegiac form. Probably the reverse statement is also true, and there are strong hints that other meters should be included in this general statement. Notice, for example, the use of the iambic trimeter in such strongly contrasted types as IV and XXIX.

We now see why Reitzenstein, starting with a knowledge that the little elegiac poems would naturally have been called epigrams, nevertheless did not restrict the term to elegiacs only. He refrained in fact altogether from defining the meter of the epigram in Catullus. He saw that mere metrical difference was not a safe criterion; that there were certainly good epigrams among the poems in lyric meters.

As we have seen, the history of the text supplies strong evidence that our collection does not, except in a very slight degree, represent the arrangement made by Catullus himself. Our present study supports this conclusion. Catullus himself may have published a part of the elegiac pieces as a unit, but in addition it is probable that he published units consisting of short poems in both lyric and elegiac meters. It is improbable that when he was ready to publish a *libellus* he sifted out the elegiac trifles reserving them for a separate book. I hazard the conjecture that each of those rolls, if he published more than one, resembled more closely a book of Martial's epigrams than any other ancient book of which we have full knowledge;[24] each roll or booklet (*libellus*) was made up of little poems (rarely perhaps an abnormally long poem) in elegiacs, hendecasyllables, and choliambics with a sprinkling of less common meters.[25]

However this may be, we must repeat that within certain rather wide limits Catullus did not regard the metrical form of his short poems as a distinction of the first importance. He was living in a period in which there was considerable freedom in the choice of meters. I have already emphasized this and it is equally evident in the all too meager fragments of his immediate predecessors, especially Laevius, and of his contemporaries, such as Calvus. Nevertheless the force of tradition was still so strong that in all cases we must base our conclusions strictly upon the actual practice of the poets, and this I have tried to do in the case of Catullus. We must not assume that in this respect he enjoyed the freedom of a modern poet. He would not have ventured to compose an epyllion, for example, in any meter but the hexameter.

The little elegiac pieces are very often connected with the other little poems by bonds of identical or very similar content, tone, and purpose, and the difference in meter does not imply that Catullus regarded them as a separate kind of poetry. How is it with their style? The language and style of the poems have been studied minutely, but I must limit myself to a few general results which concern my present purpose.

It has long been recognized that there is a marked difference in style between the eight long poems considered as one group and the short poems considered together as another group. The style of the long poems is in general dignified, elevated; the style of the short poems is much less elevated and often sinks to the opposite extreme, the vulgar. In each group there are variations and gradations as might be expected in such a mass of miscellaneous poems; among the long poems the elegies (LXV–LXVII) and the wedding poems (LXI especially) are less elevated than the epyllion (LXIV); of the short poems some have a style of decided dignity, e.g., XXXIV, the hymn to Diana.

But on the whole the two groups are very different. At present we may omit details and consider one point only. The most striking feature of the style of the short poems is colloquialism (often vulgarism), an element which is infrequently present in the long poems (e.g., LXI, LXVII). Now this colloquial element is not confined to one group of the little poems as against the other, but pervades them both alike—the elegiacs and the lyric group. Moreover the short elegiacs differ in this respect from the long elegiacs. Here then is still another indication that Catullus regarded the short elegiacs as essentially like the rest of the short poems. Certainly the two groups are connected by the bond of a common style.

In my effort to learn something about the attitude of Catullus toward his work I have already had occasion to touch on the terms which he and others applied to poems and poetry, especially to short poems. Two of these terms have been discussed: *nugae*, "trifles"— primarily a descriptive term—and *epigramma*, "epigram," a generic term. By extending our inquiry to other terms used by Catullus and other writers we shall make some further progress.

If Catullus had only told us what term or terms he applied to his little poems as a group he would have saved us much trouble. This group did not constitute a *genre*, but it contained members which could be generically classified. Yet Catullus uses only one generic term, *iambi* ("invective"), which fits any part of the group.

In avoiding generic terms he is like all the rest of the ancient poets. Unless they are writing an avowedly critical work such as Horace's *Ars poetica* they avoid technical terms. Catullus composes epic, elegy, epigram,

epithalamium, several kinds of lyric, etc. Undoubtedly
he knew the technical terms for all these *genres* and for
others also, but he uses only two which have a technical color; *iambi* (just mentioned) and *hymenaeus*
(LXII. 4), "wedding song," the latter not in the
strict generic sense. In general the poets leave technical terms to technical writers—the grammarians and
critics. This perfectly natural tendency explains why
the generic terms occur rarely and sometimes at a relatively late period in the poets.[26]

The poets then do not like to call a spade a spade.
Whenever they mention or even discuss their own
poetry or that of others they greatly prefer terms which
are not out of harmony with the particular style in
which they are writing. There is a wealth of these;
they range all the way from words like *versus, carmina*,
which are usable in poetry because they have no more
technical color than the English "verse," "verses,"
"song," to highly figurative terms such as Pliny's
passerculi and *columbuli*, "little doves." These descriptive and figurative terms throw much light upon the
attitude of poets toward poetry.

In Catullus there are a number of the colorless terms,
e.g., *versus*, "verses," *carmen*, "song," "a poem" (or
in the plural *carmina*, "verses"), *poema*, "a poem,"
"composition," *scripta*, "writings," *charta*, "paper,"
"page." He uses other terms, however, which are
more instructive.

There was a strong tendency in antiquity to employ
formal nomenclature. Terms derived from meter were
especially common both in Greek and in Latin. Two of
these terms, *iambi* and *hendecasyllabi*, occur in Catullus.
The ability and the fame of Archilochus established
the iambic as the leading meter for lyric invectives as

early as the seventh century before Christ. Through
the centuries, however, this meter was used for many
other purposes and we have seen that Catullus continues both its narrower (XXIX) and its wider functions
(IV). But he knew the technical use of *iambi* and it is
interesting to note that by his time, and probably long
before, it had lost its strictly metrical implication.
The term occurs five times in Catullus, all in hendecasyllabic passages, and it includes not only the actually
iambic invectives (XXIX, etc.), but also invectives in
other meters, especially Catullus' favorite hendecasyllables.

Hendecasyllabi is another term which was originally
metrical only, but it is not a generic term. Catullus
gave it an impulse toward the sense of "invective";
in fact he invokes his *hendecasyllabi* to aid him in
making an attack (XLII. 1 ff.) and he used the meter
again and again for this purpose. But the process was
never completed, as it had been in the case of *iambi*.
This meter had been used by Sappho and in the fourth
century Phalaecus gave it such currency that it was
often called Phalaecean or Phalaecian. But unfortunately the surviving examples of it from the period
before Catullus are so few that its history cannot be
traced. Catullus uses the hendecasyllable for a great
variety of themes and, after the elegiac couplet, it is
his favorite meter for short poems.[27] Could *hendecasyllabi* as a literary term be used in the time of Catullus
as in that of Martial to designate a collection of poems
most of which, though not all, were written in this
meter? I think it improbable. *Elegi*, a term which had
had a much longer life and much wider vogue, had
certainly not been divested of its metrical implication,
as one may see by studying the passages of Augustan

poetry (Horace, Tibullus, Ovid) in which it occurs. For similar light on *hendecasyllabi* we are forced to turn to a still later generation.

The whole question of terminology and the attitude of the Romans toward the small poem are illuminated by the Letters of the Younger Pliny.[28] Pliny ardently admired Catullus and imitated him in the composition of poetic trifles. He even gave them a touch of that naughtiness which Catullus regarded as essential to their piquancy and their success (XVI), and he was a bit afraid that the resultant taste in the mouths of his readers might ill comport with the dignity of a staid Roman gentleman. The passages in which he speaks of these indiscretions are amusing as well as instructive. He finds it necessary to justify himself by citing a long line of distinguished Romans who had indulged in the same amusement. He admits a fondness for comedies, and mimes, and all kinds of "harmless relaxation" (*innoxiae remissionis*). In short he makes his own the Terentian principle "I am human!" (*homo sum!*). Pliny's little poems were in various meters and he emphasizes the variety of their content and tone. "In them," he says, "I jest and play, I display love or grief or anger, I complain, or I describe something now briefly, now more fully."

Their purpose, he says, is to entertain. Though they are a bit broad at times he refrains from those lewd subjects and those naked words (*nuda—verba*) which Catullus (Pliny quotes him) had laid down as a law of the type (*opusculi—lex*)—a phrase which shows that for Pliny all such little poems belonged to one group. All this, except Pliny's timidity about the element of coarseness, is an excellent description of Catullus' own work. How welcome at times are the words of those writers who like Ovid and Pliny are not afraid to be even redundantly explicit!

But when Pliny decides to publish some of his verse he is puzzled about a title. On this question also he is refreshingly explicit. His trouble is that there are too many possibilities. He admits that any one of half a dozen will serve: "Call them epigrams or idylls or selections or little poems (*poematia*) or anything else you prefer!" And there are in fact plenty of other terms which he himself employs: *versiculi*, "versicles," "little verses," *scripta*, "writings," *lusus*, "playful verse," *nugae*, "trifles," *ineptiae*, "nonsense," "follies," *passerculi*[29] *et columbuli*, "little sparrows and little doves." Collectively they are an *opusculum*, "a group of bagatelles," and a book of them is a *libellus*, "a booklet," although in this case we should not emphasize the diminutive.

Truly an embarrassment of riches! And yet all terms which would have emphasized the lyric aspect of these trifles are conspicuous by their absence. Pliny never thinks of calling them "odes" or "lyrics" or anything of the sort. This is the more significant since his favorite meter, the hendecasyllable, had once been lyric. In fact he is seeking a title for a book of poetry intended for recitation and reading. Finally he decided to follow the example of many others and publish one book of hendecasyllabic poems separately. To this, on account of the meter, he gave the title *Hendecasyllabi*, but he characterizes these *hendeca-syllabi* as *nugae*, "trifles." To his thinking they did not differ essentially from the poems in other meters.

In the time of Pliny and Martial then, at the end of the first and the beginning of the second century of our era, "many" (Pliny says) had published separate books

of *hendecasyllabi* and had used the word as a title.
The certain inference from this statement is that there
were also books in which the hendecasyllables were not
separated from other meters.[30] "Many" had used
poematia, "little poems," as a title for a book. Pliny
expressly implies this. But no single term had won
its way to exclusive prominence. All told there are at
least a dozen specified by Pliny which might have
served, or a poet might have invented something
entirely new.

It is a certain inference, I think, from these facts
that no predominant term for this type of poetry
existed in the time of Catullus. The number of terms
in Catullus is considerable; by Pliny's time it is many
times greater. Almost every one of the terms used in
the earlier period occurs again later. Let us note some
other parallel details.

Pliny says that the composition of his little poems
was a form of harmless relaxation; that they were the
product of spare moments during journeys, at the
baths, at dinner. Knowing Pliny we feel sure that he
polished them before he published them, but we have
no reason to suspect that he is merely posing when he
speaks of their origin. Many of Catullus' little poems
originated in the same fashion. In the fiftieth poem he
describes a contest in verse composition which he had
with his friend Calvus. The two friends are at leisure,
otiosi (Pliny's "relaxation"); they are at dinner (Pliny's
inter cenam). Each wrote *versiculi* "little verses"
(Pliny uses the same term), playing now with this
meter now with that. Perhaps they were trying the
same theme in different meters. We do not know.
But their work is twice spoken of as "playing," *ludere*.
Pliny uses not only the verb but also the noun (*lusus*)

of light poetic composition. These words reflect even better than *nugae, ineptiae*, the Roman attitude toward this type of poetry: it was a "play," a "sport," a *jeu d'esprit*, no serious matter.

Many kinds of lighter poetry are called *lusus:* the bucolic, the epigram, the lighter odes of Horace, elegy. But the term is used relatively, not absolutely, and the contrast is almost always epic. Elegy, for example, is much more serious and elevated than epigram or satire, but in contrast with epic it is a *lusus*.[31] Collectively the term *lusus* is especially applied to little poems of various types, no matter if a few of them are very serious.

It is a striking fact that in antiquity no single term for these little poems ever attained supremacy. Pliny's testimony on this point is explicit and serves as an excellent supplement to that of Catullus. The situation is in fact the same today. Not many years ago I remember reading (in the American *Bookman*, I think) an appeal by Carolyn Wells, one of our modern composers of *nugae*, for a better term than *vers du société*, "versicles," and the like. The thing itself has remained much the same in all ages. But it is not surprising that no single term for it has become established. Its bewildering variety resists anything like exact terminology. No term is able to cover all the types of poem which may be members of such a group. Catullus had no precise term. If he had used such a term, Pliny would not have been puzzled what to call his own efforts in the same field, for he was avowedly following the example of Catullus. For once the argument *ex silentio* is convincing. To Pliny only one generic term was possible: epigram. But it is not probable that Catullus would have called all his little poems epigrams. The preponderance of so-called lyric meters over the elegiac couplet is too great, and there are too many poems which are not epigrams unless we stretch the term unduly: X, XI, XVII, XXIII, XXIX, XLII, LV, and others.

But although there was no precise term for such a group of little poems there was nevertheless a group— an *opusculum*, to use Pliny's term. To the ancients the chief bonds of kinship were the brevity of the poems, the fact that most of them were suggested by events of everyday life—*poesie de circonstance*, as Lafaye says,—and the predominantly colloquial style which is the natural garb of such themes.

Brevity is merely external, nevertheless it is the only universal characteristic. To call the group "little poems" or "short poems" as I have done may seem to be a counsel of despair, and yet the term is more significant than is at first sight apparent. Many of the terms applied to such poems emphasize their "littleness:" *versiculi*, "little verses," *passerculi* and *columbuli*, "little birds," *poematia*, meaning precisely "little poems"—one of the most popular terms according to Pliny and others. A book of such pieces was often called a *libellus*,[32] a "little book," and I think that it is not fanciful to infer that the diminutive meaning was not entirely lacking when Catullus calls one of his books of "trifles" a *libellus* (I. 1).[33] Moreover the group includes real miniatures, poems which are brief examples of types which normally appeared in much longer form. The third poem, for example, the lament for Lesbia's sparrow, is a miniature epicede in lyric meter. The thirty-fourth poem is a miniature hymn or cult song. The tenth and the seventeenth are brief narratives or anecdotes. In these instances we detect the poet, so to speak, in the act of condensing longer types, and there are other instances, for example, the eighth,[34] in which we may strongly suspect the same method.

But the terms are of importance only so far as they throw light on the nature of the group. The important point is not what he called the little poems, but how he viewed them, and the conclusion which emerges from all the evidence is that Catullus viewed all the little poems including the elegiacs as constituting one general group. He was fully aware that in this group there were poems which could be classified under more definite *genres* or types—the invective, the epigram, the hymn, etc., but these were not so numerous or, in the case of the epigram, so different as to lead him to make more minute divisions. He was writing poetry which was to be read or recited and he was free to use any one of a considerable number of meters which had once been lyric in the proper sense. The polymetrical books of his predecessor Laevius display the same tendency and he had called his poems, if the citations correctly represent him, *erotopaegnia*, "erotic playthings," a term closely akin to Catullus' *nugae*, cf. *ludere*. There are strong hints, although we lack explicit evidence as to details, that the Alexandrians published similar groups of poems. We hear of παίγνια composed by Philetas, for example, but the two extant fragments are elegiac. The term was applied by Hephaestion to the pattern poems of Simias—the *Egg*, the *Axe*, etc.: τὸ Ὠιὸν τὸ Σιμίου καὶ ἄλλα παίγνια. Here we are tempted to translate "other stunts of the sort." Wilhelm Kroll mentions Callimachus' *Iambi*, which included quite possibly iambics, choliambics, and trochaic tetrameters, and Mnasias, who wrote παίγνια and was so varied that he was called a "Salpe," a kind of variegated fish.[35]   We may add that the Alexandrians arranged the poems of Sappho, Alcaeus, etc., in books which often displayed considerable metrical variety,[36] and lastly we must not forget the certain precedent afforded by Meleager, who grouped both elegiacs and lyrics together in his *Garland*.   We do not possess any book of short poems in the form published by Catullus himself, but in our collection we have the *disiecta membra* and in them we detect the continuance of the later Greek point of view.

In Catullus the group of short poems is of first importance because it contains the pieces on which primarily his fame as a poet rests.   In bulk also the short poems comprise over half of the total number of lines.   These facts explain why I have taken so much pains to show that in spite of differences there are bonds which link all these little poems together in one group and that this represents the attitude of Catullus, derived in all probability from his Greek predecessors.   It is misleading to separate the little elegiac poems from the rest merely because they are so separated in our manuscripts and because metrically they are more clearly epigrams.   It is still more misleading to arrange all the poems in metrical groups and study them, as Lafaye has done, as if they were in separate compartments.   Catullus did not go about his work in this way and I have tried to show that in searching for poems of the same type, poems that belong together, we approximate his point of view far more closely if we regard metrical differences as secondary to identities and similarities of content, tone, and purpose.

The effort to comprehend as fully as possible what kinds and types of poetry Catullus himself distinguished has necessarily involved many references to the work of his predecessors. Both Greek and Roman poets influenced him, but the two influences differ greatly in kind and in degree. Every reader of Catullus perceives at once many indications of Greek influence. The Roman influence is not so obvious, but it is there, and certain aspects of it will be examined in the next lecture.

CHAPTER III

THE BACKGROUND IN ROMAN POETRY

The poetry of Catullus and his contemporaries would have been impossible if the way had not been prepared for it by a long line of Roman predecessors. In order to understand the work and the position of Catullus it is necessary to sketch in this Roman background, but in so doing I shall limit myself to those parts of it which have the most direct bearing upon Catullus and in particular to verse which in any way foreshadows the types which he composed.

When Catullus began to write—about 70 B.C. or a few years later—Roman poetry for a century and three-quarters had been serving that apprenticeship to the Greek which was initiated by the Greek slave and Roman freedman, Livius Andronicus. In all these years the effort to Romanize Greek technique had gone on apace and Roman skill was constantly improving. When once the pioneers, of whom Ennius was the most influential, had completed their work, the Romans had a double heritage, so far as tradition and conscious art were concerned, the one Greek and the other Roman. But the Roman tradition because of the constant use of Greek literature was itself full of Greek elements. Thus the Roman poets were soon receiving the Greek inspiration by two channels: directly, through their own reading and study of Greek literature, and indirectly, through earlier Roman literature which held in solution so much that was Greek.

In ancient literature there was a much greater respect for tradition than there is today. Nevertheless there were occasional reactions against it. One of these reactions occurred in the age of Catullus and I must allude to one feature of it here in order to show at the outset of my review of his predecessors that their influence—the influence of *Roman* tradition upon him— was much limited: Catullus and many of his contemporaries neglected—Cicero's word is "despised"—that part of their heritage which was Roman.[1] Catullus mentions Greek poets of many periods, he mentions contemporary Roman poets, but he is uniformly silent about his Roman predecessors. He does not even mention one of them by name. There is no evidence that he took the slightest friendly interest in their work.[2] When he sought aid from the past, he turned directly to the Greeks.

And yet no poet by mere assumption of such an attitude can free himself entirely from connection with those who have helped to develop the poetry of his native land. If he thinks himself to be an absolutely free lance, an ultra-modern, he is self-deceived. If the earlier Roman poets had not striven for generations to improve Roman poetic art even as Catullus in his own generation strove, he himself could not have achieved so great a degree of success. If for a moment we could imagine Catullus without Roman predecessors, we could only conceive of him as a very different poet. In spite of himself he built upon foundations which they had laid and we must take their work into account.[3]

It is obvious, for example, that without the work of Father Ennius and other earlier poets many of Catullus' meters, all of which are adapted from the Greek, could not have reached so high a degree of perfection. The same statement holds true of his poetic style in spite of the fact that he was the first genius who appeared in Roman poetry. But these are topics on which I can touch only in the most cursory fashion. I must confine myself to a few others which are more general and perhaps more important. It is nevertheless possible to gather within a brief space enough evidence to show that in the older poetry there existed a very real Roman preparation for the work of Catullus.[4]

We need not go back to the few scraps of Latin which have survived, often in garbled and later form, from the pre-literary period.[5] For the most part these are not literature; they are merely Latin writing or at most the germs of literature as, for example, the songs of the Salian priests and the Arval brethren. Moreover Catullus was not an antiquarian and his only hymn (XXXIV) is a Romanized Greek type. He displays none of that interest in the remote past of his country which characterized his contemporary, Marcus Varro, and which became so prominent a feature of Augustan poetry.

The one clear connection between Catullus and the pre-literary period is found in the Fescennines which he inserted in his first wedding poem (LXI. 119 ff.), but it would be an error to suppose that he was there consciously reviving an old Latin form of poetry. None of the pre-literary *versus Fescennini* survive, but we know that they existed even after the Greek literature was introduced, that they were often scurrilous and were employed at weddings as a means of reducing the envy which the gods might feel towards the supreme happiness of the bride and groom—"to take off the curse," as we say. The first wedding poem was written for an actual Roman wedding, the wedding of a Manlius Torquatus to Vinia Aurunculeia, and Catullus has made an interesting effort to combine the features of the Greek hymeneal with the customs of the Roman wedding. The employment of abusive Fescennines was one of these Roman customs, probably not common in Catullus' time when most of the old nuptial forms had been abandoned, but still well known and understood. Catullus made use of the *Fescennina iocatio* as an element which would increase the Roman flavor of his poem rather than as a revival of an early form of native literature. In the same way a poet nowadays might insert in a wedding poem a passage on rice and old shoes in order to reflect a current wedding custom. Similarly the old Latin dirge (*nenia*) had no real connection, so far as we can tell from the scanty evidence, with the beautiful lines in which Catullus poured forth his grief for his dead brother. Here also the significant antecedents of our poet's work are Greek.[6]

It is not until long after the Roman writers had definitely turned to Greek models that we find evidence bearing more directly on the work of Catullus. From the beginning of this movement in 240 B.C. to the earliest date at which Catullus may have begun his career (*ca*. 70 B.C.) some one hundred and seventy years elapsed. For our purposes it will be convenient to regard as Catullus' predecessors all the poets whose literary activity ceased by the year 70 B.C. although we have not sufficient information to establish a definite chronology in the case of every one, and to regard as his contemporaries all whose literary activity began *ca*. 70 B.C. or later and also those who were writing both before and after that date, e.g., Valerius Cato. The earlier period, the period of Catullus' predecessors, ends therefore with Laevius, who seems not to have been active later than the time of Sulla, *ca*. 78 B.C.

Such a division is somewhat arbitrary, as the limits of all literary periods are apt to be, but in this case there are two considerations which point to the years 70–68 B.C. as a good dividing line. In the first place it is pretty certain that Catullus, like Ovid, began his literary career when he was very young, at about the time in fact when he assumed the toga of manhood.[7] If he was born, as I believe, *ca.* 87 B.C., and if he matured at the normal age of sixteen or seventeen, we arrive at the year 70 B.C. as the year of his maturity. Those who accept 84 B.C. as the year of his birth will prefer 68 or 67 B.C. as the earliest date of his literary career; the difference, for our present purpose, is unimportant. In the second place the extant evidence indicates that there was a marked improvement in poetic art after the year 70 B.C. even if we make every allowance for the meagerness of the remains of poetry which may be dated before that year.

The most significant and important preparatory work of the earlier poets lies in the field in which Catullus particularly excelled, the field of the very short poem both in elegiac and in lyric meters. Catullus, as we have seen, refers to those pieces as *nugae, ineptiae, versiculi,* or when they were invective, iambics, but he seems not to have been bound by distinctions based on metrical forms.[8] We cannot hope to find among the meager fragments of the older poetry representatives of all or even approximately all the many types of short poem which appear in Catullus, but fortunately there are examples of the two largest and most important groups, the invective and the erotic. Upon these we shall concentrate our attention, beginning with the erotic pieces because in these we have the most illuminating material.

There are hints that Ennius, Accius, the tragic poet, Quinctius Atta, the author of *togatae*, and perhaps Lucilius, the great satirist, attempted the small erotic poem.[9] The earliest extant examples, however, occur considerably later than Ennius and their preservation is due to that ardent admirer of the early literature, Aulus Gellius, with a little aid from Cicero. The passage of Gellius is at once so valuable for my purpose and so characteristic of its author that I shall translate it almost in full.

The date may have been *ca.* 150–160 A.D. The scene is a birthday dinner given by a rich young knight from the province of Asia not only to his friends but to his teachers, a highly commendable method of securing that intimate association of teacher and student which we are nowadays attempting to revive. It will be remembered that young Marcus Cicero understood very well the value of this method; how he remarks in a letter to Tiro[10] that he is inviting one of his teachers, Cratippus, to dine with him as often as possible; that his relation to Cratippus is that of a son rather than a pupil, and that at these dinners the said Cratippus throws off the professorial mask and jests quite like a human being!

But this is digression. At the dinner described by Gellius there was present among the teachers a noted rhetorician of Spanish birth, Antonius Julianus. This gentleman asked the host to bring in a band of young slaves of both sexes who were trained singers and musicians, and when they had presented a series of Greek poems, mostly erotic, ranging from Sappho and Anacreon to the work of recent poets, certain Greeks who were present started a controversy with Antonius Julianus on the comparative merits of Greek and Latin

erotic poetry, with the obvious intention of stirring up
the Spaniard. Fortunately for our knowledge of early
Roman poetry Julianus took the bait. From this point
I will let Gellius tell the story.[11]

Then [says Gellius, after a pretty poem of Anacreon had
been sung] several Greeks, who were present at the banquet,
men of charm and well read in our literature as well as their
own, began a nagging attack upon Julianus, hinting that he
was an utter barbarian and rustic, that having been born in
Spain he was merely a bawler (*clamator*), practicing a rabid
and quarrelsome type of oratory and teaching in a language
which possessed no grace, nothing of the soothing sweetness
that comes from associating Venus with the Muses. Again
and again they asked what were his feelings about Anacreon
and the other poets of his type and whether any one of our
poets had equalled his flowing and delightful verses. "An
exception is Catullus," they added, "who perhaps has composed a few, and the same may be said of Calvus. For the
verse of Naevius is involved, that of Hortensius lacks charm,
Cinna's has no grace, Memmius' is stiff, and so with all the
rest; their compositions are immature and discordant."

Then Julianus, roused to indignation on behalf of his native
tongue as if it were his altar and his hearth, answered: "I
ought indeed to grant that you beat the devil at such worthless folly and that you surpass us in erotic song just as you
do in the over-refined pleasure of living. But I would not
have you condemn us men of Latin race of a total lack of
erotic feeling as if we were some kind of wild men lacking
the power of sex sensation, and so permit me, pray, to
conceal my head with my cloak, as they say Socrates did
when he was making some remarks rather lacking in deli-
cacy;[12] listen and learn that we have had poets even earlier
than those whom you have named who were real lovers."

Then leaning back on the couch and veiling his head he
delivered in a very winning voice certain verses of Valerius
Aedituus, an old poet, and others of Porcius Licinus and

Quintus Catulus—verses than which nothing neater, more charming, more polished or more refined can be found, in my opinion, in Greek or Latin. These are the verses of Aedituus:[13]

My Pamphila, when I would tell the secret of my heart,
The yearning that I feel for thee, no word my lips will part,
My breast is damp with sudden sweat, and passion stills my
        breath;
So wordless, shamed, I seem to feel in love the touch of death.

He added other verses of the same poet not less pleasant, by Hercules! than the foregoing:[14]

> O Phileros, a torch for me why bearest thou?
> The road's aglow from flame within my heart.
> Thy flame the savage force of wind can blow
> To nothingness, or drops of rain may quench,
> But this of mine will yield to naught but her,
> The Lady Venus, from whose power it came.

Likewise he declaimed the following verses of Porcius Licinus:

> Ye guardians of the soft sheep's tender young,
> If flame ye seek, come hither; man is flame.
> With but a finger's touch I'll fire the grove.
> The flock's all flame—all things whereon I gaze.

The verses of Quintus Catulus were as follows:

My soul has fled; 'tis gone, methinks, to Theotimus' fold.
'Tis so in truth, for there it has a refuge as of old.
And yet I did command him to shut out the runaway.
I fear to go a-questing lest I myself betray.
I stand in doubt. What shall I do? Dear Venus, point the
        way.[15]

So far Aulus Gellius. A second epigram of Catulus is preserved by Cicero:[16]

> Constiteram exorientem Auroram forte salutans,
>   cum subito a laeva Roscius exoritur,
> pace mihi liceat, caelestes, dicere vestra,
>   mortalis visus pulchrior esse deo.

The meaning of this is that to Quintus Catulus the youthful Roscius seemed fairer than the dawn—and this despite the fact that he was cross-eyed!

These five little poems are the earliest extant Roman examples of the type, and so it is important to date them as accurately as possible. It should be noted at once that apparently little or nothing of the sort had preceded them. The passage of Gellius proves that they were earlier than the work of Catullus, earlier even than Laevius. Julianus' main point is that there had been poets earlier than Catullus and Laevius who deserved to rank with the Greeks, and when we bear in mind that both Julianus and Gellius were enthusiastic archaizers, it seems certain that they would have selected examples from the period of Ennius if any had existed.

The latest probable date is fairly easy to establish. One of the poets was Quintus Lutatius Catulus, the great soldier and orator who was consul 102 B.C. and died 87 B.C. His epigram on Roscius betrays a youthful admiration and must have been composed some years before he became consul—not later, let us say, than 102 B.C. and probably nearer 130 B.C.[17]

The earliest possible date is not so easy to infer. Porcius Licinus was a critic who wrote about Ennius, Terence (†159), and other early poets, but his serious error in dating the beginnings of Roman literature in the Second Punic War shows that he must have flourished considerably later than the period he was describing and his work is generally assigned to the period of the Gracchi, which was also the period of Catulus, ca. 130–120 B.C. The date of Valerius Aedituus' activity cannot be so closely fixed, but the order of the three poets—Aedituus, Porcius Licinus, Catulus—is the same

in both Gellius and Apuleius.[18]   This suggests a chronological arrangement—perhaps an anthology in which
these epigrams were preserved[19]—and scholars are
agreed that Aedituus and Porcius Licinus were older
contemporaries of Catulus, who, as a prominent and
wealthy man, interested in literature, may have gathered about him a coterie like that of the contemporary
Scipionic Circle.

These little pieces are not great poetry, but in the
history of Roman literature they have great significance.[20]   They prove that in the last half of the second
century B.C. cultured Romans were attempting to
transplant the Alexandrian erotic epigram, a type of
poem of which the *Greek Anthology* has preserved
hundreds.   Indeed the source of Catulus' epigram on
the soul of the lover fleeing to the loved one is an
epigram of Callimachus which is still extant.[21]   The
Anthology also preserves close parallels to the two
epigrams (one by Valerius Aedituus and the one by
Porcius Licinus) on the lover's heart aflame.[22]   And
finally Valerius Aedituus' little piece on the physical
symptoms of love—the speechless tongue, the starting
perspiration, the feeling of dissolution—is clearly based
on some late Greek variation of Sappho's famous
poem, the poem which Catullus adapted to his own
case in LI.   These Romans are not translating their
Greek models; they are freely adapting them in Latin.
They are even taking over the Greek custom of writing
several poems on the same theme—in this case the fire
in the lover's heart.[23]   Furthermore, they are trying
to reproduce certain refinements of the later Greek
erotic style—the decency of vocabulary, the plays on
words, the rather fantastic imagery; cf. especially the
comparison of the youthful Roscius to Aurora.[24]   All

this strongly reminds us of the tortuosities of contemporary Greek epigram, especially of Meleager.[25] Clearly, so far as style is concerned, these Romans found their ideal not in the age of Callimachus but in the Greek epigrammatists of their own day, and in Latinizing this style they achieved considerable success although they did not quite catch the trick.

But the excellences or defects of the Roman attempts are relatively unimportant. To one who scans earlier and later Roman poetry the important thing is that here in the last third of the second century B.C., not more than a generation or two before Catullus, occur the first serious efforts of the Romans to transplant the modern type of Greek erotic poetry—the type which Catullus brought to perfection in Latin. It is the impulse lying behind these efforts that interests us, for the impulse implies an appreciation of the Greek. From the very beginnings of Roman literature the Romans had had the same general kind of erotic writing at their disposal in Callimachus and in many others, but if the extant evidence does not deceive us, a hundred years passed by before they were moved to utilize it. The fullest evidence is preserved in the formal comedy of the Romans. Here also they had at their disposal the same general type of Greek erotic with the important difference that the dramatist was not presenting his own love but the loves of his characters. Even so the Romans shrank from placing before their audiences, except to make fun of them, the more subtle and romantic details of love. Throughout the entire period of the formal comedy as we know it from the twenty-six plays of Plautus and Terence, no appreciable portion of "the wild race of Romulus"— to use the phrase of Porcius Licinus—was ever able to

appreciate the subtleties of Menandrian erotic. The
most popular Roman plays were precisely the coarsest
plays—the *Eunuchus* of Terence and the *Casina* of
Plautus. Let us remember that the *Casina* was actually
selected as the first play[26] with which to begin the
revival of Plautine comedy some time about 150–140
B.C. and that Plautus, who was far less refined than
Terence, was also far more popular. The cultured
element was but a very thin veneer upon the mass of
the Roman population.

In the drama the personal inclinations of the authors
were obscured by the form in which they wrote and
by the necessity of catering to an audience in which
there were but few of the cultured. No such inhibitions
rested on the writers of epigram, satire, or other forms
which allowed free play to the writer's erotic sentiments.
And so it is all the more striking and significant that
Roman appreciation of the finer forms of Greek erotic
art was so slow in manifesting itself. When at last
the impulse came, the Romans naturally attempted
first the favorite erotic form of contemporary Greek
poetry, the small poem or epigram in elegiac verse.

Meanwhile some progress had been made in other
varieties of the small poem in elegiac meter. The invective, the commonest type represented in Catullus, had
appeared as early as the famous controversy between the
poet Naevius and the Caecilii Metelli about 206 B.C.
The good old democratic poet's scathing remarks about
these aristocrats who were destined by fate to hold office
at Rome,   fato Metelli Romae fiunt consules,

was probably made in one of his plays,[27] but the rejoinder of the Metelli was cast in the form of Saturnians.
Naevius lost the fight and was clapped into jail, as we

know, and his fate illustrates the danger that lay in
making personal attacks at Rome. Lampoons and
satire there were, especially at times of political unrest,
but there were libel laws also, as the old jurist Trebatius
warned Horace.[28] Unless the poets attacked nonentities—and it was safer to attack dead nonentities—or
veiled their intent under a cloud of pseudonyms, they
had to have strong support, as Lucilius had, before
they could venture upon those open personal attacks
of which the Italians have always been so fond. Indeed
there are few traces of the invective or satiric short
poem earlier than the age of Catullus. The best
illustration is an *epigrammation*, as Varro calls it,[29]
by a certain Papinius or Pomponius,[30] which may have
been written as early as 150 B.C. It is a coarse personal
invective anticipating the most drastic style of Catullus
and his contemporaries, and it is noticeable that the
old Saturnian verse has been supplanted by elegiacs,
the favorite meter among the later Greeks for such
attacks. There is some evidence also that the lyric
forms of Archilochus and Hipponax were being attempted at Rome, but the dates are not very certain.
Varro cites two iambic invective lines from a certain
Manilius. Gellius, Macrobius, and Priscian cite a
number of choliambics from Gnaeus Matius, one of
which is certainly erotic.[31]

In addition to the erotic and invective types there
are in the early literature a few other short poems
which clearly foreshadow the work of Catullus. I can
do little more than enumerate these scattered bits of
verse. Omitting those which are either actually or
possibly epitaphs, omitting also the traces of dedicatory epigrams,[32] we find in Ennius a little poem glorify-
ing Scipio Africanus[33] which is of the same general type

as Catullus' complimentary poems, LXXXVI (on
Lesbia's charms) or LIII (on Calvus' oratory). Another
piece which in its expression of the poet's own feeling
reminds one of Catullus is that in which Pompilius
(*ca.* 150 B.C.?) presents himself as a tragic poet.[34]

> Pacui discipulus dicor, porro is fuit Enni,
> Ennius Musarum. Pompilius clueor.

Practically all the little poems that have been mentioned are written in elegiac couplets, the favorite
meter of the Greek epigram and commoner in Catullus
than any other meter. It is not until we arrive at the
years immediately preceding Catullus' boyhood—very
likely during his boyhood—that we find a writer who
attempted to Romanize Greek lyric meters for use in
the shorter forms of poetry. This writer was Laevius,
about whose life scarcely anything is known. He has
generally been identified with Laevius Melissus.[35]
Whether this identification is correct or not and
whether, as Leo suggests, Laevius, like Terence and
Horace's father, was a freedman we do not know. He
may even have lived on into the time when Catullus
was writing, but it is an almost certain inference from
the crudities of his technique that his work belongs to
the early part of the first century, *ca.* 100–75 B.C.

Laevius is said by Porphyrio to have written lyrics[36]
and his work must have been extensive since Charisius[37]
mentions a sixth book of his *Erotopaegnia*, "Erotic
Playthings." Perhaps all his poems were grouped
under this title. At any rate the rather numerous fragments prove that in many ways he was striving to
work along the lines which Catullus and his contemporaries followed. Like them he showed great interest
in meter. He was probably more polymetrical than

Catullus, for even the fragments comprise twelve or more meters. Most of these occur here for the first time in Latin and among them there are examples of Catullus' favorite hendecasyllables and choliambics.

In language and style he was nothing less than fantastic even if we make due allowance for the fact that many of the fragments are cited by the grammarians who are interested in oddities, which probably give a wrong impression of his work as a whole. Gellius, however, testifies clearly to this aspect of his work.[38] Such monstrosities occur as *silentus, meminens* (an effort to render μεμνημένος), *pudoricolor, trisaeclisenex,* and *subductisupercilicarptores,* cf. ὀφρυανασπασίδαι.[39] There are also many diminutives and Greek loan-words. Obviously Laevius was an innovator trying to overcome that *patrii sermonis egestas* of which not many years later Lucretius complained. He went much too far, but several of his principles were sound. The use of diminutives, of compounds, and of Greek loan-words are all striking characteristics of Catullus.

In other respects also Laevius was breaking ground for Catullus and other poets of the following generation. Like them he turned away from Ennius and the older Roman poets to the Hellenistic and Alexandrian Greeks. Like them he preferred the shorter forms of poetry,[40] and his subjects were to a large extent erotic; cf. the titles *Adonis, Alcestis, Helena, Ino, Sirenocirca,* and especially *Protesilaudamia*—the same story which Catullus used as an illustration in the sixty-eighth poem. There are glimpses of technique common to the Alexandrians and Catullus: the speech made by characters (Helen addressing Paris); Hector as a lover apostrophizing the wreath woven for him by Andromache.[41] Did Laevius advance beyond this objective treatment of erotic myths to the expression of his own love? Leo thinks this possible and compares a number of fragments with Catullus XXXII (to Ipsimilla or Ipsithilla).[42] But this interpretation of the fragments is hardly justified. The chief difficulty is that Laevius certainly put speeches into the mouths of his characters. In brief fragments, therefore, it is never possible to be sure whether Laevius himself or a character is speaking. We need more context.[43]

Laevius was making a serious attempt to Romanize the lighter poetry of the Greeks—the favorite domain of Catullus—and like Catullus he was employing for this purpose a variety of lyric meters. The absence of the elegiac distich from the fragments is probably a mere accident and yet it may indicate that Laevius rather avoided this meter. Most of his Greek models were probably in elegiac form, and it may be conjectured that one of his innovations consisted in substituting for the Alexandrian Greek elegiacs of his direct models a variety of lyric meters which he Latinized from the early Greek melic poets. If this was his method, he again anticipated Catullus and, indeed, Horace.

Thus in many ways Laevius was a true forerunner of Catullus but on the whole the fragments create an unfavorable impression of his skill. He seems to have been a schoolmaster turned poet—one who knew his material from the technical side, but who lacked the ability and the taste to accomplish much that as art was worth while. It is probably not to be held against him that he was subjected to criticism[44]—so were Catullus, Horace, and many another good poet—but it is significant that he attracted little attention. Nobody speaks of him with praise, not even Gellius, who would not have failed to find something admirable in a poet of that (to him) ancient period if anything admirable was to be found. In date and in the crudity of his work Laevius belongs with an earlier generation, but in point of view and in the kind of work he attempted he must certainly be classed as a pioneer in Catullus' own school.

With Catullus and his contemporaries Roman poetry suddenly leaps close to maturity. In some departments it achieves a perfection never afterward surpassed; in all departments it displays a remarkable improvement. This great leap forward was, as I have already remarked, probably less sudden than it seems to us for the reason that we are not able to trace all its details, but it remains almost unparalleled.   In the age of Sulla, *ca.* 80–75 B.C., we have the crudities of Laevius; only twenty to twenty-five years later we have Catullus, and the greatest successes which he and his contemporaries achieved were won by extending the kind of work begun or developed by the erotic epigrammatists and by Laevius. We must not forget, however, that side by side with these newer tendencies ran an older tradition going back in general to Ennius.   To this tradition Catullus also owed a debt, especially in matters of style and meter, but a much smaller debt and one of which he was hardly conscious. Nevertheless just as his lyric meters, for example, could not have reached so high a degree of perfection without the work of such predecessors as Laevius, so his hexameters and his distichs could not have been developed without the work of Ennius and other pioneers.

In the age of Catullus, then, there were two main schools of poetry, if we may venture to call them schools: an older school following in general the Ennian traditions, and a new school following in general the lines laid down by Laevius (although they neglected Laevius himself) and the erotic epigrammatists. The dividing line between these schools was not always sharply drawn—certain individuals, for example Varro of Atax,[45] seem to have shared in both—but in many respects the two were quite distinct. The newer school exerted much greater influence upon Catullus and I shall examine briefly its characteristics.

My text is an illuminating remark of Cicero's. The great orator was fond of poetry, at which he often tried his own hand, and he was particularly fond of Ennius whom he frequently quoted. To one of these quotations he subjoins the remark, "O poetam egregium quamquam ab his cantoribus Euphorionis contemnitur." The words occur in the *Tusculan Disputations* (iii. 45) and must have been written about 45 B.C., some eight or nine years after the death of Catullus. Cicero recognizes clearly that there was at that time a group of contemporary Roman poets who despised Ennius and admired Euphorion, the representative of a certain type of Alexandrianism. Cicero himself still persists in his lifelong devotion to Ennius[46] and stigmatizes the old poet's contemptuous opponents with a contemptuous phrase of his own, "these singers—this choir—of Euphorion's."

Cicero names no poet whom he regarded as a member of Euphorion's choir, but two other remarks of his have been universally taken to be references to the same group. Describing his crossing of the Adriatic on the way home from his province, 50 B.C., he writes to Atticus (VII. 2. 1):

flavit ab Epiro lenissimus Onchesmites.

Hunc σπονδειάζοντα, si cui voles τῶν νεωτέρων, pro tuo vendito.

"You may have this spondaic line and sell it to any one of the moderns you please." Thus Cicero characterizes the spondaic line as an affectation of certain poets whom he calls the "younger ones," the "moderns," and it cannot be accident that the use of the spondaic line is a striking characteristic of Catullus' short epic (LXIV) in which spondaic lines are relatively much more common than anywhere else in Latin.[47]

Cicero's last remark concerns another bit of metrical technique. In his *Orator* (§161) he remarks that the *novi poetae*, the "new poets," avoid the elision of a final -s, as in *optumus*, before a following consonant. Again it cannot be accident that there is only one certain example of this phenomenon in all Catullus,[48] though his great contemporary Lucretius, who in general followed the Ennian tradition, often makes use of it. Furthermore, we should exclude this single example because it is evident that Catullus is here mimicking and mocking his enemy Gellius for retaining a device which he himself regards as crude.[49]

In both these details of technique, then, Catullus falls into line with the poets whom Cicero calls "moderns" and *poetae novi;* in both he stands opposed to Ennius and his followers. The "singers of Euphorion," whom Cicero mentions as despisers of Ennius, must be identified with these "new poets," these "younger ones," these "moderns," who were in revolt against the older school. Many of our literary historians of Rome have borrowed for the rebels Cicero's term νεώτεροι. Cicero in turn borrowed it from the earlier battle of the books of Alexandrian days in which Apollonius and the followers of the older tradition were called "the Homerians," while their opponents under the lead of Callimachus, whom Catullus particularly admired, were called νεώτεροι, the "moderns," the "young poets."

Even without Cicero's testimony, however, we should be able to infer that there were two opposing camps of poets in the Rome of Catullus' day. Catullus wholly avoids the longer kinds of poetry and there is good evidence that many of his contemporaries were of the same mind. Like Catullus, and still earlier like Callimachus, they prefer the small poem, whether in distichs or in lyric meter, the elegy, the epithalamium, and especially the short epic or epyllion. In fact the young poets adopted and transferred to Latin literature Callimachus' famous principle μέγα βιβλίον, μέγα κακόν,⁵⁰ "big book, big bore." The battle raged most fiercely about the epyllion. The composition of one of these miniature epics became a mark of caste. The only complete extant example of the period is Catullus' *Wedding of Peleus and Thetis*, but the titles of several others are known: the *Zmyrna* of Helvius Cinna, the *Io* of Calvus, the *Lydia* of Valerius Cato.⁵¹ The importance of the epyllion was due not only to the fact that it symbolized the difference between the current schools as it had done in the days of Callimachus, but also that it afforded to the young poets the best field for the display of their principles. The subjects of these epyllia were always Greek myths, often rather obscure and generally erotic. The Romans found these stories already worked out with refined art in many kinds of late Greek literature. Their object was not to translate, but to produce equivalent artistic compositions in Latin. They wished to be Roman νεώτεροι. The successful accomplishment of this object required knowledge not only of the myths, but above all of the literary methods and technique of later Greek poetry. The Romans had come to appreciate and understand this refined art, but appreciation is one thing and technical skill is another. The acqui- sition of the latter meant work, and these young poets did not shrink from work; they gloried in it. Catullus epitomizes the situation in a sentence when he says (XCV) that the *Zmyrna* of his friend Helvius Cinna was published nine years after it was begun.[52] From the point of view of the young poets the epyllion represented the pinnacle of artistic effort. The author must be a *doctus poeta*, one who possessed both learning and technical skill in addition to inspiration, and his composition must not be hasty hack work, but a real *carmen vigilatum*, a poem resulting from midnight toil.

The watchword of the young poets was, in brief, artistry, with all that the word implies. They saw that Roman poetry greatly needed improvement in artistic technique; on this they concentrated their efforts and with success. They hated the slovenly work which could hardly be avoided in long-winded compositions. This was one of their reasons for pre- ferring the shorter forms of poetry. In the ninety- fifth poem Catullus sneers at the "five hundred thou- sand verses" of Hortensius in contrast with the few hundred to which Cinna's *Zmyrna* must have been limited; in the twenty-second he sneers at the "ten thousand or more" of that "goat milker" Suffenus, who was to him the very personification of the poisonous versifier (XIV. 19). The young poets emphasized quality against quantity with a vigor equal to that of Horace in the next generation.

Thus the epyllion afforded the young poets the best opportunity for the display of their principles, but of course they extended these principles to the rest of their favorite forms. Of these forms they had no monopoly, for some of them were practiced by poets of the older school.   Apart from the epyllion a preference for the shorter forms may be a hint, though it is not a proof, that a given poet belonged to the new school.   Any poet might write elegy, or epithalamium, or the very short poem in lyric or elegiac verse.   The real criterion was a difference in artistic treatment, and since very little survives of the work of Catullus' contemporaries, it is impossible in many cases to apply this test.   If then we attempt to name the members of the modern school, we must rely chiefly upon ancient statements which serve to affiliate each poet with one group or the other.

Valerius Cato has usually been regarded as the leader of the moderns.   Not only was he considerably older than any other poet who can possibly be designated for this position—he was born not later than 100 B.C.— but also he was both poet and teacher.   As a teacher he had a reputation for his lectures on poetry and his help-fulness to those of his pupils who were interested in poetic composition.   Among these pupils were probably Furius Bibaculus, Ticidas, Helvius Cinna, and possibly even Catullus, although there is no specific evidence for this last conjecture.   Cato's own compositions included erotic poetry and at least one epyllion, the *Lydia*,— *doctorum maxima cura liber*, as Ticidas says.[53]   He lived to a ripe old age and died perhaps as late as 25 B.C.

In addition to Valerius Cato it has been the custom of historians of Roman literature to classify almost all the poets of Catullus' day as "moderns."   No doubt the new movement was all the rage and many were trying their hand at the favorite *genres* of the young poets.   But in order to prove a given poet an adherent of the school we need to know something about his

literary opinions and on this point the scanty evidence
at our disposal rarely gives us a reliable hint. We are
sure, however, of Catullus' friends Calvus, Helvius
Cinna, and Caecilius, and fairly sure of Furius Bibaculus, Ticidas, and Memmius.[54] Fortunately there is no
doubt that Catullus himself was one of the group,
and indeed the greatest of them all. A part of the
evidence for this statement has already been given and
indeed it could be proved without any other evidence
by the nature of Catullus' poetic art which I shall study
later. But it happens that Catullus was not a silent
partisan; his literary opinions are often clearly stated
or implied in his own words, as, for example, in the
praise of Cinna's *Zmyrna* which I have already mentioned. In that poem, it will be remembered, Catullus
not only approves this epyllion and the long, careful
toil which his friend had expended upon it, but also
he contrasts the poem with the long-winded verses of
Hortensius, which to him represent the opposite qualities. He contrasts also the *Annales* of Volusius and
emphasizes the brevity of the epyllion.[55] And finally
he states his own fondness for the epyllion in opposition
to popular liking for long-winded poetry as typified
by Antimachus. There is a biting quality in the poet's
criticism of the long-winded poets—Hortensius, Volusius,[56] and Antimachus—which proves that Catullus
is here not merely sympathizing with the ideals of his
friend Helvius Cinna; he is himself an active partisan.
He is issuing a manifesto against those who, like
Cicero, were rather contemptuous of that kind of
poetic art which was best illustrated in the short epic,
and it must not be forgotten that Catullus himself
wrote one of these pieces. His tone indicates that
whether he himself had been criticized or not—we do

not know the date of LXIV or indeed of Cinna's *Zmyrna*—he felt himself to be under the fire of those who disliked the short epic. Moreover his words echo two well-known principles of him who led the young poets of Alexandria: the "big book, big bore," and the dislike of common hackneyed things (including the long epic)—the things liked by the mass.[57] "Culture," as Arthur Twining Hadley once said, "is the opposite of absorption in the obvious." Unlike Lucilius, Catullus did not write for the "man in the street."

When Catullus speaks of the "swollen Antimachus" (*tumidus*) he is using an example of the "big book" which Callimachus had used, for the latter had characterized the *Lyde*, the long, elegiac work of Antimachus, as a "big, dull, and obscure composition."[58] Thus Catullus adopted certain definite tenets from the creed of Callimachus.

His admiration of Callimachus is further attested by his translations. Only one of these survives, *The Tress of Berenice* (LXVI), but it is probable that he made others.[59] His attitude toward the older school repeats the attitude of Callimachus toward the older school of his day, although the respective reforms of the two poets were not in all cases the same; Catullus had to do much in the way of reforming immature technique, while Callimachus was reacting against a technique that was over-mature. Both were, however, seeking to revivify by novel methods the poetry of their times and in this also Catullus secured valuable hints from his great predecessor.

Catullus believed that a poet needed the knowledge and careful training in his art which can be acquired only by hard work. This is evident from his praise of Cinna's *Zmyrna* and Caecilius' *Magna Mater* (XXXV);

it is evident from the fact that when he is asked to compose a poem of consolation, one of his reasons for refusal is his lack (at the time) of enough books (LXVIII. 33 and 36); it is evident everywhere in his own work, of course; but I am speaking at present of the poet's explicit or implicit opinions. In this respect also Catullus held the same view as Callimachus who was one of the scholar poets of Alexandria. At Rome the word for a poet of this type was *doctus*. A *doctus poeta* was not merely a poet of native ability, but one who *knew*, one who could use his gift and knowledge to good effect.[60] *Doctus* in the literary sphere corresponded very closely to *urbanus* in the social sphere; both words imply the possession of adequate knowledge together with skill and taste. Suffenus, who was socially *urbanus* but in literature the opposite of *doctus*, was to Catullus a weird mixture, a gentleman in society but a boor in literature. To the *doctus poeta* the Muses were of course *doctae*—Catullus calls them *doctae virgines* (LXV. 2)—and in complimenting the girl who was filled with admiration upon hearing Caecilius read from his *Great Mother*, Catullus calls her *Musa doctior* (XXXV. 17); she can appreciate the work of a poet who knows how to write.

Posterity gave Catullus a place among the *docti poetae*, as he himself would have wished. The epithet is applied to him eight or ten times—no other occurs more than once or twice—and it is especially significant that Lygdamus uses it in a passage ([Tibullus] III. 6, 41) referring to the *Peleus and Thetis*, the poem in which Catullus' *doctrina* is most obvious.

It is then in the sphere of narrative poetry, especially in the short epic, that the modern tendency of Catullus and his circle is clearest. But the same tendency strongly affected all their poetry. In recognizing this we should guard ourselves from thinking that these young poets closed their eyes to the beauties of early Greek poetry—Homer and the lyric poets especially— and confined themselves wholly to Callimachus and his successors. Such a view would be very far from the truth; Catullus himself greatly admired Sappho, and it was not Homer against whom Callimachus fulminated but those who in his own time were still trying to be Homeric in the fashion of Homer. If we except the epyllion, Catullus and his friends did not learn from the later Greeks new kinds of poetry; they learned to attempt old kinds in a new way. They learned to look at all Greek poetry through modern Greek—often contemporary Greek—glasses. And this point of view was precisely what Roman poetry needed at the time— to throw away its stilts and plant its feet upon the solid earth.

In this lecture I have sought to show in general terms how the earlier Roman poets prepared the way for Catullus and what part he took in the literary controversies of his time. The attempt has led us inevitably from Roman poetry to the Greek, but in both cases we have been dealing for the most part with the influence of literary tradition. In the next lecture an effort will be made to complete the background by a brief study of the poet's life, for together with the influence of tradition his own experience also is constantly reflected in his work.

CHAPTER IV

THE POET'S LIFE AND TRAINING

In an effort to sketch the historical background of Catullus' poetry I have already touched upon a number of topics—for example his opinions on poetry—which might well have been included in a lecture on his life. Those elements of the background which belong rather to literary history merge, in the case of Catullus, with others which are more directly biographical and a knowledge of both is indispensable to the interpretation of his poetry. I have carried the account of Roman literary tendencies into the lifetime of the poet. With many of these he was intimately concerned, for he was strongly influenced by them and probably he helped effectively to guide them. All this is reflected here and there in his verse. But side by side with these things and not everywhere to be separated from them there is the influence of life in the ordinary sense—his birth, his training, and all the more or less accidental events which befell him during his brief existence. With some of these I intend to deal in the present lecture.

It is not my intention to write in full the life of Catullus, but rather to touch upon those aspects of it which are most helpful in interpreting his poetry. Incidentally it may not be amiss to discuss a number of points which are not certain, for writing the biography of Catullus and especially the story of his love for Lesbia has been a favorite pastime not only of philologists but of men of letters generally and the resultant disquisitions are but too often composed without due regard to the strict interpretation of the ancient evidence. This evidence consists for the most part of the poet's own statements, to which must be added a number of references, some of them of great value, in other Latin writers.[1]

The poet's full name was probably Gaius Valerius Catullus. The names Valerius and Catullus are certain; and there is not much doubt about Gaius, which rests upon better authority than Quintus.[2] He was often called by later writers Catullus of Verona (*Catullus Veronensis*). The dates of his birth and death cannot be established with certainty. Saint Jerome says that he was born in 87 B.C. and died at Rome in the thirtieth year of his age (*XXX aetatis anno*). This notice is placed under the year of Abraham 1959 or 1960 (58–57 B.C.) in the good Saint's *Chronicle*, and since "thirtieth year" or "fortieth year," as the case may be, regularly signifies in Jerome the completed thirtieth year or fortieth year the latest date indicated for the poet's death is 57 B.C. But this date is certainly wrong. The poet refers to the invasion of Germany and Britain by Caesar in 55 B.C. (XI, XXIX, XLV), to the second consulship of Pompey, 55 B.C. (CXIII), to Pompey's portico, which was opened in 55 B.C. (LV). Catullus was still living therefore in 55 and probably in 54 B.C. Saint Jerome, or quite possibly Suetonius, who was one of his chief sources, may have followed a statement that Catullus died at the age of thirty which through some error he attached to the year 87 as the birth year, although the correct year was 84 B.C. If this is correct the poet was born in 84 B.C. and died *ca.* 54 B.C. The only difficulty in accepting this conclusion is that it increases the difference between the ages of Catullus and Lesbia—if Lesbia was Clodia, the wife of Metellus Celer. On this hypothesis she would have been ten or eleven years older than the poet, for she was born probably *ca.* 95–94 B.C. This is not a serious difficulty to anybody who remembers the many Pendennises of life and literature and especially the fact that Marcus Caelius Rufus, who could not have been more than a year older than Catullus and may have been younger, had a violent love affair with this very Clodia when she was drawing dangerously near the age of forty.[3] Clodia was undoubtedly very attractive to young men, and the cases of Catullus and Caelius exemplify the truth, that

> Sixty takes to seventeen,
> Nineteen to forty-nine!

But how shall we account for Saint Jerome's statement that Catullus was born in 87 B.C.? One of the consuls of 84 B.C., Cornelius Cinna, had also been consul in 87 B.C., say the theorists, and so Jerome (or Suetonius who may have been his source) confused the two years. This is a favorite method of accounting for the good Saint's numerous errors. Indeed it has been used so often that one grows skeptical—especially when we have not two pairs of similarly named consuls to explain the confusion but only half a pair and that half (Cinna) was consul every year from 87 to 84!

Another explanation is more attractive. Let us suppose that Suetonius (or some source of his) took LII as the latest poem in which Catullus speaks of immediate death as preferable to the sight of such scoundrels as Nonius in public office and Vatinius perjuring himself by his consulship.[4] Then, knowing that Catullus was born in 87 and that Vatinius was consul in 47 B.C., he noted that the poet was forty years old at the time of his death. The numeral was expressed by the customary symbol xxxx and by the omission of one symbol became xxx, a type of error which is very common in Latin manuscripts. Hence arose the wrong "thirtieth year" which in turn caused the erroneous statement that the poet died 57 B.C. On the whole it seems more probable that Catullus was born in 87 B.C., but certainty cannot be attained unless additional evidence is discovered, and 84 B.C. will always have its champions.

Catullus came from a prominent and wealthy Veronese family. His father was a friend of Caesar's and repeatedly entertained that great man when duty and politics brought him to Cis-Alpine Gaul in the winters between his campaigns beyond the Alps. The family[5] had a villa on the promontory of Sirmione at the southern end of the Lago di Garda, and Catullus speaks of another villa, probably his own, on the confines of the fashionable town of Tibur (now Tivoli), about eighteen miles east of Rome.[6] The poet's life in Rome affords the best proof of his social position and his means or rather his father's generosity. He was a young man about town, supported undoubtedly by a generous allowance from his father, and knowing many persons of rank and position, for example at least one of the Manlii Torquati, Quintus Hortensius, the orator, Licinius Calvus, the orator and poet, Helvius Cinna, the poet, Asinius Pollio, Cornelius Nepos, and many others. He must have worked hard at his poetry but apart from this his only semblance of an occupation was the position which he held for a year on the staff of Memmius during the latter's propraetorship in Bithynia. His duties in this capacity were probably not very onerous and certainly he made no money (X. 9 ff.).

The chief events of his life were his unfortunate love for Lesbia, the death of his dearly loved brother, his journey to Bithynia, and his hostility to Caesar and his henchmen. From these events spring much of his best verse and all of them except the last are linked with one another.

I have not time to discuss in full the poet's affair with Lesbia, but it is necessary to make a few remarks about certain aspects of it. Ovid tells us that Lesbia was a pseudonym and Apuleius reveals her real name, Clodia. In the sixteenth century Victorius[7] suggested that this Clodia was identical with the Clodia who was a sister of Cicero's inveterate enemy, Publius Clodius, and the wife of Quintus Caecilius Metellus Celer, who was consul 60 B.C. and died 59 B.C. This identification has been accepted by the vast majority of scholars particularly since 1862 when Ludwig Schwabe published his very thorough and careful *Quaestiones Catullianae*. All that is known from Catullus about Lesbia tallies so closely with all that is known from Cicero and others about this particular Clodia (the second of three sisters) that very strong arguments are necessary to refute the conclusion that the ladies were one and the same. Such arguments have not been forthcoming and yet there have always been and will continue to be skeptics. The most thoroughgoing in recent years is Max Rothstein, who in 1923 revived the old view that Lesbia was not Clodia, the wife of Metellus Celer, but possibly her younger sister, the divorced wife of Lucullus, and that the unnamed lady of rank with whom Catullus shows that he was desperately in love (LXVIII) was some other person whom we cannot identify at all.[8]

Rothstein merely multiplies hypotheses and it would be easy, if there were time, to refute or rebut his arguments point by point. One point indeed must be considered, for it concerns the chronology of the poems. If Lesbia was not Clodia, the wife of Metellus Celer, the earlier part of the chronology so carefully worked out by Brunér, Schwabe, and others falls to the ground. But the identification provides a chronology that works, and the test of a good theory is that it works, i.e., it accounts for the facts. Let us see. The sixty-eighth poem proves that the husband (*vir*) of the lady mentioned in the poem was alive in the early stages of Catullus' love.[9] If this husband was Metellus Celer, then the love affair began a considerable time before his death, 59 B.C.[10] He was in Cis-Alpine Gaul 62 B.C., but he must have come to Rome in 61 B.C. to sue for the consulship which he held in 60 B.C. Furthermore Lesbia was beginning to be unfaithful to Catullus when the sixty-eighth poem was written (135 ff.) so that we must date the poem rather late in the affair, and since Caelius Rufus' affair with Clodia was at its height in 58–57 B.C. and Catullus had broken with Lesbia by the time he went to Bithynia (57 B.C.) we may assume that LXVIII was written about 59 B.C. and (with Schwabe) that Catullus' love began not less than two years earlier, *ca.* 61 B.C.

Moreover, the sixty-eighth poem enables us, on the generally accepted hypothesis, to date approximately the death of Catullus' brother. When this poem was written the brother had recently died in the Troad;[11] the poet was utterly crushed by the loss. This sad event occurred, then, toward the end of the Lesbia

affair, *ca.* 60–59 B.C., and the affectionate duty of performing the last sad rites at his brother's tomb (CI) was
one of the chief reasons for the poet's journey to Asia.

Thus the sixty-eighth poem supplies very important
chronological evidence—if the lady mentioned is
Lesbia-Clodia. All this is cast aside by Rothstein,
who finds no reliable chronological references in the
poems until 56 B.C. (XLVI the earliest), about a year
and a half before Catullus' death; a conclusion which
will be rejected, in my opinion, by anybody who will
examine the evidence point by point. Indeed several
scholars have already rejected it.[12]

But to revert to Lesbia—whether she was or was not
the infamous *Clodia quadrantaria*[13] makes no difference
in our estimate of the poetry which she inspired. To
Catullus she was beautiful, witty, altogether the most
charming of women, but alas! she was fickle and faithless. At last he was forced with a sore heart to recognize her for what she was. Whatever the moralists
may say, we must not forget that to him his love
seemed pure. He loved her at first, to use his own
words, "not as the common herd love a mistress, but
as a father loves his sons" (LXXII). But this love
became a torment to him, ruinous he calls it, and like
some fell disease. The effort to tear it from his heart
nearly cost him his life, but he succeeded, and his
heart was not utterly broken, for there are poems
written after he had torn himself away from Lesbia
which prove that he was once more captain of his soul
and that his old gaiety had returned.

The story of Catullus and Lesbia is one of the world's
famous passions. Countless writers have tried to
present it in prose form but with very indifferent success. He who would tell it really well needs more

insight than has yet been applied to it.   But why transpose it into prose?   The real lovers of poetry will always turn to him who felt it all and laid bare his heart for all to read, Catullus himself.

We may condemn Catullus, we may even condemn Lesbia, forgetting that she cannot defend herself—for no words of hers have survived, but we cannot forget that Catullus' thankless passion stimulated some of the world's finest love poetry, to say nothing of some of its most revolting invectives.   The rôle which the affair plays in his poetry is indicated by the fact that some thirty of his poems,[14] more than a quarter of them all, owe their existence to his love or hate of Lesbia.   It was, in his own words, a "long love" (LXXVI) and we can still trace it from its inception through periods of happiness, disagreement, reconciliation, doubt, torture, and almost utter despair to that final prayer for release (LXXVI) which the kindly gods granted.   The passion must have lasted for at least three years, *ca.* 61–59 B.C. Later still there was a final echo, for after Catullus had broken away, had spent a year abroad, and had become once more master of himself, Lesbia made a last appeal to him for one more reconciliation.   This appeal he answers in a poem unexcelled for high irony and scorn, and for beauty—a poem which proves that there could indeed be nothing more between himself and Lesbia.   Furius and Aurelius have come with Lesbia's appeal and the eleventh poem is the poet's answer to her envoys:

> Furius, and thou Aurelius, pledged to be
>   Catullus' comrades whether he explore
> The farthest Indies, where the Eastern sea
>   With far-resounding billow pounds the shore,

Or travel to the Parthians, armed with bows,
   The languid Arabs, Scythians of the plain,
Or to the land where Nile's dark water flows
   Through seven mouths and dyes the level main,

Or scale the lofty Alps, where Caesar passed,
   And view the landmarks that he left behind—
The Gallic Rhine, the raging sea, and last,
   The Britons, most remote of humankind;

Prepared with him to meet and brave them all,
   Whate'er the will of heaven may provide,
Pray bear unto my love this message small
   And far from gracious—nothing else beside:

Let her live on and thrive in love unchaste,
   Holding her countless paramours in thrall,
She who is true to none, but who doth waste
   Again and yet again the strength of all.

But my love let her now regard no more,
   For that has fallen through her sin alone
As some fair flower the ploughshare passes o'er
   Droops on the meadow's edge where it has grown.[15]

Again I have outrun chronology, for the eleventh
poem, as the references to Caesar's invasions of Germany and Britain show, must have been written in
55 or 54 B.C. Just before this period occurred Catullus'
journey to Bithynia. He was a member of the governor's staff, and the governor was Gaius Memmius, a
man well versed in literature, especially Greek literature,[16] and himself a poet. It is natural enough that
such a man should have included among the members
of his suite two poets, Catullus and his friend Helvius
Cinna. Memmius, who had been praetor in Rome

during the year 58 B.C., governed Bithynia from the latter part of 57 to some time in 56 B.C.[17] The paramount motive to Catullus for this journey was undoubtedly, as I have already said, the duty of performing the last rites at his brother's tomb in the Troad. We may indeed feel certain that his father and the rest of the poet's relatives were as anxious as the poet that these rites should be performed. The first four lines of the one hundred and first poem express this purpose. This poem, which was so deeply impressed on the heart of Tennyson, is not a grave epigram although it is related to this type and also to the elegy. It reflects a situation and a mood: the poet stands by his brother's tomb making offerings to the dead and giving vent to his own grief:

Over many a land, and over many an ocean
  Here to thy desolate grave, brother, oh brother, I come!
Only on thee to bestow death's last forlornest bestrewments,
  Only in vain to conjure thy unanswering dust.
Woe is me for the doom that of thee so untimely bereft me,
  Hapless brother, when thou wert so relentlessly ta'en!
Now meanwhile the tribute our fathers from ages primeval
  Gave in their sorrow to those whom in life they had loved,
Take, all drenched with the tears of brotherly anguish; and,
          brother,
  Ever be blessings on thee—fare thee well evermore![18]

One must assume, I think, that the poet visited his brother's tomb as soon as possible after his arrival in Asia in 57 B.C.[19] Nothing is known of the route followed on this outward journey, but the customary one by way of Brundisium, the Adriatic, and Macedonia would have afforded Catullus a good opportunity for the visit to the Troad, which was close to the western border of Bithynia, the province in which he was to serve.

Nothing more is known of his activities until the spring of 56 B.C. when he was about to leave Nicaea on his homeward journey, as we learn from the forty-sixth poem. The gaiety and eagerness to be off which characterize this pretty little piece are quite inconsistent with the view that he was just about to visit his brother's tomb. If, on the other hand, he had already paid that sad visit some months earlier, the tone of the poem presents no difficulty.

> Warm spring is here: the cold is gone:
>   Before the Zephyr's gentle breeze
> The equinoctial rage has flown:
>   Ah, 'tis on days like these
> I long to leave the sultry plain
> And breathe a clearer air again.
>
> "O for the road, the open way"—
>   I hear a voice within me cry:
> My eager feet brook no delay.
>   Good-bye, dear friends, good-bye.
> Far have we travelled from our Rome,
> But diverse paths will lead us home.[20]

This poem informs us that the members of Memmius' suite left home together but are returning by different routes. Catullus bids his comrades farewell, expressing his intentions to "fly to the famous cities of Asia." From this we need not infer that he parted at Nicaea from absolutely all his comrades or (because he declares that his "feet are tingling with eagerness") that he contemplated a journey chiefly by land. To go home from Nicaea, which was inland, he had to journey both by land and by water and it is more than probable that a congenial friend or two accompanied him, for example Helvius Cinna, who as we know in his own words returned at least part of the way on "a Bithynian ship."[21]   Was this Bithynian ship identical with the yacht (*phaselus*) whose voyage, described in the fourth poem, so exactly reproduces one of the routes which Catullus may very easily have followed and on which he himself, according to the traditional view, returned? The suggestion has been made and it is a tempting one.[22]

Whether the famous old *phaselus*—"pinnace," Munro called her—was in fact the property of Catullus, whether she carried him first to those "famous cities of Asia," then through the Cyclades and the Adriatic, and finally whether he actually took her or had her taken into the Lago di Garda (*Benacus*), there to be laid up and dedicated to the great twin brethren, are questions still being debated by scholars.   To recount to you all the suggestions which have been made to clear up the difficulties of this single poem would require more than the time at my disposal for this entire lecture.   I must, however, say a word or two.   But first the poem:

> Stranger, the bark you see before you says
> That in old times and in her early days
> She was a lively vessel that could make
> The quickest voyages, and overtake
> All her competitors with sail or oar;
> And she defies the rude Illyrian shore,
> And Rhodes with her proud harbor, and the seas
> That intersect the scattered Cyclades,
> And the Propontic and the Thracian coast,
> (Bold as it is) to contradict her boast.
> She calls to witness the dark Euxine sea
> And mountains that had known her as a tree,
> Before her transformation, when she stood
> A native of the deep Cytorian wood,

Where all her ancestors had flourished long,
And, with their old traditionary song,
Had whispered her responses to the breeze
And waked the chorus of her sister trees.

Amastris, from your haven forth she went,
You witnessed her first outset and descent,
Adventuring on an unknown element.
From thence she bore her master safe and free
From danger and alarm through many a sea;
Nor ever once was known to lag behind,
Foremost on every tack, with every wind.
At last, to this fair inland lake, she says
She came to pass the remnant of her days,
Leaving no debt due to the Deities
For vows preferred in danger on the seas:
Clear of incumbrance, therefore, and all other
Contentious claims, to Castor or his brother
As a free gift and offering she devotes
Herself, as long as she survives and floats.[23]

These lines are full of the liveliest personal interest:
the route followed by the pinnace is one by which the
poet may very well have returned, the pinnace lies
on the bank of a "clear lake," and we know from the
thirty-first poem that Catullus not only loved the
Lago di Garda but that he returned thither—to Sirmio
—before he went to Rome. And yet he does not give
the name of the lake or the name of the man whom
he calls "owner" (*erus*) of the yacht. How careless of
him! Why could he not be as explicit as Ovid, who
carefully describes much of his voyage into exile and
clearly states that he traveled on three different ships.
In this respect unfortunately Catullus differed from
Ovid and we must do what we can with him.

Today it is impossible to take even the smallest sea-
going craft by water up the Mincio into the Lago di
Garda. At Peschiera by the lake in 1924 I questioned an
Italian sailor on this point. "Non c'e acqua," was
his reply, and conditions, so far as the natural features
of the river are concerned, could hardly have been
very different in antiquity. Because of more extensive
forests on the Alpine watershed there was probably a
somewhat greater and steadier flow in the Mincio.
In our day the depth from May to January (Catullus
must have returned within these months) varies between .78 and 1.18 meters[24]—a depth sufficient on the
average for a small sea-going yacht of the ancient
type. The fall of the river in the twenty-seven miles
from the lake to the lagoons of Mantua is about one
hundred and fifty-four feet,[25] or a little over five and a
half feet per mile, not an excessively rapid descent.
The real difficulties must have been shallows necessi-
tating dredged channels or portages. If, as Count
Montanari thought possible,[26] there was an ancient
canal from the Adige near Verona to the Valeggio on
the Mincio (about seven miles by the river below the
lake), most of these difficulties were avoided. Lacking
proof of the existence of such a canal or of an improved
channel we are forced to assume that the pinnace was
dragged over portages and up a stream which was
often very shallow. The assumption is not entirely
impossible, however, as we shall see presently. Meanwhile I suggest a second possible route. The Adige,
the fine river on which Verona is situated, parallels the
eastern shore of the lake. In pre-glacial times the
river actually flowed into the lake near the present
town of Garda toward the southern end.[27] Now directly
east of the peninsula of Sirmio, where Catullus had

his villa, there is a low divide only three and a half
miles wide between the lake at Lazise and the river.
At that point the river is about 100 feet above the lake
so that a ship way—if there was one—had to rise only
about 170 feet over the divide and then descend to the
lake—by no means an impossible thing when we
remember ancient feats of transportation, for example
the hauling of ships across the Isthmus of Corinth.[28]

Furthermore there was a motive for such transportation. Verona was on the trade routes from north to
south, from east to west. In a new country water
routes are the first to be utilized for heavy transportation. These routes (to the north) were (1) from
Verona up the Adige or up the Lago di Garda, (2)
from the Po up the Mincio and up Lago di Garda, and
it seems to me probable that one or both of them had
been so improved that a sentimental young man
actually had his faithful old craft brought home into
his favorite lake. The fact that he gives no hint of the
route by which the pinnace entered the lake creates a
presumption that there was a familiar route.

Or can we really believe that this *limpidus lacus* was
any other lake? Cichorius has tried to show that it
was Lake Apollonia in Bithynia, a lake connected
with the Propontis by a navigable stream (the Rhyn-
dacus), and that the entire poem is reminiscent of a
visit paid by Catullus to some guest friend there.[29]
But we read the poem, as the ancients read it, among
the poems of Catullus of Verona. Catullus had a
deep love for the Lago di Garda (XXXI) and he
mentions no other. His contemporaries must have
inferred, as we infer,[30] that the lake mentioned in this
poem was the lake to which he returned so thankfully
from his long journey. If he meant some foreign lake

and some friend's pinnace,[31] then he wrote a puzzle for his contemporaries and this particular kind of puzzle seems entirely out of harmony with his manner. The poem would be almost as much a puzzle if it referred, as some scholars believe, not to the actual pinnace, but to a model or a picture of her which he had dedicated at Sirmio.[32]

But whatever may be the truth about the pinnace, Catullus was home once more, probably in the summer or early autumn of 56 B.C. His homecoming needs no description of mine, for we have the poet's own words:

> Dear Sirmio, that art the very eye
> Of islands and peninsulas, that lie
> Deeply embosomed in calm inland lake,
> Or where the waves of the vast ocean break;
> Joy of all joys, to gaze on thee once more!
> I scarce believe that I have left the shore
> Of Thynia, and Bithynia's parching plain,
> And gaze on thee in safety once again!
> Oh, what more sweet than when, from care set free,
> The spirit lays its burden down, and we,
> With distant travel spent, come home and spread
> Our limbs to rest along the wished-for bed!
> This, this alone, repays such toils as these!
> Smile, then, fair Sirmio, and thy master please,—
> And you, ye dancing waters of the lake,
> Rejoice; and every smile of home awake![33]

But even Sirmio could not hold him long. Soon he is back in Rome—Rome where, as he had said at an earlier day (LXVIII. 35) he "plucked the blooms of life" (*illic mea carpitur aetas*). It is but a scant year and a half before the silence is to descend upon him. This is the period in which he makes the largest number of certain references to contemporary events and many of his activities are revealed. In 55–54 B.C. he rejects with scorn, as we have seen, Lesbia's final appeal for a reconciliation (XI). In the same period he continues his attacks on Caesar and Mamurra (XXIX, LVII), but his formal reconciliation with the great man must have occurred very soon afterward. In the same period he was renewing with old friends the associations which had been interrupted by his journey to Bithynia. Prominent among them were Veranius and Fabullus, otherwise unknown to us but dear to the poet. At an earlier date they had been in Spain[34] together, and at about the same time the poet was in Bithynia they had served on the staff of a certain Piso, probably the dissipated gentleman whom Cicero violently attacked in his speech *In Pisonem*. This Piso, Lucius Calpurnius Piso Caesoninus, was governor of Macedonia 57–55 B.C., and if we may believe Catullus, he had treated Fabullus and Veranius as scurvily there as he himself had been treated by Memmius in Bithynia.[35] Catullus uses unspeakable terms of abuse against both Piso and Memmius. Both of them, to judge by other evidence, were far from being admirable characters, but as to their scurvy treatment of the hungry retainers who flocked into the provinces one sometimes wonders.[36] Perhaps the motive which led Memmius, for example, to prevent the members of his suite from enriching themselves (X) was not wholly selfish. Perhaps the poor provincials were grateful. At any rate we should bear in mind that abuse from the mouth of a hot-tempered poet and a hostile advocate should be heavily discounted.

Many other poems reflect the poet's life at this period and show at the same time that he had entirely regained his spirits.

The fifty-third poem is a *bon mot* in verse. Gaius
Licinius Macer Calvus, the closest friend of Catullus,
delivered at least three swingeing attacks upon Caesar's
henchman Vatinius. Calvus was a great orator, but
physically he was a little man—*parvolus statura*, says
Seneca the Elder—and Catullus' anecdote combines
both facts in a compliment to his friend:

> Oh how I laughed the other day
> When into court I chanced to stray.
> Our Calvus in his peroration
> Consigned Vatinius to damnation
> And some one cried out:—"Strike me dumb,
> Can't he just talk, that Tommy Thumb!"[37]

The forty-fifth poem is a different type. The Roman
name Septimius coupled with the Greek Acme suggests
possibly a real love affair as the basis, but the poem may
be wholly imaginative. It is a little tableau: the lovers
protest their undying devotion as they clasp each other
in fond embrace, while Cupid flits about in the background, an amused and ironic eavesdropper. The poet's
light grace is at its best:

> Septimius cried, as on his breast
> His darling Acme he caressed,
> "My Acme, if I love not thee
> To madness, ay, distractedly,
> And with a love that well I know
> With time shall fonder, wilder grow,
> In Libya may I then, my sweet,
> Or India's burning deserts meet
> The green-eyed lion's hungry glare,
> And none be by to help me there!"
>
> As thus he whispered, Love was pleased
> And on the right propitious sneezed.

Then bending gently back her head,
And with that mouth, so rosy-red,
Impressing on his eyes a kiss,
His eyes, that drunken were with bliss,
"Oh, Septimillus, life!" cried she,
"So love our only master be,
As burns in me, thine Acme true,
A fire that thrills my marrow through,
Intenser, mightier, more divine,
Than any thou canst feel in thine!"

As thus she whispered, Love was pleased
And on the right propitious sneezed.

Now hallowed by such omens fair,
Each dotes on each, that happy pair.
He, sick with love, rates Acme's smiles
Above the East or Britain's isles;
Whilst Acme, to Septimius true,
For him, him only, doth renew
Love's first delights, and to her boy
Unfolds fresh treasuries of joy.

Were ever souls so lapped in bliss!
Was ever love so blest as this![38]

The time at my disposal has allowed me to give
only a few illustrations of the manner in which Catullus'
own poems contribute to our knowledge of his life.
To complete my sketch you must read a large majority
of the poems. Obviously much of their content,
especially the content of the shorter poems, is derived
from his own experience and observation. But this
fact is not enough to explain his poetry even if we
add to it his poetic inspiration. If we imagine for a
moment a Catullus richly endowed by nature with the
poetic instinct but uneducated and totally ignorant of

literature, he might indeed have produced poetry, but it would have been something entirely different in kind from that which he actually produced. In the tenth poem, for example, he works up a trifling anecdote into a delightful bit of verse. In the thirteenth he takes as his theme an invitation to dinner. If he had been without education or knowledge of literature, he would never have thought of such themes at all.[39] As we read his poetry our first thought is, "Here is a poet whose whole life is revealed in his verse."[40] Much of his life is indeed revealed there, and yet his literary biographer finds the material very incomplete.[41] I would gladly consign to oblivion more than one-quarter of his poems if I could gain in exchange a few others containing some information about his ancestry, something more explicit about life in the Verona of his day, something—anything—about his schooldays and youth down to about 61 B.C. Again we sigh regretfully when we compare Catullus with Ovid or with Horace. But again we must do the best we can.

Of what blood was Catullus? Reliable information on this point would be very helpful. The mere fact that he was born in Verona, which was not in Italic territory, does not prove that his blood was not Roman or not Italic. Verona apparently became a colony with Latin rights in 89 B.C.[42] and much earlier it must have been a busy trading place,[43] for it lay at the junction of important trade routes east and west, north and south. Possibly the poet was descended from some colonist or trader from the south who had settled in Verona. The family's wealth and importance suggest that for a generation at least it had been domiciled in the region of Verona. Perhaps they had grown rich through trade or as landed proprietors through their proximity to a trading center. On the other hand, the poet's genius seems un-Roman, un-Italic. Certainly he lacked the reserve and the self-restraint which are generally regarded as characteristic of the ancient Italic stocks. He was decidedly temperamental. And yet Catullus, like Pindar among the Boeotians, may have been one more exception to the general rule. Both Cicero and Ovid, for example, were temperamental, yet both were of Italic stock, the former Latin, the latter Paelignian with probably some Latin admixture.[44]

There is considerable basis, however, for the conjecture that Catullus had at least some Etruscan and Celtic blood. His *gens* name was Valerius, a common one, as inscriptions prove, in many parts of Italy, especially about Verona.[45] Valerii play important parts in the traditional accounts of Rome's early history and some have believed that the name was originally Sabine and therefore Italic. Much more probably it was Etruscan. W. Schulze, in his monumental book on Latin names,[46] compares Valerius with the older forms Volusius (Etruscan *velusna*) and Volesius[47] (Etr. *vlesi*). Both Vergil and Ovid knew traditions which point to an Etruscan origin. Vergil mentions a Valerus as an Etruscan ancestor of the Valerii. The intervocalic *r* shows that this is a comparatively late invention. Ovid speaks of a Volesus as the "founder of the ancestral name."[48] But if in the region of Rome the Valerii were once of Etruscan stock, there had been ample time for their original racial characteristics to reach the vanishing point before the birth of a Valerius Catullus. The Italic stocks became dominant there at a very early period. The conditions about Verona, as we shall see presently, were very different.

How is it with the cognomen Catullus?   Cognomina
of this type do not antedate the first century B.C.[49] If
then the poet's family was native to the Po Valley, it is
probable that Catullus' father in the final process of
Romanizing the family name added Catullus to Valerius.   Or the process may have been the reverse; Catullus
may have been the earlier of the two names.[50] Certain it
is that the poet always (over twenty times) calls himself
Catullus, never Valerius.   In this there may be a hint
that Catullus was the more important, the older name.[51]

Schulze regards the name Catullus as Celtic although
he admits that it may be connected with the Etruscan
catu.[52]   The names Valerius and Catullus certainly
suggest that the poet had both Etruscan and Celtic
blood in his veins, whether some ancestral Valerius
came from the south or not.   This conjecture becomes
plausible when we study the ethnography of the region
in which the poet was born.

Pliny calls Verona a town of the Raeti and Euganei,
and the statement seems to represent a reliable tradition.[53]   These peoples were of Etruscan stock and were
later overcome by the Celts—the Cenomani—coming
from Brescia (*Brixia*).   Catullus alone preserves the
tradition that Verona was founded from Brescia.   In
the sixty-seventh poem the door of a certain Veronese
house speaks of

Brixia Veronae mater amata meae.

But the Cenomani, indeed the Celts in general, did
not entirely destroy or expel the earlier peoples; they
broke their power, settled among them, and gradually
amalgamated with them.   The name Verona is probably
Celtic, but there must have been an older Etruscan
settlement on or near the site.   Raetian inscriptions

have been found in the hills nearby, and there are traces of cults which appear to have been Etruscan.[54] Thus Verona and the surrounding district including Sirmio, which belonged to the domain of Verona, were racially Etrusco-Celtic. Catullus knew the tradition that Verona had been founded by Celts. He also knew that Etruscans had once dwelt on the shores of the Lago di Garda, for, if the text (XXXI. 13) is correct, he calls its waters "Lydian,"

O Lydiae lacus undae,

referring to the belief, common in antiquity, that the Etruscans came from Lydia.

But of course neither an individual's name nor the predominant racial character of his native place establishes the racial affinities of that individual—especially when the native place is a center of thriving trade for men of several different stocks. Not long after Catullus' time Verona was the most prosperous town in that section of Italy, having far outstripped her neighbors Mantua and Brixia.[55] This was undoubtedly due to her favorable situation for trade. Indeed at a much earlier period, when Rome was subduing the Gauls of the Po Valley toward the close of the third century B.C., the Cenomani as a state sided with Rome against the other peoples of their race. Even then civilization advancing from the south and east along the trade routes had made some progress, and during the second century this progress became rapid. The importance of Verona as a center of trade provides a natural explanation of the wealth and prominence of Catullus' father, a citizen who repeatedly entertained Julius Caesar. In that generation at latest the family had become thoroughly Romanized.

Verona and other towns of the region beyond the
Po supplied Catullus with a considerable number of
themes for his verse. Of this fact we have already had
proof. But from his own words we can form but a
very inadequate conception of the Verona of his day.
When at the age of twenty-five or more he had come
to know Rome, he felt of course that Verona was
provincial (LXVIII. 27–30), no place for a young man
of fashion. Rome was the place in which to enjoy
life to the full (*ibid.* 34–35). This is natural enough;
no other town in Italy could be compared with Rome.
But was there sufficient culture at Verona to require
the existence of a good school for the sons of the wealthy
and prominent citizens? Or did Catullus' father, like
the fathers of Horace and Ovid, send his boys to Rome
or even to Athens for at least the more important
part of their training? Was Valerius Cato one of the
poet's teachers? It is impossible to answer these
questions. So far as Verona is concerned we can only
say that the town was probably much richer and more
populous than Venusia or Sulmona, the native towns
of Horace and Ovid, but this does not prove that it
possessed a good school. As for Rome—the fact that
Catullus moved in good circles there proves that he
must in some way have secured the proper introduction;
mere wealth even when united with great literary ability
could hardly have been sufficient for this. Perhaps he
had attended a Roman school with some of the boys
of good family. There is, however, not a single direct
statement about the poet's education. As Bernhard
Schmidt says, *De educatione eius nihil est traditum.*[56]

And yet somewhere, somehow Catullus obtained an
excellent education. The poems prove beyond a doubt
that he was exceptionally well grounded in Greek and

that he knew rhetoric well. How much of his knowledge he acquired in school and how much later by his own efforts, it is impossible to say, for he was all his life a student. Study was in fact one of the cardinal points in his poetic creed. This studious habit of the man is of primary value to one who attempts to define his position in the development of classical poetry. In addition to his expressed or implied opinions about poetry on which I have already touched, the poems often give clues to the sources which he read or studied, to the technique which he sought to make his own, and to the methods which he followed.

It is a safe assumption that Catullus began the practice of at least three of these methods—translation, imitation, rhetoric—while he was still in school. They had been common tools of every poet's craft from the very beginnings of Graeco-Roman literature, and Catullus' teachers, particularly in connection with his exercises, must have had a good deal to say about them. Under them a great many details of his art may be summarized, and since they formed part of his equipment both in the preparatory years which I have attempted to outline and in his mature work which I am about to examine, it is fitting that a brief general account of them should be given here as a preliminary to many details which will appear in the ensuing chapters.

Catullus' translations from the Greek range in extent from a complete poem (LXVI) to short passages, single lines, phrases, and words occurring in poems which as wholes are not translations.[57] These briefer instances should be dealt with as part of the process of imitation rather than translation, since here the poet has his own work—his own purpose—primarily in mind and

he may often distort the thought and purpose of the
Greek author. The fifty-first poem is an excellent
illustration. Much of this poem is translated from
Sappho but as a whole the Latin poem is not a translation. Catullus omits at least two of Sappho's
stanzas, substitutes a stanza of his own, and adapts the
rest to his own situation. He intended to honor
Sappho, for all cultured readers would have recognized
his chief source,[58] and at the same time produce a
Latin poem of his own. It is the method which prevailed among the early Roman poets. Plautus and
Terence, for example, based their plays in the main
upon Greek plays, but by omissions, expansions, sub-
stitutions, and in many other ways they dealt very
freely with their originals because their purpose was
to compose Roman plays for Roman audiences. Both
poets speak of their work as translation (vortere)—
Terence even uses the phrase "word-for-word translation" (verbum de verbo exprimere),[59] but even the
meager remnants of Terence's originals preserved by
Donatus suffice to prove that as wholes the Latin plays
were not, from our point of view, translations. They
contained translations, even here and there word-for-
word translations, like the fifty-first poem of Catullus,
but as a whole such a Roman play was not a translation; it was an imitation or adaptation. The Roman
playwright did not everywhere respect the integrity,
the art, the language, the meter of his Greek model;
he freely altered or modified them in order to adapt the
play to Roman conditions.

Catullus understood the difference between a real
translation and more original work. In answer to the
request of Hortensius for a poem, he writes (LXV)
that he is so overwhelmed by the death of his brother

that he is unable to compose and so sends a translation from Callimachus (*expressa* . . . . *carmina Battiadae*)— clearly not such a poem as the great orator wanted but the best substitute the sorrowing poet could offer at the time. There can be no doubt that the translation sent to Hortensius was the poem which immediately follows in our manuscripts (LXVI), a Latin version of the great Alexandrian's elegy, *The Tress of Berenice,* and from the one hundred and sixteenth poem we gain the impression that Catullus made other translations from the same Greek poet which are now lost. It is interesting to find the greatest poet of the age willing to devote himself to poetic translation. He must have thought the task worth while, at least so far as the sixty-sixth poem is concerned, for he sent that translation to a man of mark and we shall not be far wrong if we infer that he thought rather well of the translation itself.

The *Tress of Berenice* affords the best opportunity of studying Catullus' work as a translator. In contrast with his purpose in the fifty-first poem he is here single-mindedly bent on presenting Callimachus in Latin verse with due respect for the Greek author's thought and art. But he is not trying to make a close translation. As we have seen in the case of Terence, the Romans believed that a translation which was itself to be a work of art should not everywhere reflect closely the words of the original; it should render the thought and content rather than the words.[60]

The fortunate discovery of some twenty lines of the Greek original, *The Tress of Berenice,* has enabled us to discern much more clearly than before how Catullus proceeded.[61] We now see, as we had before conjectured, that the Latin poem is as faithful a rendering as can

be expected when one poet translates another into the
same metrical form.   Indeed, as poetic translations go,
it is often an accurate translation; in some passages
even the peculiarities of Greek syntax, vocabulary, and
order are closely rendered; in others the Latin version
is free, there are omissions and expansions, and once
at least there is obscurity where the Greek is clear—
the famous *crux* in which Catullus speaks of the
"brother of Aethiopian Memnon, Arsinoe's winged
steed." If he had only translated the words θῆλυς
ἀήτης, we should have known that this strange creature
was one of the winds, not a divine ostrich, and the
commentators would have been spared many pages of
discussion. On the other hand, Catullus often succeeds
in finding the *mot juste*, and although he does not translate line for line or even couplet for couplet, there is
reason to believe that he limited his version to the
same total number of lines as its original.[62]

Translation, as I have already remarked, was one
of the elements, though not a necessary element, of
the broader method called imitation, or, to state the
relation somewhat differently, poems or passages which
are in general imitations often contain more or less
translation, generally limited to a word or two or at
most a line. Imitation was so widely practiced in
antiquity that a comprehension of it is essential to
the understanding of ancient literature.[63] Students
were trained to imitate the best models. The theorists
gradually evolved and laid down various principles
which are exemplified, sometimes with certain individual modifications, by the writers of both prose and
verse. Catullus is no exception to the rule. Subject
matter was regarded as common property. Any poet
was free to write on a theme which had been used

again and again. Two of these themes appear in the
sixty-fourth poem, the wedding of Peleus and Thetis
and the fortunes of Ariadne. So far there was no
question of imitation. But if a poet chose the story
of Ariadne and wished to imitate the work of a predecessor upon the same theme, he had to follow certain
principles unless he wished to be charged with plagiarism, which both Greeks and Romans called by the
forthright term, "robbery" (κλοπή, *furtum*). Imitation
was a perfectly legitimate and praiseworthy method.
It concerned not the content or the thought, but rather
the technique. Dionysius of Halicarnassus defines imitation as not the use of the thoughts but a similar
artistic treatment of earlier writing, and again, not
the repetition of what Demosthenes composed but
writing in the manner of Demosthenes—the single
Greek word Δημοσθενικῶς contains the gist of the whole
matter. But the similar artistic treatment of the
imitator meant that he must not adopt the treatment
of his model, but must so express the passage in his
own technique that it became his own though it
recalled the model. Hence the many passages about
"rivalling" or "improving" the model.[64] If there was
not sufficient alteration or improvement the imitator
laid himself open to the charge of "theft." The line
between imitation and plagiarism was a narrow one
and the poets often lacked the skill (though their
purpose might be above suspicion), just as the critics
lacked the insight, to draw the line clearly. And
so charges of plagiarism were rife though often unjustified, as in the case of those eight books which a certain
Quintus Octavius Avitus is said to have written about
the thefts of Vergil. The same Vergil illustrates the
proper method of imitation when he alters Catullus'

description of the labyrinth, *inobservabilis error* (LXIV. 115) to *inextricabilis error* (*Aen*. VI. 27). Vergil's phrase is in the manner of Catullus but he gives it a touch that is all his own.

This example suggests two other principles which were commonly accepted. In the first place Vergil, though he does not name Catullus, expected his cultured readers to recognize that he was borrowing from his great predecessor.[65] Again he might have taken the phrase *inobservabilis error* bodily, without alteration, into the *Aeneid* with the purpose of honoring Catullus by a complimentary citation. This practice also was a common one and there are undoubtedly in Latin poetry a great many of these complimentary citations (from works now lost) which we cannot now recognize.[66]

The Greek system of imitation—and indeed the tendency to make charges of plagiarism which so often grew out of it—was borrowed by the Romans. It concerned originally the imitation of one Greek writer by another. As soon as the Romans began to develop a literature, a double relation necessarily arose: a Roman writer might imitate a Roman writer or he might imitate a Greek writer. Curiously enough, charges of plagiarism seem for a long time to have been limited to relations between Romans. As for the Greeks—they were, in Fielding's phrase about his own relation to the Classics, "a rich common, whereon every person who hath the smallest tenement in Parnassus has a right to fatten his muse."[67] But as time went on there are hints that some critics took a juster point of view. Afranius, the author of comedies on Roman themes (*togatae*), was accused of robbing not only Roman poets but also Menander. Probably he did not acknowledge or did

not sufficiently improve his borrowings. At any rate
he stood to his guns, admitted that he had taken material from Menander, and any other things that suited
him even in Latin poets.[68] This incident must have
occurred in the second half of the second century B.C.
At a much later period Vergil was accused of robbing
Homer and is said to have replied that if his critics
would attempt the thing they would find it easier to
steal the club from Hercules than a verse from Homer.[69]

Here then were critics who wished to put Greek and
Latin poetry on the same footing so far as the principles
of imitation were concerned. The view did not prevail,
but it is possible that Catullus had a certain sympathy
with it. We have seen that one Greek poet could make
a complimentary citation from another, not naming
his predecessor but expecting the citation to be recognized. In the same way a Roman poet could compliment another Roman poet. In Catullus there are at
least two passages which suggest that translations from
Greek poets were thus employed. The first is the
translation of some lines of Sappho which Catullus
includes in the fifty-first poem. Catullus does not name
Sappho, but any reader who was even halfway cultured
would have "recognized" the source. The second is the
single line from an unknown Greek poet (probably
Callimachus) which is closely translated (LXIV. 111).
Cicero also quotes the line—in its Greek form—as
one that was well known and would be recognized by
his friend Atticus.[70]

Enough has been said by way of introduction about
translation and imitation. A few words must be added
about rhetoric. The poetry of Catullus reveals here
and there the influence of rhetoric. In the seventh
poem he wishes Lesbia's kisses to be as many as the

sands and stars—an old rhetorical comparison; in the thirtieth the faithless one allows the winds to carry his vain words away—an equally common rhetorical touch; in the sixtieth it is suggested that a cruel being may have been the child of the lioness or Scylla. All these passages and many more smack of rhetoric.[71] Did this influence come to Catullus from Greek poets who had made use of rhetoric, or was it in part at least the result of his training in school?[72] Had the poet been grounded in rhetoric in his youth and so won a basis for use of the same methods in his maturity? Undoubtedly both of these possibilities must be borne in mind. Certainly the rhetoricians taught imitation, trained their pupils to make paraphrases and (at Rome) translations, supplied lists of *sententiae* and illustrations, taught the principles of arrangement, the use of commonplaces, descriptive passages, and the like. In formulating principles and collecting illustrations they made use of poetry as well as prose, and their pupils were often trained in the composition of both. The two forms were mutually helpful, and rhetoric was useful (and often injurious!) to both.

Fortunately Catullus cannot be called a rhetorical poet in the sense that Ovid is rhetorical. But wherever he obtained it his knowledge of rhetoric was considerable. The rhetorical element is there and it must be taken into account as one of the explanations of certain resemblances between his work and that of the Greeks.

The foregoing outline supplies a number of valuable clues to one who is interested in the relations between Catullus and earlier Greek and Roman poets. In this respect as in others his work must be considered from the point of view of general ancient theory and practice.

But when we have applied to our problem a knowledge of ancient methods and points of view in translation, imitation, and rhetoric, much still remains to be done. The material with which we have to deal in the poetry itself consists of a large number of resemblances (sometimes identities)—let us not call them "imitations" or "reminiscences" or "borrowings" or the like until we know more precisely what they are—between Catullus and one or more of his predecessors. These resemblances range all the way from translations of single Greek words to similarities in thought between some poem or passage of Catullus and a poem or passage of some earlier writer. Between the two extremes the resemblances assume a great variety of forms. It is our task to account as far as possible for these phenomena and so to understand better the nature of Catullus' poetry and something of his methods. It is well therefore to begin where the material is richest, not with the short poems in which, considered as a group, the Greek influence is not very obvious, but with the long poems which have so many Greek elements that Ellis has called them not unfittingly "Greek studies." Of these the sixty-fourth, the short epic or poetic tale, is probably the best example of studied art. Certainly it is by far the longest poem and contains the fullest and most varied material for the purposes of our study. Moreover we have at our disposal more Greek material for the study of poetic narrative than we have for any other kind of poetry practiced by Catullus with the possible exception of the epigram. There are, then, good reasons for beginning the more detailed work with a study of the sixty-fourth poem, and that poem, ordinarily known as *The Wedding of Peleus and Thetis*, will be the subject of the next lecture.

CHAPTER V

THE POETIC TALE

The sixty-fourth poem is the best surviving example of the brief narrative in hexameters which was much practiced in the Alexandrian period and especially in the period of Catullus. This variety of narrative belonged to the epic *genre* and although it differed in many ways from the long Homeric type neither the Greeks nor the Romans, during the centuries in which it flourished, seem to have given it a distinctive name. But there are advantages in a term which at least implies certain differences, and in modern times the short epic has come to be known as the epyllion or epyll.[1]

The epyllion was brief, but there was nothing new in brevity as such. Brief narratives had existed from pre-Homeric times and many are woven into the fabric of the Homeric poems. One, the so-called *Shield of Hercules*, attributed to Hesiod, has come down to us as a separate poem although it was once imbedded in a longer context. But until Callimachus led the revolt against it, the long epic had been dominant, and even the success of Callimachus by no means eliminated it. Nevertheless it was his example more than anything else which resulted in establishing by its side the short epic. He chose deliberately the short form and above all he applied to it many a principle of modern poetic art. Thus he produced something not in all ways new, but new enough to set a literary fashion which culminated two hundred years later in the time of Catullus.

Of the *Hecale*—"the finely wrought story of Calli-machus," as Crinagoras calls it—time has spared seventy or eighty more or less broken lines. In addition several complete or nearly complete poems of the same general type survive in the Theocritus collection. We need not discuss the authenticity of these pieces since they are all earlier than Catullus. They are the *Baby Hercules* (138 lines) and *Hercules the Lion Slayer* (281 lines) attributed to Theocritus, the *Europa* (166 lines) and the *Megara* (125 lines) attributed to Moschus. There are moreover about a dozen titles of lost poems which are believed with some reason to have been epyllia, but the fragments are too meager to be helpful. And finally we must not forget that examples of the Alexandrian art of narrative occur in other forms of poetry, for example the genuinely Theocritean *Cyclops* and *Hylas*, or the *Hymns* of Callimachus. In these one must be on the lookout for differences from the modern epic art, but they have at the same time many of the same features. The proof of this state-ment will be found by anybody who will compare the long papyrus fragment of Callimachus' *Cydippe* (some 80 lines) with the epyllia. The *Cydippe* was Callimachus' most famous elegy, but it was a narra-tive elegy—and a love story—and its technique is in many details identical with that of the epyllion, the tale in hexameters.[2]

All told, then, there is considerable material from which to infer the characteristics of the Alexandrian epyllion. A comparison of Catullus' sixty-fourth poem with this material, together with earlier Greek narrative poetry, shows very clearly what he was trying to do. But since the poem is over four hundred lines long, it is impossible in a brief lecture to cover all the interesting

topics.   Certain results of a comprehensive study may
be stated, but my treatment must be summary.

The title usually given to the poem, *The Wedding of
Peleus and Thetis*, is misleading because no less than
two hundred and twelve of the four hundred and nine
lines are devoted to another tale—that of abandoned
Ariadne—in which the poet feels a deeper interest
than in the ostensible theme.   Both tales are old and
both had been common subjects of Greek literature and
art long before the time of Catullus.   The poet had
therefore abundant material from which to select, but
many of the sources open to him are lost to us.   A brief
summary of the two stories, as Catullus tells them, will
show his attitude toward his material and reveal the
features in which his version is unique.[3]

The poem opens with an introductory portion (1–30)
in which the events preceding the wedding are briefly
recounted.   The Argo, built by Athena, set forth upon
her voyage to Colchis with a picked crew of heroes in
quest of the golden fleece.   In the crew was Peleus.
The ship had scarcely begun her voyage when the
Nereids appeared in the waves wondering at the strange
new craft.   Then Peleus and Thetis fell in love, and
Jupiter, perceiving that they must wed, yielded his
own love to the mortal.   (Here begins the narrative
of the wedding, 31 ff.) When the wedding day came,
all the people of Thessaly flocked to Pharsalus, where
they gazed with wonder on the splendors within the
palace of Peleus and particularly at the wedding couch
of the goddess with its ivory adornment and splendid
coverlet, embroidered with heroic figures (50–57).   (At
this point the story of Ariadne, one of the figures
depicted on the coverlet, is inserted, 52–264.   Let us
go on with the wedding.)   When these mortal guests

having gazed their fill departed (267–277)[4] the divine
guests arrived: Chiron with gifts of flowers, the river
god Penios with beeches and other trees, Prometheus,
Jupiter with his wife and children (278–298) except
Phoebus and Diana, who would not attend (299–302).
The gods sat down to a splendid feast and the aged
Fates (Parcae), spinning the while, sang the prophetic
wedding song (303–322). They sang of the love of
Peleus and Thetis, of the birth of Achilles, of his
glory in life and death (323–383). The poem closes
with a reflective passage in which the poet contrasts
the happiness of that early age, when the gods showed
themselves to mortals face to face, with the degenerate
later ages in which the world became so steeped in
crime that the gods no longer deigned to reveal themselves (384–408).

Catullus follows in general that version of the old
myth in which Peleus weds Thetis not through his own
efforts, but by divine decision: Jupiter yields her to
him (*concessit amores*, 27). But he supplies a new
motive for Jupiter's act, the love of Peleus and Thetis
for each other (18–21). He hints at the love of Jupiter
himself for Thetis (27)—this throws Peleus' good fortune into higher relief—but he says nothing of the well-
known oracle which, according to many earlier writers,
chilled Jupiter's passion, or of that rebuff which,
according to others, caused the father of the gods to
decree a mortal husband to Thetis as a punishment,
or of the chastity of Peleus, which was rewarded by
the gift of an immortal bride. In fact Catullus both
by his omissions and by his treatment emphasizes the
love. Peleus and Thetis fall in love at first sight
(19–20), Jupiter realizes that they must wed (21) and
yields his own passion (27), Thetis' relatives consent

(29–30), the wedded bliss of the pair is guaranteed by the Fates (328–336, 372–380, cf. 28 *tenuit*). The erotic is the outstanding feature of Catullus' version of the story. This is part of the general transformation of many old myths into love stories which was practiced in the Alexandrian and later ages[5]—even Hercules and Polyphemus became lovers—but this particular myth does not appear thus transformed in any extant version earlier than Catullus. He probably knew late Greek erotic versions, but they are lost to us. In the versions known to us Thetis is an unwilling bride who at best endures marriage with a mortal. Of the writers who preceded Catullus, Apollonius alone, so far as I have been able to discover, seems to imply a version that gave the pair at least a brief period of wedded bliss. In the fourth book of the *Argonautica*, when Hera summons Thetis to aid the Argonauts, Apollonius tells at some length the story of the Nereid. In important respects this version differs from that of Catullus, but when Hera reminds Thetis (805–806), "I gave the best of mortals to be thy husband that thou mightest find heart-rejoicing[6] marriage," there is at least a hint that Thetis was not unwilling, and when later (885 ff.) Thetis is represented as having deserted Peleus in anger because he had misunderstood her efforts to render the infant Achilles immortal, we may perhaps assume that Apollonius knew a fuller version in which their union was for a short time a happy one. Catullus is for us, however, the earliest poet who lays any stress upon the love: Peleus finds in Thetis a divine bride filled with human passion; her divine relatives and even Jupiter himself display human feeling. This is part of the humanization of the divine which is so characteristic of the Alexandrian poets.

An examination of the other details strengthens one's conviction that Catullus is modernizing the ancient tale. This is shown by the variants which he adopts. The wedding occurs after the Argonautic expedition, and the scene is the palace of Peleus at Pharsalus. These details appear only in Catullus; in the other versions the wedding precedes the expedition and takes place on Mount Pelion, in Chiron's cave, in Phthia, etc. Catullus makes Peleus lord of all Thessaly, even of the outlying Isle of Scyros—if the text of v. 35 is correct—and he modernizes the geography, avoiding the Thessalian names given in Homer. There are several striking variants in our poet's account of the guests. In other versions only gods—"all the gods," says Homer,—attend the wedding. In Catullus not only are present two deities, Penios and Prometheus, who are not specified elsewhere, and two absent, Phoebus and Diana, whose presence is specified elsewhere, but mortals also bring gifts, although the nature of their gifts is unknown and they do not remain for the ceremony (267–277). Catullus is the first to speak of these mortals. Many gifts are mentioned in other accounts, but Catullus specifies two (flowers and trees) unknown elsewhere. In Catullus the Fates (Parcae) sing the wedding song; elsewhere this rôle is assigned to Phoebus, to the Muses, or vaguely to "the gods."

Some of these variants probably have no special significance. The mention of Penios and Prometheus among the guests, for example, is not surprising in view of the tradition which made "all the gods" attend. Flowers and trees as gifts are merely two more in a list which shows considerable variation in the different accounts of the wedding; it is rather the use to which the trees are put (292–293) that is significant, and of this I shall speak presently.

A survey of these new features of the story reveals the modernizing tendency of Catullus. He removes the scene of the wedding from the wilds of Pelion and gives it a human setting by placing it in the palace and introducing human guests. He uses modern names for the Thessalian towns. He represents the ceremony as occurring in a bower of greenery (292–293) which, together with the figured coverlet and the glitter of gold and silver and ivory within the palace (43 ff.), suggests the splendors of the potentates of Asia and Egypt, described for us in the *Adoniazusae* of Theocritus— splendors at which their subjects were allowed to gaze on festal days.

There is another hint that Catullus is making use of late versions of the story. There was in the neighborhood of Pharsalia a Thetideion, a precinct, probably including a building, sacred to Thetis. Pherecydes states that "Peleus went with Thetis to Phthia on a chariot . . . . and lived in Pharsalus and in Thetideion."[7] Reitzenstein suggests that the "palace" in Catullus was, in his source, the Thetideion. However this may be, it seems certain that the placing of the wedding at Pharsalus has some connection with the Thetideion, and this in turn suggests that there was probably a version of the story accounting for the origin of the Thetideion. Such an etiological version would have gained special currency in the Alexandrian Age when etiology was a fad.

It is clear that the differences which appear in Catullus' version as compared with earlier forms of the story are for the most part such as to adapt it to a modern dress. It is very improbable that he invented or dealt arbitrarily with the main points of the tale. He hardly invented, for example, a new place and time for the wedding or substituted the Fates for Apollo or the Muses, although it is easier to believe that he may have brought the erotic motive into greater prominence or even that he was the first Greek or Roman poet to give it any prominence whatever. But although this is possible, it is much more likely that he found this, as he almost certainly found the apparently novel points of his story, in that later Greek literature which is lost to us. He was a *doctus poeta*—is called *doctus*, in fact, with reference to this very poem— and the *doctus poeta*, bearing in mind Callimachus' principle of relating nothing that was unattested,[8] respected his material and the sources on which it rested. This scrupulosity of the "moderns" has been substantiated by the long fragment of their master's *Cydippe* in which he names his source (Xenomedes) for the love story of Acontius and Cydippe and for many other curious details concerning the island of Ceos. The manner in which Catullus presents the most curiously unique detail of his story of the wedding, the absence of Phoebus and Diana, still further substantiates the principle. They alone of the gods were absent, he tells us (299–302), for they looked with scorn on Peleus and would not attend the wedding. This is a learned reference, in the manner of the *docti poetae*, half telling or merely alluding to a tale which the reader is left to complete for himself. But the very manner proves that such a tale existed and that Catullus did not invent the mere allusion to it with which we have to content ourselves. What motive the divine twins had for their disdain we do not know, but Catullus knew an authority which explained the puzzle. He did not treat myths with that arbitrary independence with which he is credited by one of his editors.[9]

The results obtained from a study of the story of Ariadne (52–264) are similar. Catullus follows the version in which Ariadne falls in love with Theseus, who had come to Crete for the purpose of slaying the Minotaur and ridding his native land of the tribute paid in the form of a sacrifice to the monster, flees with him by sea, is abandoned by him in the Isle of Dia while she is asleep, and is finally consoled by Bacchus. Here we have all the elements of an unfortunate love story and Catullus handles it with much more zest than the story of Peleus' wedding.

Here again the most striking difference between the version of Catullus and earlier forms of the story is the stress laid on the erotic element, which in this case pervades almost every part of the narrative. Ariadne was depicted as an eloping princess even as early as Homer, so that it was unnecessary for the poets of the later ages to supply the erotic motive. And yet so far as our extant sources indicate, the germ lay dormant for centuries. There is nothing like a developed erotic treatment until we reach Catullus himself, but we may feel certain that so excellent a theme was not thus overlooked by his Alexandrian predecessors even though we have no direct proof that any of them made use of it.

It is unnecessary to recount the many details and variations of the myth omitted by Catullus with the exception of one or two which may have had some connection with the motives in which he is interested. His omissions and the slightness of his references to some details are significant. He concentrates our

attention on the figure of Ariadne, for whom he wishes
to arouse sympathy and pity. He dwells at length
upon her beauty and her distress, and he puts into her
mouth a long lament (132–201) in order to paint her
desperate situation in the most effective way. Of her
beauty, earlier writers tell us only that she was "fair-
tressed" (καλλιπλόκαμος) or "fair-haired" (ξανθή); and
there is no hint that she uttered a lament, except the
phrase of Pherecydes that after Theseus left her
Aphrodite appeared while she was "lamenting"
(κατολοφυρομένης). If Ariadne is to be pitied it will not
do to palliate Theseus' desertion. Catullus accordingly
omits all reference to the various excuses that were
made for the Athenian hero—that Dionysus took her
from him, that like Aeneas in later time he received
divine orders to abandon his sweetheart, that he left
her on the island intending to return but was prevented
by the wind, that he returned to Naxos after her
death and instituted a festival in her honor. In these
versions it is easy to detect the touch of Athenian
patriotism and there is some reason for believing that
Catullus was not entirely insensible to this aspect of
the story. The positive description of Theseus as
handsome (98) and brave (81 ff., 101 ff.) is indeed
essential to a love story, as Catullus conceives it, but
it is noticeable that in the narrative portion of the
tale he gives scant space to the baseness of Theseus:
the youth was "thoughtless"; he fled, leaving his "vain
promises" to the blast (58 f., cf. 123, 248). Is this
merely because the poet wishes to concentrate such
reproaches in the lament of his heroine, or is the thrice
repeated *immemor*, a weak word for such a caddish
lover, a reflection of the stories which made Theseus a
puppet in the hands of higher powers?

In another respect also Theseus had been represented as "forgetful": he forgot to raise the white sail which had been agreed upon as a signal of his safe return. Thus he caused his father's death. Retaining this feature of the story, Catullus makes it serve a double purpose. Aegeus, parting with the child of his old age whom he is sending to almost certain death, utters a speech full of parental love and anguish and thus becomes a far more pathetic figure than he had been in earlier versions of the tale. The feeling of pity already aroused by the picture of Ariadne is therefore continued and enhanced by that of Aegeus. Furthermore, Catullus satisfies the requirements of poetic justice by attributing the son's forgetfulness (which causes the old king's death) to the curse of her whom that son has abandoned; Catullus is the first to connect the abandonment of Ariadne with the death of Aegeus.

The tale of Ariadne is sad, as the poet wishes it to be, but at the very end he allows one ray of light to pierce the gloom that shrouds his heroine. He will not destroy the tragic effect that he has produced and so he does not narrate at length how Ariadne became the bride of Dionysus, but as she stands, the very figure of grief, upon the shore (249–250), the god and his followers approach, and the one line,

> te quaerens, Ariadna, tuoque incensus amore

hints at happier days to come for her. This is Alexandrian art at its best.

Both stories, then, are presented from the modern point of view and this fact conditions the selection of the elements and the motives which accompany them. But why are stories so different combined within the limits of one poem? Have they any inner connection? This is a question which has always puzzled scholars, for, as Friedrich says, the faithlessness of Theseus to Ariadne is a rather strange subject for the coverlet of a marriage couch.[10] This is especially true when, as in this case, the marriage is a happy one.

Various explanations of the puzzle are offered by the commentators. Ellis, who remarks that the episode of Ariadne "seems to have absolutely nothing to do with the main subject of the poem," quotes Shadworth Hodgson to the effect that "a connecting link is to be found in the common theme of the two stories, the glory of marriage." "The theme of the poem," says Hodgson, "the glory of marriage, is exhibited by the two contrasted stories, which thus properly assume almost equal importance—the circumstance that the union of Peleus and Thetis was a union between a mortal and an immortal finds its counterpart in the advent of Bacchus." But as Ellis says, "This view does not lie on the surface." If Catullus had emphasized the marriage of Ariadne with Bacchus we might discern some such connection as Hodgson finds, but the poet gives a mere hint of this: it is the unfortunate side of Ariadne's fate on which he dwells.

Lafaye, remarking on the tendency of Alexandrian poetry to avoid unity of composition, sees only an aesthetic reason for the juxtaposition of the two stories: to obtain an agreeable and affecting contrast, to oppose the despair of a deserted sweetheart to the joy of a wedding festival. This is equivalent to a statement that the stories have no inner connection, and this has been the general opinion of scholars. The contrast is in fact so striking that it has suggested the theory, which has found some favor, that Catullus has combined two separate Greek poems, and it must be admitted that no satisfactory link between the stories has been discovered.

But if we abandon the effort to discover some internal connection between the tales and turn our attention to the pretext, the device of the *vestis*, by which they are externally connected, it will be possible to answer the general question satisfactorily. From the structural point of view one must bear in mind that the story of Ariadne is an example of the tale within a tale; it is inserted in the story of the wedding of Peleus and Thetis; also it is the description of a work of art, because the figures of Ariadne, Theseus, Bacchus, etc., are depicted on the *vestis*. Thus Catullus combines two well-known forms of poetic technique. Both are as old as Homer, but Catullus is the first poet to combine them in this way. A brief outline of their history will make this clear.

Catullus begins the story of Ariadne as if he were going to confine himself to a description of the figures on the coverlet. It was purple, he tells us, and marvelously ornamented with figures of men of the olden time (49–51). Then eighteen verses are devoted to a picture[11]—for it is really a picture—of Ariadne on the wave-beaten shore, distractedly gazing after Theseus as he flees in his ship. She is just roused from sleep, she can scarce believe her eyes, and like a nude Bacchante she stands there gazing, gazing, while the waves make playthings of her snood and her raiment (52–70). In this passage there is nothing which really mars the pictorial effect, but there are hints of what is to come. Theseus flees *irrita ventosae linquens promissa procellae* (59). He had made promises, then. The poet expresses his sympathy by the ejaculation *eheu* (61), and he

apostrophizes Theseus directly (69) as he describes
the desperate plight of Ariadne.

With v. 71, however, the poet begins to transcend
description and pass to narrative. It is as if his feeling
were too strong for him, as if he were carried away by
an irresistible impulse to tell Ariadne's story. He pities
her[12] (*a misera*) for the ill-starred love "which the
Lady of Eryx cast upon her when"—and here (v. 73)
we are fairly launched upon the tale, which proceeds in
narrative and speech with here and there a bit of vivid
description for nearly two hundred lines. The description of the coverlet has developed into a narrative.

Now if Homer or any of his followers had wished to
insert into an epic on another subject the story of
Ariadne it is safe to say that he would have put it into
the mouth of a character or related it as a digression
from the main narrative.[13] In fact both Homer and
Apollonius give brief versions of this very tale, the
former as a digression, the latter through the lips of
Jason. These methods were customary also, so far as
our evidence allows us to judge, with those who professed to oppose the Homeric School—the "moderns,"
whose leader was Callimachus.

But since Catullus chooses to attach his narrative to
the description of a work of art, let us see how the earlier
poets managed this device. Examples are numerous.

The earliest example is Homer's description of the
shield of Achilles (*Il.* XVIII. 478 ff.), but the best analogy
from the early period is Hesiod's *Shield of Hercules*
because this poem was regarded in the Alexandrian
Age as a short epic and therefore from the ancient point
of view more closely resembles the sixty-fourth poem.[14]

Hercules arms himself for the fight with Cycnus with
greaves, breastplate, spear, etc. Last of all he took up his

shield (139 ff.), "a wonder to look upon" (θαῦμα ἰδέσθαι). It gleamed with enamel and white ivory, with electrum and gold, and there were bands of cyanus (dark blue) upon it. So much for the opening description.

Then the poet describes the objects depicted upon the shield: Fear was in the middle (ἐν μέσ λσῳ---ἔην, 144); Advance and Retreat were wrought upon it (ἐν - - - τέτυκτο, 154); there were twelve heads of snakes (ἐν . . . . ἔσαν, 168); there were herds of boars and lions (ἐν . . . . ἔσαν, 168), etc. Everywhere the reader is reminded by the repetition of these or similar formulae that the scenes were on the shield. Materials (gold, silver, tin, bronze, etc.) and colors are frequently mentioned. The description is rendered vivid by the use of imperfect tenses, progressive participles, inceptive verbs and such phrases as "like to those who are singing" (Μοῦσαι . . . . μελπομένῃς εἰκυῖαι, 206), "as if alive" (ὡσεὶ ζωούς, 194). The artist, Hephaestus, is kept constantly before us, cf. 219, 244, 297, 313, 319, and the poet frequently utters admiring comment upon his work; "a wonder to see" (140, 224, 318), "works of wonder" (165), "a great wonder to tell of" (218). The poet keeps to his theme, the description of a work of art. He is aware that the various figures are vividly motionless, so to speak; indeed he naïvely remarks after describing the charioteers that "they had unending toil and for them the victory was never accomplished; the contest was undecided" (310–311). And yet the desire for vividness causes him here and there to add a bit of sound and motion to his pictures: "the serpents would gnash their teeth when the son of Amphitryon fought" (164), "the shield echoed" to the tread of the Gorgons (232), "the women . . . . were uttering shrill cries" (243), but the poet adds at once "like those who are alive" (244). The best illustration occurs where repeated acts of the Fates are mentioned (289 ff.): "they strove for the men who were falling. When a man lay prostrate or was falling, a Fate would seize him. When they had sated their souls with blood, they would hurl the man behind them and again take part in the battle. . . . . And they all fought over one man."

Once the poet digresses for three lines into a bit of comment. He has been describing Eris, who aided Hercules against his foes, and he adds that the souls of these foes enter Hades but their bones rot and molder away upon the earth.

The poet therefore holds in general very closely to what is proper in description. I have given a rather full outline of his method because it is the method which persists unchanged in any essential way until we come to Catullus. At the same time his description of the shield contains in its occasional references to sound and motion and in its meager scraps of comment the germs from which the treatment found in Catullus must have developed.

In Greek poetry from Hesiod to the time of Catullus there are many descriptions of works of art: Aeschylus (*Septem*, 374 ff.), Euripides (*Phoenissae*, 1104 ff., *Ion*, 1141 ff., *Electra*, 1254 ff.), Apollonius (I. 721–768, Jason's mantle), Theocritus (I. 27–56, the cup), Moschus (II. 37–62, Europa's basket), and others. In all these passages—even the latest—the older technique persists, and this holds true of narrative poetry as well as other kinds. If, then, Catullus learned the technique which he employs in the sixty-fourth poem from the Greek, his model must have been very late, perhaps as late as his own century.[15]

From these larger matters of content and structure I turn to some illustrations of the manner of Catullus in details. In connection with the hundreds of Greek parallels to be found in editions, dissertations, articles, etc., one often finds the assertion that Catullus "translates" or "imitates" a definite passage, phrase, or word.[16] A careful study of these resemblances has convinced me that it is not often proper to use the term "translation" or even "imitation" in this connection. It must be admitted that a poet may be imitating (consciously using) a definite passage in another poet even where the imitation is so different from the original that the relation cannot be detected without explicit testimony from the poet himself or from some other ancient source.[17] But in the absence of such testimony we cannot base any conclusions on these tenuous resemblances. We must exclude them from our material. We must exclude also a mass of cases which may just as well be due to other causes as to imitation in the proper sense.[18] In short we must limit our material to the certain and probable cases if we expect our inferences to be reliable. Even then scholars will not agree concerning every detail, but in the sixty-fourth poem after excluding doubtful material there will always be a sufficient residue on which to base results.

Catullus was trying to reproduce in Latin certain characteristics of Greek narrative poetry. Many of these were common enough, a few were rare, or even to the best of our knowledge unique. Sometimes he borrowed Greek words or used Greek words which his predecessors had borrowed, but these loan-words lie outside the limits of the present investigation. More often he translated or imitated—the line between the two methods cannot always be clearly drawn—a Greek word or phrase, but almost always he had in mind *types* of expression (epithets, metaphors, etc.) employed by several Greek poets, very rarely the definite words of a single poet.

In passages of considerable extent—a line or more—it is often possible to detect the predominant influence of a single Greek poet, e.g., Homer in the description of the nod of Zeus (204–206) or Hesiod in the contrast between the degenerate present and the Golden Age (384 ff.), but it is very rarely possible to feel sure that Catullus was making direct use of one Greek poet. Certainly when the dominant poet belonged to the archaic period the versions of Catullus are so modern that we must assume either that one or more late Greek poets were his more direct models or that he himself has greatly modified Homer or Hesiod, as the case may be, by modern Greek methods. But before this question can be decided the foregoing general statements require some illustration.

Let us examine first some of the single words and brief phrases. When Catullus calls Athene *diva* . . . . *retinens in summis urbibus arces* (8), "the goddess who keeps the citadels in the heights of cities," he clearly has in mind such epithets as ἀκρία, πολιάς, πολιοῦχος—it matters not which one—and the same statement holds true of *magnanimum* (85), "great souled," cf. μεγάθυμος, etc., of *cultricem montibus*, "mountain-dwelling" (300), cf. οὑρεσίοικος, of *flavo* (63, cf. 98), "golden haired," cf. ξανθός. These are translations of well-known Greek epithets or conventional adjectives. Similarly Peleus is the *Thessaliae columen* (26), "the prop of Thessaly," cf. κίων; the Argo is a *currus* (9), "a car," cf. ὄχημα, etc.; Ariadne "tosses on mighty billows of woe" (*fluctuat*, etc., 62, *fluctibus*, 98), cf. κλύζεσθαι, etc., "she hung with

her whole soul" on Theseus (*pendebat*, 70, cf. κρεμάννυμι)
—both are figures from later Greek erotic. The palace,
adorned for the wedding, "laughed" (*risit*, 284, cf.
γελάω, etc.). These figures, rare or unique in Latin
though not uncommon in Greek, are translated by
Catullus, but in no case can we name a definite passage
as his source, and this is his normal method. In one or
two cases, however, a definite source may be named.
Homer represents the river Scamander as saying that
his waters are choked ("narrowed") by the corpses of
those whom Achilles slew (*Il.* XXI. 220). Catullus,
speaking of the same event, renders στεινόμενος by the
rare word *angustare* (359). Again, Homer speaks of
the spear "which Chiron gave to Achilles' father from
the peak of Pelion," τὴν πατρὶ φίλῳ πόρε Χείρων Πηλίου
ἐκ κορυφῆς (*Il.* XVI. 143–144). In Catullus (278) the
situation is not the same and there is nothing striking
in the phraseology, but it is probable that the words,
e vertice Pelei . . . . *Chiron*, represent a Homeric
phrase which the poet remembered from his schooldays.
Finally we may feel certain that the curious *nutrices*,
meaning "breasts" (18), cf. τίτθη, is a translation from
some lost Greek poetic passage since the usage is
unique in Latin and very rare in Greek. This particular
attempt of Catullus to enrich the elevated style was
not approved by other Roman poets.

In addition to single words and brief phrases there is
one complete hexameter which Catullus clearly translated (v. 111), intending that his translation should
remind his readers of the original Greek.[19] The story
of the Greek line is interesting—and tantalizing. Early
in the year 49 B.C. Cicero had a rather heated interview
with a temperamental Greek named Dionysius, who
apparently was hoping to secure the position of tutor

to the orator's son, young Marcus. Dionysius left
the house in high dudgeon and, as Cicero wrote to
Atticus (VIII. 5. 1), he went cursing along the road;

πολλὰ μάτην κεράεσσιν ἐς ἠέρα θυμήναντα,

"of raging with his horns in vain upon the air." To
describe the futile gestures of the angry Greek Cicero
quoted a line which he knew would be familiar to
Atticus, and so he did not name its author. Too bad!
For modern scholars have assigned it to all possible
authors! The mention of "horns" suggests the ineffec-
tive thrashing of some horned monster, and the best
conjecture, in my opinion, is that of Moritz Haupt,
who believed that the Marathonian bull is meant and
assigned the line to the *Hecale* of Callimachus. Others
assigned it to some lost Greek poem describing the
death of the Minotaur because Catullus uses it for this
purpose. But whoever wrote the Greek line, Catullus
certainly renders it rather closely:

nequiquam vanis iactantem cornua ventis.

Every Greek word has some equivalent in the Latin
version, but for once Catullus neglects the opportunity
to write a spondaic verse!

This is translation, but in the entire poem it is the
only case, extending beyond a word or two, in which I
feel certain that Catullus is translating. His normal
method is something quite different, and we shall best
illustrate it by means of some passages comprising
more than single words or even a single line. Let us
consider for a moment the comparison, a device common in epic poetry from Homer onward. There are
two developed comparisons in the poem: the fall of the
Minotaur is compared to the fall of an oak or a pine
(105–111), and the departure of the throng of wedding

guests is compared to the inception and movement of
waves upon the sea (269–277). In both, the central
idea and a number of details are Homeric, but it is
interesting to note the modifications. The first passage
runs as follows:

As an oak waving its arms on the summit of Taurus or a
cone-bearing pine with sweating bark is overthrown by the
indomitable gale which rends with its blast the tough wood,
and the tree (*illa*) torn from its roots falls afar and prone,
breaking everything that lies in its way, so Theseus over-
came the savage monster and laid him low as he lashed with
his horns in vain the empty air.

Homer often likens the fall of heroes to the fall of
trees—even the same kinds of trees that appear in
Catullus: "he fell as falls an oak when cut" (or a poplar
or a fir, *Il.* XIII. 389, *ibid.* V. 560). The tree is sometimes
pictured as growing on a mountain: "he fell as a beech
or an ash falls which grows ὄρεος κορυφῇ," *Il.* XIII. 179;
cf. Catullus' *in summo* . . . . *Tauro*. Catullus uses a
spondaic line to enhance the effect; cf. Homer, *ibid.*
IV. 482 αἴγειρος ὥς.

The main idea and at least four of the details are
Homeric. Possibly we should add to these the detail
that the tree in Catullus is torn from its roots (*radicitus*),
for Homer mentions this detail though not in a comparison: πρόρριζοι πίπτουσιν (*Il.* XI. 156–157, trees falling in a forest fire); cf. XXI, 243 ἐκ ῥιζέων—where
Achilles grasps the elm.

Catullus applies the comparison to the Minotaur, a
monster. This detail, not a very important one,
appears first in Apollonius (IV. 1682–1689) where the
bronze giant Talos is slain by Medea's enchantments
and "falls as a fir (πεύκη) on the mountains falls when
it is left half-cut," etc.

In Catullus the tree is overthrown by the blast. Apollonius has this detail (III. 1374–1376): the sons of the dragon's teeth "fall as pines or oaks fall which the blasts overthrow."

But several details remain for which there are no Greek parallels. Catullus imagines his trees to stand on the top of a definite mountain—Taurus. They are not vaguely "tall" or "great," as in Homer or Apollonius, but the oak is waving its arms, the pine bears cones and drips with resin, the bark "sweats." The devastating effects of the crash are described with a vividness which does not occur in the Greek. There is, then, a strong tendency, not simply to expand the Homeric motive, but to give it a minute concreteness of detail—to individualize it—as though some Dutch landscape artist had retouched a scene by Corot. The forest would still be Corot's, but it would be recognized as a grove near the Hague with each tree and leaf distinct!

The lines of Catullus have more points of contact with Homer than any other Greek writer, and yet one is forced to cite several passages from Homer in order to accumulate all the Homeric details. If Catullus followed Homer directly, he did not confine himself to one passage. Nor did he confine himself to one passage of Apollonius. There is, in fact, no single extant passage to which he could have gone for all the details. Some of the best touches do not occur at all in his predecessors— and of course the last line, in which he translates the line quoted by Cicero, occurs neither in Homer nor in Apollonius. If then he had for the whole passage a single model—the poet, for example, whom he translates in v. 111—that model is now lost. But the hypothesis of a single model is improbable. The significant

feature of the passage is the character of the art, especially the tendency to embroider. The passage
demonstrates the vitality of the Homeric comparison,
but the technique is neither Homeric nor Apollonian;
it is the product of an age later even than Apollonius.
The result is a Homeric comparison in modern dress.
For Catullus a suggestion from Homer was sufficient
and it is unnecessary to attribute the variations from
Homer—except, of course, v.111—to definite passages
of later Greek poets. Catullus, as his entire work
proves, had mastered the later technique and we may
safely assign most of the variations to him. He wished
to adapt Homer's invention to the rest of his poem and
so he wrote not Ὁμηρικῶς, but νεωτερικῶς.

   To be more explicit—Catullus in describing the
fall of the Minotaur bethought himself of Homer's
habit of comparing the fall of the mighty to the fall
of trees; he did not need to look up the passages.
He worked out his comparison in neoteric fashion,
specifying Taurus as the mountain, visualizing the
tree minutely (*quatientem brachia . . . . conigeram
sudanti cortice*, etc.), adding finally as a complimentary
citation v. 111, which he knew his cultured readers
would recognize in its Latin form just as Cicero knew
that Atticus would recognize the original Greek. For
these touches Catullus did not need to consult books.
They demonstrate indeed his general indebtedness to
later Greek poetic method—which probably he extended in his vivid picture of the tree—but not (except
in v. 111) to definite passages.

   A study of the second developed comparison (269–
277) leads to the same general conclusion but it is
even more interesting because the Greek poets who
must be brought into the discussion are more numerous.

An even better idea however of the poet's method can be given by a brief examination of Ariadne's lament (132–201).

The situations of Ariadne and Medea are very similar. Each has fallen in love with a young prince who has come on a dangerous mission; each has aided her lover to accomplish his task and has saved his life; each has fled with her lover in a ship, sacrificing for him home, parents, and a brother. Each makes a speech full of reproaches, although the speeches occur at different points in the stories: Medea (Apollonius, IV. 355–390) reproaches Jason because she fears that he will abandon her, and wins her point; Ariadne utters her plaint after Theseus has abandoned her.

The speeches of Medea in Euripides and Apollonius have many thoughts in common with Ariadne's lament. Comparing Medea's speech in Apollonius, IV, 355–390, we find that both heroines reproach the lover with neglect of promises and oaths, and with cruelty; both recall their own abandonment of home and kin; both admit the commission of foul deeds to save a lover. Neither can return to her father. Both would follow the lover, if not as wife, then as sister or as slave. Both dwell on their loneliness, and finally both call down a curse on the lover, invoking the Furies against him.

Ariadne utters almost all the content of Medea's speech, but she utters much more. The mood of the abandoned heroine is much more fully developed in her speech and it is twice as long as Medea's. An obvious reason for this is that Apollonius, writing the long epic, has ample space elsewhere in which to characterize his heroine; Catullus, writing the short epic, is hampered by narrow limits and must use Ariadne's speech not only to present her mood but also as a vehicle for details of her story which he has not the space or has not chosen to narrate elsewhere, for the reader must know enough of her story to appreciate her feelings.

But apart from the limitations of his form Catullus displays a notable tendency to dress up the thoughts, to expand. The lover's promises, for example, are merely alluded to by Medea and are known beforehand to the reader (III. 1128–1130; IV. 95–98), but Ariadne not only specifies *conubia* . . . . *hymenaeos* (141), she generalizes for six lines concerning the faithlessness of all men—a purely rhetorical expansion (143–148).

The thought that the heroine will follow her lover in some guise—as slave or as sister if not as wife—is given but one verse in Apollonius; it is given six verses in Ariadne's speech (158–163). The loneliness touched on by Medea (362–3) is, in view of Ariadne's situation, more strongly emphasized by the latter (133, 152–3, 168, 178–9, 184–187).

Numerous parallels for every one of these passages occur in Greek poetry. I must limit myself to a few illustrations.

Ariadne dwells upon the charge of cruelty, cf. the questions (136–138): "Could nothing influence your cruel mind? Had you no mercy in your heart for me?" In her present mood she thinks of Theseus as one who from the first had "hidden his cruel designs within a handsome person" (175). In vv. 152–157 she expands the charge:

> pro quo dilaceranda feris dabor alitibusque
> praeda neque iniacta tumulabor mortua terra.
> quaenam te genuit sola sub rupe leaena,
> quod mare conceptum spumantibus exspuit undis,
> quae Syrtis, quae Scylla rapax, quae vasta Charybdis,
> talia qui reddis pro dulci praemia vita?

"What lioness bore thee 'neath a lonely crag? What sea conceived thee and spewed thee forth from its foaming waves? What Syrtis? What ravening Scylla? What dread Charybdis?"

This method of emphasizing cruelty has its beginnings in Homer, cf. *Il.* XVI. 34–35, where Achilles, because of his cruelty, is called "child of the sea and the crags." In the *Medea* of Euripides (1342–1343) Jason calls Medea (after she has murdered her children) "a lioness, not a woman, with a nature more cruel than Scylla's," cf. 1358 f., 1407. In the *Bacchae* (988–990) the chorus says of Pentheus: "Who can have borne him? He was not born of the blood of woman, but of some lioness or Libyan Gorgon." In Theocritus also (III. 15; XXIII. 19—both erotic passages) the lioness is typical of cruelty. The figure of the sea "spewing" something forth occurs in Homer (*Od.* XII. 237 and 437).

The central idea and many details in these lines of Catullus are Greek. But he has more than any single Greek passage, for example the Syrtis, Charybdis. If he produced his lines by combining details from a number of Greek passages—a patchwork method which has been assumed in such cases by too many scholars— we must believe that some of the Greek material is lost. This assumption however must be rejected. The crowding together in one passage of so many traditional details, together with the questions and the emphatic repetitions, points to the influence of rhetoric.[20] The passage is a widespread poetical commonplace (I have not cited all its occurrences) beginning in Homer, developed by Euripides and others, and first applied to the hard-hearted lover, so far as we know, by Theocritus (XXIII. 19). The rhetoricians had seized upon it, and

Catullus, wherever he got his original suggestion, certainly works it up in rhetorical fashion. He tries his hand at it in the sixtieth poem: "Can it be that some lioness in the Libyan hills or some baying Scylla bore thee to be so cruel hearted," etc. This poem reads like a school exercise and it may quite possibly have been a preliminary study for the passages which I have been discussing.

Lines 158–163 contain a similar commonplace which we might entitle "The devoted girl would follow the lover in any guise." "If," says Ariadne, "thou didst not desire marriage with me, because thou didst dread the stern commands of thy father, yet couldst thou have taken me to thy home to serve thee as bondslave —to wash thy feet, to spread thy couch."[21]

The germ of this idea also is in Homer. In the *Iliad* (III. 409) Helen, the original eloping heroine, suggests bitterly to Aphrodite that Paris may make the goddess "either his wife or his bondslave." In a fragment of the *Andromeda* of Euripides (133 N.) the heroine thus addresses Perseus: "Take me, O stranger, either as wife or as servant."

In Nonnus, a Greek epic poet centuries later than Catullus, Ariadne addresses Theseus: "Take me as a servant for thy chamber . . . . , I will spread thy couch, ... as a servant I will weave for thy happy bride" (*Dionysiaca* XLVII. 386 ff., 404). The expanded form of this commonplace appears first in Catullus, but comparison with Nonnus shows that it must have occurred in Greek poetry also—probably earlier than Catullus. Furthermore, Ariadne did not monopolize it. Other heroines express their devotion in the same way, as, for example, Scylla (*Ciris*, 438 ff.), Tarpeia (Propertius, IV. 4, 33 ff.), and Briseis (Ovid, *Her.* III. 69 ff.).[22]

Nobody can read these passages—particularly the commonplaces on cruelty, loveliness, devoted service, perjuries, vain complaints, and others—without discerning the hand of the rhetorician. The same impression is conveyed by many other details, e.g., the numerous questions, especially the question answering a question (177–183)—"Whither shall I go? . . . . Shall I seek the mountains?" etc.—the description of the Eumenides (193–4), the all-pervading anaphora, the self-address (196), etc. Some of these details are not in themselves exclusively rhetorical, e.g., the questions and the anaphora, and the latter is very sparingly used by Apollonius; their excessive use is the striking feature.

This tendency to dress up the thoughts, almost to play with them, is the great difference between Catullus and Apollonius. It is characteristic of an age much later than Apollonius, when rhetoric had become obvious in poetry; of a style much more modern than his, for he, as a partizan of the old Homeric method, in many ways lags behind the newer tendencies of his age.

One must conclude that Ariadne's lament is not based directly upon the words of Medea as given by Apollonius and Euripides. To a real poet the content of the lament could have been suggested by either of these Greek writers, but if Catullus had either of them in mind, he expressed their thoughts in a very different manner. Ellis is not correct in saying that Apollonius and Euripides "closely resemble Catullus in expression," for in matters of technique Catullus differs markedly not only from Euripides and Apollonius but from any extant Greek poet earlier than his own age.

A complete presentation of all the material would merely amplify in great variety the tendencies which have already been illustrated. It remains to state certain conclusions based upon a study of all the important aspects of the poem.

The results throw light upon the vexed problem of the sources. On this question various theories have been formulated which for the sake of brevity may be grouped under two heads. First there is the view that the sixty-fourth poem is a translation or an imitation of a single Greek poem now lost. Bernhardy suggested a poem of the Hesiodic school, i.e., a very early Greek poem or one which followed the early style. Bergk believed the lost model to be a poem of Euphorion, i.e., in late Greek style (*ca.* 200 B.C.), and he assigned to this poem the single Greek line which Catullus translates in v. 111. On this hypothesis the Greek line is the only surviving remnant of Catullus' original. Riese suggested that the original was a poem of Callimachus, but later he withdrew this suggestion. Hertzburg, Teuffel, Reitzenstein, Wilamowitz, and others have believed that a single Greek poem was the model, but they have refrained from naming a definite poet, although Reitzenstein favors Callimachus and Wilamowitz suggests some Greek *Spätling*.

In this group we may place Drachmann and Pascal,[23] who have suggested two lost Greek poems as models. This theory would account for the combination in Catullus of two stories which have no organic connection. Pascal, for example, believes that the sections on Peleus and Thetis are based upon a poem of Hesiod, whereas the part on Ariadne comes from some Alexandrian poem.

The scholars of the second group have held that the poem is a composition in Greek style by Catullus himself in which he has not limited himself to one or two Greek poems but has made free use of many.[24]

This view, with various differences of detail, has been held by the majority of scholars—M. Haupt,[25] K. P. Schulze, Magnus, Lafaye, Ellis, Friedrich, and many others. Some scholars of this group have found in the poem many details which they have considered as imitations of Roman poets (Plautus, Ennius, Lucretius, etc.); some have held that in certain parts of the poem, especially the lines describing Ariadne on the shore (52–70),[26] Catullus was influenced primarily by sculpture or painting,[27] not literature.

When doctors disagree, we should not at once assume that all of them are wrong! One of them at least may be right or approximately right, although his view has not been sufficiently supported to carry conviction. The present study of the technique renders it possible to eliminate a number of hypotheses and indicate at least that a certain type of solution has probability.[28]

The general view that Catullus translated or closely imitated a definite Greek poem (or two poems) would be refuted if we could believe (with Ellis and others) that he translates or imitates here and there many Greek passages from Homer, Hesiod, Euripides, Apollonius, etc.—that in fact the sixty-fourth poem is to a considerable extent a mosaic of imitations. But it is very difficult to prove that Catullus translates or closely imitates many definite Greek passages. I feel justified in using the terms translation or close imitation only of v. 111. To this I would add a good many single words and a few phrases in which Catullus is probably Romanizing Greek poetic technique, epithets, figures, and the like, though in each particular case one cannot say that he has a definite passage in mind. In other cases the differences from the suggested original are such that one cannot properly term them translations.

If then he had one definite model, we shall be forced to assume that it is not extant, that the resemblances between the work of Catullus and extant Greek are due to the lost Greek poet, and that Catullus' relation to extant Greek is therefore indirect.

If, however, it could be proved that a considerable number of characteristics are Roman, one could accept without hesitation the second view: that the sixty-fourth poem is a free composition by Catullus himself. But since the content and atmosphere are Greek, as they should be in a Greek tale, it is difficult to feel sure of Roman elements.[29]   And yet the present study of the technique supplies an argument of considerable weight in support of this view.   I have called attention to the modern character of the poem as shown in the versions of the two stories, the peculiar structure, the treatment of the device of the *vestis*.   All these might easily be attributed to some late Alexandrian, but taken together with the details of technique they suggest a different solution.

A very large number of the details can be paralleled in Greek; Catullus is working in the Greek manner. But the point which distinguishes his work from that of any preceding Greek poet is the superabundance of mannerisms: the pictorial passages, the use of prophecy to narrate the deeds of Achilles,[30] the learned allusiveness, the intrusion of the poet's personality, the use of apostrophe[31] and speech for purposes of vivid narrative, the rhetorical commonplaces and expansions, the excessive anaphora and questions, and many others. The accumulation of all these things in one poem of moderate length is the strong argument.   In the sixty-fourth poem we have in a late and exaggerated form an example of that modern narrative art with

which the name of Callimachus was connected in the
time of Catullus—is in fact still connected. But
Catullus goes far beyond Callimachus. I know of no
Greek poet before the time of Catullus who tells a
story thus. Certainly neither Alexander of Aetolia
nor Apollonius nor Hermesianax worked in this way.[32]
Not even Callimachus in the long fragment of the
Cydippe, which most clearly reveals his art in telling a
love story, is modern to the same degree. There is in
the poem a *nescio quid nimii*, as Ellis vaguely feels
(282), and for this I believe that Catullus himself is
chiefly responsible. The only other possible solution
is the view that he is translating or closely imitating
some very late Greek poet, some *Spätling*, as Wilamowitz puts it. How priceless would be the discovery of
some complete erotic poems or long passages of
Euphorion, Nicander, or Parthenius, that we might
know exactly how these later poets wrote! And yet
since the Greek poets whose work is much later than
Catullus—Nonnus, Quintus Smyrnaeus, Musaeus—
differ markedly from him, the assumption that the
kind of art under discussion is the work of some lost
Greek—a sort of Greek Catullus—is improbable and
unnecessary.

In fine, Catullus' epyllion contains in detail both
translation and imitation, but it is not as a whole a
translation or a mosaic of translations and close imitations. It is a real *carmen vigilatum*, probably very
similar (except in the comparative absence of obscurity)
to such poems as the *Zmyrna* of Catullus' friend
Helvius Cinna, filled with resemblances to passages
in many Greek poets. But the character of these
resemblances indicates that the original motives have
passed through a period of evolution, and opposes in

general the view that Catullus is consciously following definite passages of extant Greek. The art of Catullus as a story teller is here ultra-modern—an effort, not always highly successful, to Romanize and improve the latest Greek technique. This art is the product not only of the poet's reading and study but also of his rhetorical training, and in many ways it anticipates the methods, more perfect in some respects, of the Augustan poets. Such poetic art may be called Roman, but a more expressive term for it is Graeco-Roman.

CHAPTER VI

THE ELEGIES

In elegy the Romans achieved one of their greatest literary successes. Three quarters of a century after the death of Ovid, the last of the great Augustan elegists, Quintilian, a sober critic, comparing the Roman achievement with the Greek, briefly expresses his verdict in the words, *elegia . . . . Graecos provocamus,* "in elegy we challenge the Greeks." It is a verdict from which the modern critic, after studying all the remains of Greek and Roman elegy—and the material is abundant—is not likely to dissent. Undoubtedly the Romans possessed a remarkable gift for this kind of poetry,[1] and even if we had before us today the entire product of all the Greeks and Romans, it is probable that we should still regard the elegy of the Augustan Age, with its four great names—Gallus, Tibullus, Propertius, and Ovid—as on the whole the acme of the *genre.*

Like all other kinds of Roman poetry, Augustan elegy is compounded of both Greek and Roman elements. Among the Greeks the *genre* had a very long development and they had brought it to the highest degree of perfection of which they were capable some two centuries before the Romans began to practice it. The first Roman elegies appear in Catullus only a generation earlier than the most perfect example of the *genre* in the Augustan Age. Clearly if we would understand how it came about that the Romans achieved such perfection, it is necessary to study the elegies of Catullus, the pioneer.

But what was the general character of elegy in antiquity? We of modern times have inherited the term, but we have greatly restricted its meaning. Elegy is now defined as "a short poem of lamentation or regret, called forth by the decease of a beloved or revered person, or by a general sense of the pathos of mortality," or as "a song of grief . . . . it can look forward to death as well as back."[2]

These definitions fit only one type of ancient elegy— an important type because, in accordance with the predominant ancient view, elegy was originally a lament; the word ἔλεγοι (Latin *elegi*), "couplets" or "an elegy," and the adjective ἐλεγεῖος from which came the noun ἐλεγεία (Latin *elegeia* or *elegia*), "an elegy" or "elegy" (the *genre*), were connected, perhaps rightly, with the noun ἔλεγος, a "lament." But if elegy was ever exclusively restricted to a content of mourning, sorrow, and consolation, it must have been at a period antedating the earliest extant examples of the *genre*, which occur in Archilochus and Callinus sometime between 700 and 650 B.C. The actual (and abundant) remains of elegy reveal no such restriction. On the contrary from the seventh century to the end of the Augustan Age the lament was at some periods rare and was never the most important type of elegy. In fact so far as content and tone are concerned ancient elegy had an extremely wide range. But to an ancient nothing was elegy unless it was written in the elegiac couplet, which consisted, in the words of Diomedes, of a (dactylic) hexameter and a pentameter placed alternately.[3] In English the movement of this meter is fairly well represented by Coleridge's translation of Schiller's couplet:

> In the hexameter rises the fountain's silvery column,
> In the pentameter aye falling in melody back.

This meter was used by the ancients for such a wide range of themes that we may almost agree with Mackail that it was a meter "which would refuse nothing."[4] But we cannot fully agree, for the couplet was regarded as a weaker, less dignified, metrical vehicle than the hexameter alone. The Greeks and Romans often called the pentameter "soft," "tender" (μαλακός, *tener*), peculiarly adapted to the theme of love. Ovid wittily illustrates this conception in the second poem of his *Amores*. He had begun a lofty epic, he says, and the second verse was equal in length to the first, for he was using the regulation epic meter, the hexameter. But Cupid, who was resolved that Ovid should be a love poet, stole a foot from the second verse, thus changing it into a pentameter, whereupon the poet in his tirade against the thief exclaims, "My fresh page began with a splendid first line, but that second line removed all my vigor!" And so perforce he had to sing of love in a meter better adapted to the subject.

Efforts to reproduce classical meters in English are rarely successful, although with the employment of extreme care in the choice of words and syllables some fairly good results can be attained. In English the pentameter is bound to be monotonous and tends to degenerate into a mere jingle. Tennyson, who was in the best sense an imitator of the classics, greatly admired the hexameter and the Alcaics of Horace, but he did not like the Sapphic stanza with the little

Adonic at the end "like a pig with its tail tightly curled,"
as he expressed it, and for the pentameter he suggested
the outrageous parody:

All men alike hate slops, particularly gruel.[5]

The metrical form of ancient elegy was fixed; in
modern elegy it is free. The themes of ancient elegy
had a very wide range; in modern elegy they are rather
closely limited. The ancient elegists put some curious
subjects into elegiac form. For example, Nicander
wrote on snakes, Archelaus on plants, Xenothemis on
travel, and Ovid during the long years of his exile
wrote nine books of elegiac verse, mostly letters to his
friends in Rome. All these things were, from the
ancient point of view, elegy, but they were bypaths,
not the main highway. Anybody who will follow the
course of elegy for more than six hundred and fifty
years from Archilochus and Callinus to Ovid will be
impressed by the great variety of its content and its
purpose. He will be still more impressed by the fact
that love, for the first three hundred years an infrequent
theme, became important in the fourth and third
centuries and dominant in the Augustan Age. From
early Greek elegy—ending about 400 B.C. or somewhat
later—we have remains of over thirty elegists, but only
two, Mimnermus (*ca.* 600 B.C.) and Antimachus (*ca.*
400 and later) are really important as erotic elegists.
During most of the fourth century the history of elegy
cannot be followed; the remains are too meager. Toward
300 B.C., however, fragments become more numerous,
so that we can form some conception, imperfect though
it is, of the so-called Alexandrian elegy from Philetas
and Callimachus, its acknowledged leaders, to Parthenius, sometimes called the last of the Alexandrians.

Toward the end of this period Rome became the literary center of the world. Parthenius lived at Rome and his long life made him a contemporary of both Catullus and the Augustan poets. He was intimately associated with Gallus and Vergil, and he dedicated to the former a collection of mythological love stories in prose to be used, as he says, in the composition of epic and elegy.[6] This little book is still extant, but the poetical work of Parthenius is in tatters.

This association in Rome of Greek writers composing in Greek with Romans composing in Latin is, I think, one of the most striking proofs of the continuity of Greek and Roman literature. Parthenius was only one of many. For nearly two hundred years there had been Greek men of letters residing in Rome. A long list of these Greeks is known, including in the second century B.C. such prominent names as Panaetius, the philosopher, and Polybius, the historian, who were members of the literary circle of the younger Scipio, the conqueror of Carthage, and in the first century besides Parthenius the epigrammatists Philodemus and Crinagoras. Cicero knew and befriended a number of Greek literary men, among whom the name of Archias is known (or used to be known!) to every schoolboy. The surviving work of Archias, however, does not measure up to the estimate which Cicero gives of his ability as a poet.

From these Greeks the Romans learned much and they learned to such good effect that by the Augustan Age they had wrested from them the supremacy in most departments of poetry which were being practiced at that time. They were freed at last from Greek leading strings although they did not wish to be freed from Greek influence.

Elegy was one of the greatest Roman successes, and although other themes were by no means excluded, it was to a very large extent erotic. In the Tibullus collection, for example, there are, excluding the little erotic epigrams, twenty-eight elegies of which twenty-two belong to the thorough-going erotic type, while in four others love is an important theme, and the non-erotic themes, such as love of country life, hatred of war, are often intimately connected with the erotic. In Propertius and Ovid there is greater variety, but love continues to be by far the most important theme. Gallus wrote four books of elegies of which only one line survives, but there is not the slightest doubt that they too were predominantly erotic.

It is not surprising then that when the ancient critics of this and later periods spoke of elegy they thought first of erotic elegy. Fine elegies were written on other themes, for example the seventh of Tibullus' first book celebrating at once the Aquitanian triumph and the birthday of the great Messalla, or Propertius, III. 18, mourning the untimely death of young Marcellus; but such elegies were outside the main current. And so we find that when in the first century of the Empire Quintilian alludes to elegy he has in mind primarily erotic elegy. In his famous canon of the elegists he characterizes Ovid as *lascivior*, "more wanton," a word which applies only to the erotic elegies of that poet. Elsewhere he remarks that elegy is not suitable reading for schoolboys.[7]

At the outset we must distinguish two main groups of erotic elegies: (1) those in which the poet deals with his own love; (2) those in which he deals with the love of others—friends, mythological characters, etc. The first variety is often called by the clumsy but expressive name subjective-erotic elegy, and it is by far the more important because here the Romans are probably most original, certainly at their best. If we are to determine what contributions Catullus made to elegy it will be well to bear in mind what were the salient characteristics of this type in the period of its highest development. And so it is worth while to attempt a definition or concise description of the Augustan erotic elegy. In the sphere of poetry, definitions are never very satisfactory, but the attempt to define may serve to clarify our ideas.

A subjective-erotic elegy was a poem of considerable length, usually addressed to an individual or to readers, in which the poet communicates the thoughts and feelings which are suggested by some experience or aspect of his own love. It is usually serious or sad, but on occasion it may be joyous or even gay. Humor and wit are not excluded. It may be gracefully familiar, but it is rarely comic or vulgar, for it possesses a certain dignity of tone and style.[8] Some comments will make this definition clearer. The length of such an elegy may vary between some sixteen lines (Propertius, II.31) and one hundred and sixty (Catullus, LXVIII). The average is between fifty and sixty lines. Longer pieces are found among Ovid's *Heroides* or *Tristia* and of course in the three books of his *Ars amatoria*, but these are not of the subjective-erotic type and I have excluded them. When a composition is very short it tends to pass into the field of the epigram, as, for example, Propertius, I.21 or 22 (10 lines) or Tibullus, IV.14 (4 lines). This point will be considered later. Ordinarily, however, there is no difficulty in distinguishing an elegy from an epigram.

The address, which had been a common feature of elegy from the earliest times, is ordinarily to the loved

one or to friends (*sodales, amici*) of the poet, less often
to patrons—Messalla, Maecenas, etc. Sometimes no
name is used and we have a mere *amici* or *vos* or an
address to readers generally. This feature is not confined to elegy; it occurs in many other forms—lyric,
satire, etc., but it is a noteworthy characteristic of
elegy—part of its intimate nature.

The course of true love never did run smooth—it
would not be very interesting if it did—and so the tone
of elegy is usually serious or sad. Exultation there is,
but gloom and despair are far more common. Sometimes there are flashes of humor, as in Tibullus, or of
wit, as in Ovid. But Ovid's excessive display of gaiety
and wit show that in him the elegy is already beginning
to decline.

The general dignity of this type of Augustan elegy
is striking. The poet-lover maintains in general a
gallant, romantic, almost a chivalrous attitude which
lifts this love poetry far above most of the stuff which
the Greeks, so far as we know, produced. In the last
analysis this tone is due to the general attitude of the
Roman toward the Roman woman, whose position was
superior to that held by woman among the Greeks.[9]
With this attitude the style of elegy conforms; there
is a general decency, not to say nobility of language.

Elegy, says Reitzenstein,[10] speaking of the earlier
Greek period, is "talk." Solon, for example, talks to
his audience. This is much more true of Roman elegy.
It is *sermo*, often very much like the *sermones*, the
"talks," of Horace, except that its style is more dignified,
and it deals for the most part with different themes.
The elegist like the satirist often thinks or reflects out
loud. This produces a loose quasi-extemporaneous
structure, and logic often goes by the board. It is as

if the reader received only those impressions of the poet's mood which happen to become oral.

There is an endless variety in human love affairs and the novelists of our day have by no means exhausted them. If you survey the whole range of Roman elegy you will find that these ancient poets made a very fair beginning and many a passage in the modern novel, particularly if the story happens to be told in the first person, need only be translated into Latin elegiacs to become a good Roman elegy. I have noted such passages all the way from Henry Fielding to Arnold Bennett. But of course there is an enormous difference in the impression of sincerity produced by a Roman elegist pouring forth his own sentiments about his own passion and the impression produced by a modern novelist presenting the sentiments of a character —the same difference which exists between Tibullus' subjective-erotic elegies and those pretty pieces in the fourth book in which he deals with the love affair of Sulpicia and Cerinthus, or between these same pretty pieces and their sources, the startlingly sincere little elegiac letters of Sulpicia herself.

The best Roman elegies create the impression of reality and sincerity. The heroine is real flesh and blood and the poet's moods and sentiments have a real basis. At times he displays a bit of humor but for the most part he is in dead earnest. We must not forget this when we read one of those humorous summaries of the elegiac love story which it is easy for the observant bystander to compose. The scoffing bystander is indeed a character in Roman elegy, for the elegists, especially Propertius, were quite aware that their preoccupation with love was in the eyes of the average Roman folly and worthlessness (*nequitia*). This confession renders the picture of their slavery all the more convincing. The true elegist is the slave of love and he cannot help it, and it is precisely because Ovid was in reality a witty bystander that he is not so good an elegist as Tibullus and Propertius.

If you will bear in mind the importance of love to the elegist himself, it will do no harm to read the outline of a typical affair composed by one who saw at once its pathos and its humor—the late Kirby Smith.

The bacillus amatorius generally penetrates the poet by way of his eyes, and the period of incubation is ridiculously short. Among the first symptoms one of the most notable is an utter inability to sleep. It is useless to struggle. The arrows of Dan Cupid are unerring and burn to the bone. His victim is an ox at the plow, and the worst is yet to come; he is a soldier detailed for special service, always leading the forlorn hope. To overcome the girl's disdain is only one of his troubles. Frequently there is a selfish and tactless "husband" in the way. Then follow all the varieties, moods, and motives of an intrigue.

The emotional temperature is far above the danger point. Clothes torn, hair forcibly removed, faces scratched, black and blue spots—these are all marks of affection. As the observant Parmeno remarks—

> in amore haec omnia insunt vitia: iniuriae,
> suspiciones, inimicitiae, indutiae,
> bellum, pax rursum, etc.

"A bitter-sweet passion at best," says Burton, after consulting all the books in and about Oxford—"dolentia delectabilis, hilare tormentum—fair, foul, and full of variation."

Jove's book for recording lovers' oaths is running water. And "la donna è mobile"—her promises are sport for the winds and seas. The poet is always poor. His mistress however is not only a pearl, but a pearl of price. He promises her immortality in his verses; she is more concerned about

her immediate future in this life. He learns as did the
Abbé Voisenon that—

> Sans dépenser
> C'est en vain qu'on espère
> De s'avancer
> Au pays de Cythère.

He is therefore the natural enemy of wealth, greed, and
present-day luxury. His ideal is the Golden Age, when men
were so happy and so poor. He takes no part in politics, is
not ambitious to get on in affairs; war is as unpopular with
him as seafaring and similar short cuts to death. He observes
omens, frequently consults witch-wives and Thessalian moon
specialists, and generally makes them responsible for the sins
of his mistress. She herself has a decided leaning for ritual-
ism. She is devoted to Isis and sows dissension by her peri-
odical attacks of going into retreat.

She is earnestly advised not to mar her great natural
beauty by artificial means. In the course of the affair she
never fails to have an illness. The poet nurses her and after-
wards writes a poem about it. He too falls ill. Maybe he is
going to die. If so, will she see to it that the following
directions with regard to his funeral are carried out?

Like Anakreon he must love, and is made to sing of love
alone. To expect him to write epic is quite out of the question. Indeed the gods themselves sometimes serve notice
on him to that effect.[11]

Such then in outline was the most important type
of elegy at the height of its development in the Augustan Age. Its chief basis was life and experience, but
the poets were trained artists and they drew freely on
all kinds of literature, Greek and Roman, which could
help them in the artistic presentation of their love.
They did not limit themselves to elegy but made use
of epic, lyric, epigram, Greek New Comedy, bucolic
poetry, and even prose—remember, for example, the
little prose book of love stories which Parthenius

dedicated to Gallus "for use in epic and in elegy." Whatever useful material they found they poured into the form of elegy, each poet of course modifying it to suit his own purpose.

Now the most important feature of this elegy is the fact that the poet employs all his material, whether he drew it from life or from literature, in the presentation of his own love. He depicts the varying aspects of his love at length; he dwells on them. He causes the reader to grasp the elements which enter into his varying moods. Often he is highly lyric, often he narrates, describes or illustrates, still more often he reflects, as it were, out loud. Many details of this elegy have been traced to ultimate sources in Greek literature, but the whole—the developed treatment by a poet of his own love—has no counterpart there, even in elegy. If any Greek elegist wrote poems of this kind, they have not survived.

From the point of view of literary history we have here a question which has divided scholars into two camps. The Alexandrian elegists, Philetas and Callimachus, were greatly admired by Catullus, Propertius, and Ovid, and the last two often acknowledge a debt to them. Although Tibullus names no Greek poet, his obligation to the Greeks is none the less clear. Philetas is said to have written some kind of poetry concerning a sweetheart Bittis, but the few fragments of his work allow us to form no conception of it. Callimachus is called by Quintilian the leader of elegy (*princeps elegiae*). He wrote many elegies of which we have fairly numerous fragments—one of eighty-odd lines— together with the Latin translation of a complete elegy by Catullus,[12] but no sweetheart's name is mentioned in connection with him, and all his elegies seem to have been of the etiological variety, narrative poems in which it would have been very difficult to insert passages about his own love. In fact neither the fragments of Alexandrian elegy nor the numerous statements by Greek and Roman writers about it prove that any of these Greek poets composed elegies of the Roman type. And yet many scholars have believed that subjective-erotic elegies were composed by the Alexandrian poets and that the Romans found in them direct models which they adapted to their own situations. These scholars believe that the Greek elegists utilized the new comedy, lyric, epic, epigram, etc., and that the presence in Roman elegy of motive traceable to these *genres* is best explained on their assumption. When, for example, Propertius and Ovid pose as experts in the art of love, it has been asserted that they did not get the idea directly from the New Comedy where it was first developed, but from some Greek elegist who had used the New Comedy.[13]

The work of Catullus throws considerable light, in my opinion, on this central problem of elegy and I shall keep it in mind throughout the following discussion. Catullus was not generally thought of as an elegist, for he wrote few poems of this kind. Moreover, his fame as a writer of the very short types of poetry was so great that men were prone to forget the rest of his work. In the Augustan Age Propertius alone[14] connects him with elegy, placing him with Varro of Atax at the head of his list of Roman elegists. Varro was a contemporary of Catullus but he did not turn to elegy until he had completed a long epic on the Argonauts and so it is probable that Catullus is to be regarded as actually the first Roman elegist. Certainly as a poet he ranked far above Varro.

We have from Catullus only five elegies (including the translation from Callimachus): LXV–LXVIII, and LXXVI—a total of 402 lines. Two of these (LXV, LXVIII) can be dated *ca.* 59 B.C. In 59 B.C. Gallus was a boy of nine or ten, and Tibullus and Propertius began to write nearly thirty years later, about 31–30 B.C. Ovid began to make public his *Amores* about 25 B.C.[15] In round numbers a period of about seventy-five years—from the earliest datable work of Catullus to the death of Ovid, 17 A.D.—will include the beginning, the perfection, and the decline of the best Roman elegy.

When we compare the work of Catullus with Augustan elegy, we see at once that the Augustans developed the *genre* in many ways. What part Gallus took in this development it is impossible to say since his four books of elegies are lost, but his contribution was certainly important and, since he died 26 B.C. and had for some time been actively engaged in affairs, his work was probably completed before Tibullus and Propertius began to write. At any rate even the earliest elegies of the last two poets are finished products. It is with their work and that of Ovid that we must compare the elegies of Catullus. To what extent did he anticipate them in content and in form? What was his conception of elegy and how did it influence the Augustans? And, finally, what elements of Greek elegy did Catullus make his own? These are some of the questions which I shall try to answer and the result will enable us to define the position in this department of Catullus himself. He is a much more important figure, I am convinced, than most scholars have believed him to be, and even the few who have recognized in him the founder of Roman elegy[16] have not given an adequate account of his contributions to the development of the *genre*.

Meter is too technical a subject to be fully discussed here, but perhaps I can make one or two points clear. The first Roman to employ the elegiac couplet was, so far as we know, Ennius, over one hundred years earlier than Catullus. He did not write elegy, but, as we have had occasion to note again and again, the couplet was the favorite meter of epigram and in tracing the history of the meter all occurrences of it must be included. The hexameter and pentameter were adapted from the Greek and they were difficult for the Romans because their movement is dactylic (– ◡ ◡) and for this the Latin language was not by nature well suited; it had too many long vowels and syllables, not enough words and combinations of two short syllables. Moreover the Latin accent had a strong element of stress which had to be reckoned with in working out a verse agreeable to the ear. From the metrical point of view Roman poetry is a curious phenomenon. Almost every one of the meters was taken over from the Greek, which had a so-called musical accent, into a language whose accent was to a large extent one of stress. It was a transfer from one medium into another in which the original elements were not present in the same degree or the same proportions. Necessarily the results were different in kind. The Roman poets strove to compose verses which to their ears reproduced the movement of the Greek originals. The results could only be approximate since the media were different.

And so generation after generation of Roman poets contributed to the development of this meter. As we follow the history of the meters from the third century B.C. to the Augustan Age, they become more and more perfect in form. In fact the Romans rather overdid the thing and developed ideals of perfection unknown to the Greeks or at least unpracticed except as *tours de force*. To my taste the meters of Horace's odes are too perfect. They sacrifice freedom for a perfection of form which incurs the risk of artificiality.

The history of the elegiac couplet follows the usual course, and it is to a large extent a struggle to secure a dactylic movement. In this Ovid was the first Roman to succeed. The verses of Catullus are heavy with spondees. In other respects also the Augustan poets produced lighter, smoother, more flexible verses. They have fewer and less harsh elisions and they were far more successful in adapting the word order, the syntax, and the sense to the meter.

Yet we must remember that all the poets who wrote elegiac couplets were trying to perfect the meter and that the Augustans could not have succeeded in their achievement without the work of a long line of predecessors among whom Catullus was foremost. We may, I think, go a step farther. Catullus, with all his metrical skill, was unable to perfect the couplet. He came too early. But if we compare his work with that of the earlier centuries (Greek and Roman) on the one hand, and with that of the Augustan Age on the other, we see that if he could have carried out his ideas with the requisite technical skill, his couplets would have reached a perfection different from that of Tibullus and especially of Ovid whose couplets are usually regarded as the norm. His successors followed a number of the principles which he had laid down, others they rejected, and they developed some new things, notably the "Law of the Distich," in accordance with which each distich or couplet became more or less a unit of thought.

Neither the Greeks nor Catullus observed this last principle and I doubt whether it was a real improvement. The same may be said of the strong Augustan tendency to end the pentameter with a word of two syllables. Both these principles tend to make the verse schematic, monotonous. Catullus held more closely to the Greeks and as a result he strove to produce a freer couplet. The Augustans, although they had greater technical skill, restricted its freedom. It is all a matter of taste, but I agree with the greatest commentator on Catullus, Robinson Ellis, that a Vergil might have molded a better couplet than that of Ovid by following along the lines marked out by Catullus. Propertius indeed started to do this but later he went over to the camp of Ovid.

Thus Catullus helped to develop the metrical technique of elegy; but his chief contributions are of a different character. The first of these is his development of the epigram into an elegy. We have already noted that elegy and epigram run closely parallel courses in Greek and Latin. The favorite meter of epigram was the elegiac couplet and the themes were often the same as the themes of elegy. Almost all the extant collections of Roman elegies—Catullus, Tibullus, Propertius, Ovid's *Amores*—include epigrams, sometimes imbedded in an elegy.[17] Many an elegy was in a sense an expanded epigram or, if you prefer, the same theme was worked up in both epigram and elegy. The difference was one of length and especially of treatment.[18]

Ordinarily if we wish to study the difference between an elegy and an epigram on the same subject it is necessary to compare the work of two different poets. Excellent examples of this may be found in the fourth book of the Tibullus collection where some of the little

epigrams of Sulpicia are worked up by a real poet,
presumably Tibullus himself, into elegies. In each
case the elegy is three or four times the length of the
epigram on which it is based. In Catullus however
we have the unique opportunity of comparing an elegy
with epigrams on the same situation all written by
one and the same poet. Moreover these poems all
concern the poet's own love, and so they throw a great
light on one way at least in which the most important
type of elegy originated and developed.

The eighty-fifth poem consists of only two lines, but
it is one of the unforgettable things of poetry:

> Odi et amo: quare id faciam fortasse requiris.
> nescio, sed fieri sentio et excrucior.

Hate and love—torture that I do not understand—a
whole human life in a couplet, as Moritz Haupt said.[19]
But soon the poet begins to understand. In the seventy-
fifth poem the same situation is treated still epigram-
matically, but a little more fully: "My heart has been
brought to such a pass through your fault, Lesbia, and
has suffered such ruin through its own devotion that I
could no longer wish you well, should you become the
best of women, nor cease to love you, no matter what
you do." Here the hate (in the tempered form of
"not wishing her well") and the love persist, but there
is more; there is the inability to cast the feelings aside,
and above all there is some explanation: Lesbia's
faithlessness (*culpa*) and the poet's devotion have
caused his conflicting passions. The poet has begun
to reflect. He has taken the first step toward that
extended presentation of a situation and a mood which
characterizes subjective-erotic elegy in its purest form.
And in the seventy-sixth poem we have the elegy. The

situation is the same—the poet-lover convinced of the girl's faithlessness but unable to break the fetters of his love. The brief suggestions of the epigrams appear in expanded form: his devoted loyalty, her faithlessness, his persistent love and torture; the recognition that his own strength is so slight that he must appeal to the gods for pity and aid. There are many more finished poems in Latin and in Catullus, but none can approach this elegy in the gripping power and sincerity with which the torture of a human heart is laid bare. Propertius and Ovid have dealt with the same theme but their elegies are very inferior to that of Catullus.[20]

Thus Catullus had begun to work into subjective-erotic elegy by way of epigram. In this he anticipates an important method of Augustan elegy. Before Catullus no Greek or Roman poet, so far as we know, had attempted it, but it would be rash to assume that the method as a method originated with Catullus.

The only other subjective-erotic elegy is the long sixty-eighth poem. In this elegy Catullus combines three themes: his friendship for Allius, his grief for his brother's death, and his love for Lesbia. He had gone home to Verona crushed by his grief when his friend Allius, who was suffering from some misfortune in love, wrote to him requesting consolatory poetry. Catullus at first declares that his grief makes it impossible for him to write, and then suddenly he launches forth into a long poem of more than one hundred lines in which he mourns his brother and praises Allius for aid in his own love affair with Lesbia. As a whole the poem is a curious composition. Its structure, for example, is unique. The poet has three main themes: friendship, love, sorrow. He works through the friendship to the love and so to the sorrow and then back

again in reverse order: sorrow, love, friendship. The
structure may be represented by the letters A B C B A,
and the parts also of each main theme are arranged with
equal symmetry. As we read from the beginning to
the central lines we may compare the poem to one of
those nests of boxes cunningly wrought by some
Chinese workman, the sorrow representing the core of
the whole. Whether this highly artificial structure
was suggested to Catullus by some lost Greek poem,
or by the Pindaric ode, or whether he invented it himself, we do not know. To me it appears to be an extreme
development of the old Homeric digression or the tale
within the tale, but since it was never imitated it
throws no light on the development of elegy and I
need not discuss it here.[21]

The three themes—grief, friendship, love—taken in
the broadest sense all appear both in Greek and in
Augustan elegy. Catullus' lament for his brother continues one of the oldest themes of elegy—perhaps, as
we have seen, the original theme. But the other two
themes stand on a different basis. They are closely
connected with each other, and the friend (Allius) is
thanked and praised for services connected with the
poet's own love. Praise (encomium) as such is not
uncommon in Greek elegy, but nowhere is it rendered
for services in love. Catullus connects the encomiastic
element with the subjective-erotic and in this also he
anticipated Augustan elegy. Like Tibullus and Propertius he had begun to reflect in elegy the love affairs
of himself and his friends, and the services for which
he thanks Allius are of the same type as the services
which Propertius, for example, promises to Gallus.[22]

In the use to which he puts the story of Laodamia
Catullus anticipates an important feature of Augustan

elegy. He makes of the myth an illustration of his own love: Laodamia came to Protesilaus as Lesbia came to Catullus and her motive also was love. The Greeks—Theognis and Antimachus, for example—had begun this use of myth, but they had not developed it in the same way. In Augustan elegy however and especially in Propertius the phenomenon is so common as to require no illustration, but it is worth while to note that Propertius employed the same myth.[23]

Another mythological parallel occurs in vv. 138–140 and suggests an interesting point. In this passage the poet compares his own forbearance toward Lesbia's flirtations with the attitude—enforced, to be sure!—of Juno toward Jupiter. Both the attitude and the manner in which it is expressed became common in Augustan elegy, but the Augustans developed them into the principle of complaisance (*obsequium*) and made it part of their didactic system. Catullus knows nothing of such a system.[24]

I have referred above to the generally elevated tone and style of Augustan erotic elegy—one of its most striking characteristics. In this also Catullus led the way. He felt his love for Lesbia to be of the purest type—like that of a father for his children.[25] When he came to a full realization of her perfidy his epigrams and lyrics express hate and loathing in the most violent terms. Not so the elegies. In his elegies he preserves a certain decency and dignity. Lesbia possessed for him much more than physical charm. She was dearer to him than his life and he regarded their relation as bound by a compact like that of wedlock.[26] Nothing is more significant of his conception of elegy than the style in which the erotic details are expressed. The sixty-eighth poem contains many such details but they are clothed in language which does not endanger the dignity of the whole composition. Clearly Catullus felt that elegy should maintain a certain dignified level,[27] and this is all the more striking because in the rest of his subjective-erotic work he follows no such principle. In addition to the principle itself every one of the details which I have mentioned can be paralleled in Augustan elegy. But I must pass on to other things.

The remaining elegies (LXV–LXVII) do not represent the most important type, but they contribute a number of interesting points to our knowledge of Catullian elegy as a whole.

The sixty-seventh poem, the tale of a bit of Veronese scandal, lies so far outside the general course of ancient elegy that I need not dwell long upon it. It has, however, two details of form which are interesting because they appear again in Augustan elegy. The story is told in dramatic dialogue between the poet and a house door. Speaking tombstones, statues, chaplets— even, as we shall see in a moment, locks of hair—are common enough in ancient poetry, but this is the first appearance of the device in elegy. Propertius continued it in the sixteenth elegy of his first book and he employs the dramatic dialogue also in the first poem of his fourth book. But the form was exceptional. When a character was made to speak, the instinct of the elegists was correct in choosing the informal method which allowed the poet also to speak and to comment at will. The dramatic dialogue was too rigid to suit the general character of elegy.

The sixty-sixth poem, the *Tress of Berenice*, is a translation of Callimachus' Βερενίκης πλόκαμος, a complimentary elegy of the etiological type. The Greek poet told how the queen vowed one of her tresses to the gods if her husband Ptolemy should return safely from war, and how the tress, as the astronomer Conon had professed to discover, became a constellation.[28] This is the only complete elegy of Callimachus that has survived and in spite of the Latin form it throws a great deal of light upon the Greek poet's art as an elegist,[29] for Catullus' translation is on the whole so faithful that we may rely on the Latin poem as representing the structure, the run of the thought, and the general character of the Greek, though not always the verbal details.[30]

In the history of elegy the sixty-sixth poem contributes chiefly to our knowledge of Callimachus, not Catullus. But Catullus admired Callimachus; he must have seen something to admire in this elegy or else he would not have translated it. Since Callimachus was regarded by both Catullus and Propertius as the leader among Alexandrian elegists it is worth while to examine the sixty-sixth poem in order to determine what qualities appealed to Catullus. The answer is in short this: Catullus was interested chiefly in the poetic art with which Callimachus told a love story, the same art—the "modern" art—which is displayed in the long papyrus fragment of the great Alexandrian's *Cydippe*, his most famous elegy.[31] Let us glance at some of the details.

The *Tress of Berenice* is a narrative elegy. The ostensible theme is the dedication and the deification or, if I may use such a term, the "starification" of the tress. But the erotic element, which is logically subordinate, becomes in the actual telling of the story much more important than the mere narrative theme. It is the love of Berenice for Ptolemy which prompts her to make and to carry out her vow, and it is love for Berenice which is the chief feeling of the Tress as she

tells the story—for Callimachus makes of the tress a
person and puts the whole tale into her mouth. This
device is of the same kind as that employed by Catullus
and Propertius when they personify the house door.
Callimachus found in' it a convenient means of complimenting the royal pair. The elegy is court poetry, but
it has other aspects which are of much greater interest.

The elegy is full of learning, especially in the astro-
nomical passages. Some of the allusions are so obscure
that in spite of the labors of scholars they are not yet
fully understood. Callimachus knew and his cultured
readers understood him, but we do not wonder that in
later times his elegies proved to be so difficult that
they were called the "exercising ground of the grammarians."[32] Catullus and the other *docti poetae* were
attracted by this idea of inserting bits of learning into
poetry. More important is the manner in which it
was done. Often there was just an allusion; the reader
was expected to know the rest, as when Callimachus
just alludes (5–6) to the tale of Endymion. If such a
tale did not happen to be well known, obscurity might
result, but the poets were at no pains to be clear. It
was a method widely practiced by the well trained
Roman poets and they learned it from Callimachus
and other later Greeks.

Still more important is the way in which the erotic
element is managed. Berenice's feelings as she parts
weeping from her husband are analyzed—in fact the
feelings of brides in general are analyzed—by a series
of insinuating questions and answers (15–32) which
prove that her acts are due to love. The passage is
worthy of Ovid. Berenice becomes one of those heroines who, like the Arethusa of Propertius,[33] are forced
to part from their lovers. All the details are familiar

to readers of Augustan elegy—the tears, the vow, the longing for the lover's return, the parting words, although Callimachus spares us the actual speech.

Similarly the feelings of the Tress are emphasized— her unwillingness to leave Berenice, her yearnings to be once more with the queen, her despair. These reflections of feeling are skilfully connected with the narrative, and the manner in which Callimachus passes from one to the other, dwelling rather on the feeling, is a marked characteristic of Roman elegy. It is part of the modern Greek method of telling a love story which is better illustrated in the *Cydippe* of Callimachus than anywhere else because there the poet is himself telling the tale, not, as in the *Tress of Berenice*, putting it into the mouth of a character. In the *Cydippe* also the narrative advances, as it were, by fits and starts. The poet breaks off to address himself and to reflect, he apostrophizes Acontius, gives his source for the story (Xenomedes), and expresses his own resolve. In a word, the personality of the poet is constantly felt— we might almost say intruded—in this modern fashion of telling a story. Many details of this technique appear also, as I have shown, in the short epic, the hexameter narrative. But in elegy the poets made of it something more natural, and as regards style more colloquial. What a world of difference there is between this intimate, modern way of telling a story and the old-fashioned style and how quickly it developed can best be seen by comparing the long fragment of Alexander of Aetolia (*ca.* 300 B.C.), in which the story of Antheus and Cleobeia is told,[34] with the *Cydippe*, which must have been written hardly fifty years later.

Here then in the art of Callimachus we have the secret of his influence on Roman elegy. This alone is sufficient to explain why Catullus liked the *Tress of Berenice*, why Callimachus is mentioned much more often by Propertius and Ovid than any other Greek elegist. The Romans undoubtedly utilized the material they found in Callimachus, but their chief obligation was one of poetic craftsmanship. Callimachus wrote no subjective erotic elegies—he confined this content to his epigrams—but many details of the art which he employed in narrative elegy were easily transferred by the Romans to elegies and other forms in which they presented love. In this Catullus made a good beginning.

In a brief lecture it is impossible to present all the details or even all the classes of details which contribute to our estimate of Catullus as an elegist. I have omitted much—for example, all comment on the sixty-fifth poem. But enough has been said, I think, to prove that Catullus in the department of elegy was a real pioneer laying the foundations and in many ways clearly indicating the lines which his successors were to follow. In elegy as in his other work he owed much to the Greeks, but his indebtedness, stated in general terms, was an indebtedness of form, not content. The entire content of the sixty-seventh and seventy-sixth poems and the major parts of the sixty-fifth and sixty-eighth were derived from his own observation and experience. He learned from the Greeks not so much what to say as how to say it.

His own elegies are few—only four, if we exclude the translation of Callimachus—and yet they anticipate Augustan elegy in a surprising number of characteristics. By far the most important of these is the expression of the poet's own love, for this became the striking feature of Augustan elegy. It is quite possible that his services here were even more important than the meager extant evidence indicates—that he was not only the first Roman poet, but the first poet, Greek or Roman, to enter this field. As one scans the long centuries of elegiac writing from Archilochus to Catullus, searching for the beginning or at least the elements of that modern, extended treatment by a poet of his own love which is the great achievement of the Augustan elegists, several tendencies seem to converge on Catullus. From the earliest times certain elements persist to the very end, for example the address to friend, or patron, or reader—a form not peculiar to elegy but nevertheless very characteristic of it—or the mythological parallel. Such elements may be called permanent traits of the *genre;* they pass from the early to the later Greeks, to Catullus, and so to the Augustans. I have amused myself by making a collection of these permanent traits. Among the themes of elegy the lament is such a trait; love for woman is another. But the mere mention of these reminds one that during the course of six hundred years such elements were subject to modification and development. Love of woman first appears as a theme of elegy in Mimnermus *ca.* 600 B.C., then in Antimachus *ca.* 400 B.C. or later, then in a number of elegists at the end of the fourth century and the beginning of the third—Philetas, Hermesianax, Alexander Aetolus—and finally in Callimachus and his successors who lead us on to Catullus and the Augustans in the first century. "Mimnermus burned with love for Nanno," says Hermesianax, a somewhat dubious authority, "inventing amid his woes the breath of the soft pentameter." Subjective-erotic, then, in elegy. But how did Mimnermus deal with love? In almost eighty lines of fragments he touches on love:[35] life is nothing without

love; love is the tender flower of youth; let me die when
love is no longer possible for me. Love and youth are
the great blessings of humanity, old age and death are
its evils. He generalizes; his attitude is that of the
philosopher surveying human life and finding love an
important element. There is nothing of that intimate
personal treatment which characterizes the Roman
elegy.

Antimachus also dealt with his own love. The nine
broken lines which have survived from his poetry give
no hint of his treatment, but we know something about
it from the statements of other writers, especially
Plutarch. He consoled himself (says Plutarch) for
the loss of his wife Lyde by enumerating, in an elegy
named after her, the unfortunate affairs of mythology.
The *Lyde*, then, was a long composition in at least two
books, chiefly narrative, not subjective; the myths,
not the poet's love, were the main theme.[36] It was a
catalogue poem. Of its method we can form a good
idea by reading the long fragments of Hermesianax
and Phanocles who continued this form. All is objective narrative-story tacked on to the story by means of
the old formulae "such as," "or as," etc. It is certain,
I think, that these earlier elegists did not work out in
detail the vicissitudes and moods of their own love, and
I have already noted that in objective narrative the
earlier manner persisted into the third century, when
Philetas and Callimachus revolted against it. Callimachus (and Catullus too) condemned Antimachus,[37]
and Callimachus at least knew how to tell the tale of
another's love in modern fashion. His own love he
restricts to epigram, in which probably Asclepiades
had preceded him.[38] And this brings me to the second
point.

When we search extant Greek poetry for traces of subjective-erotic we find it not in elegy, but in lyric and especially in epigram, forms which did not afford opportunity for the extended treatment which is characteristic of elegy. The epigram and the lyric have something more than the mere germs of it; there the situations, the moods, the sentiments are often the same as in elegy. But the Greeks did not develop the epigram into a true elegy. Just before and during the period of Catullus certainly they were still confining their subjective-erotic poetry to the short forms, witness Meleager, Philodemus, and others.[39]

It is significant that the first attempts of the Romans in this kind of erotic—the attempts of Valerius Aedituus, Porcius Licinus, and Lutatius Catulus, which I described in the third lecture—are also in epigram, and still more significant that Catullus continued the same type of epigram. But as we have just seen, he was the first, so far as we know, to develop such epigrams into elegies. We see him feeling his way from one *genre* into another, a *genre* that is richer in every way—a better medium for the expression of a poet's own erotic feeling. It seems to me that in Catullus we may discern the chief type of elegy coming into existence. If, as many scholars have believed, the Greeks had written elegies of this type, it is difficult to understand why Catullus did not write more of them. They were an excellent form, as his two examples show, in which to express his love for Lesbia.

But Catullus did not choose to persist in elegy, and if such a course would have curtailed his other work, we may on the whole congratulate ourselves that he did not persist. The briefer and more varied forms were better suited to his genius and he used them with a much more perfect technique than he displays in elegy. Nevertheless we must not allow the brilliance of these little jewels to obscure their author's importance in the field of elegy.

The Augustan specialists developed elegy in every way. They perfected its form and they greatly extended its scope. Elegiac erotic became a system in which countless situations, countless moods were reflected in whole cycles of poems and the poet lover posed as an erotic expert able to aid other lovers although he admits on occasion that he cannot aid himself. This system does not exist in Catullian elegy but many of its elements and much of the art with which it was presented are there. Like Catullus the Augustan elegists were expressing for the most part their own experiences and sentiments. Like him they utilized any suitable material which they found in any kind of Greek literature. They greatly extended the field in which such material could be found, turning, for example, to Greek New Comedy and bucolic poetry which (in elegy) Catullus had not used. All these suggestions they poured into the elegiac mold. But, so far as the sources of elegy were bookish, the Augustans had an advantage over Catullus; in addition to the Greek writers they had at their disposal a group of artistic Roman poets among whom Catullus himself was foremost, whereas Catullus had found no stimulus in the art of his own Roman predecessors. In fact the Augustan elegists, not Horace or Vergil, were the real heirs of Catullus. They were stimulated not only by his elegies but by all parts of his work. But if we consider the influence of his elegy alone, it is fair to say that the Augustans achieved their success in this field by following the lead of Catullus.

CHAPTER VII

THE WEDDING POEMS

Before the beginnings of literature in antiquity the wedding song existed as a custom among the people. From the popular songs the poets gradually developed various compositions which may be grouped under the term wedding poem. Thus arose a kind of poetry which was always more or less closely rooted in a popular custom, for the popular and the literary forms continued side by side. By far the best and most beautiful examples of the literary form are found in Catullus: the sixty-first and sixty-second poems, together with lines 323–381 of the sixty-fourth poem, the song of the Fates at the wedding of Peleus and Thetis.[1]

The supremacy of Catullus in this department of poetry may perhaps be discounted because his work has survived whereas almost all the wedding poetry of his predecessors is lost. Only one complete poem earlier than Catullus has survived—the eighteenth of Theocritus, on the wedding of Helen and Menelaus— so that in this field anything like an adequate comparison of the Latin poet with the Greeks is impossible. Nevertheless if such a comparison were possible there is no doubt that Catullus would still hold a very high position.

Although our information concerning wedding poetry earlier than Catullus is far from complete it is sufficient for a general outline of the *genre*.[2] In addition to the single complete piece of Theocritus there are interesting

fragments, especially from Sappho. Moreover tradition within the *genre* was so strong that important
inferences about the earlier period may be made from
evidence which is later than Catullus. During the first
five or six centuries of the Empire the Latin poets
often practiced the epithalamium, and a new form of
wedding composition, the wedding oration in prose,
was developed. Both the wedding orators themselves,
for example Himerius in the fourth century, and the
rhetoricians who describe the wedding oration possessed
and utilized a long series of pre-Catullian Greek epithalamia which are now lost. All told there is considerable evidence on which to base a just estimate of
Catullus' position in the development of this *genre*
and especially the extent to which he followed tradition.
A brief summary of the history of wedding poetry
before the time of Catullus will furnish the necessary
background.

The earliest references to a wedding song are in
Homer. One of the scenes depicted on Achilles' shield
is a wedding party (*Il.* XVIII. 491–496). The bride and
groom with their friends are proceeding on foot. There
are torches and dancing, and a wedding song (ὑμέναιος)
is being sung to the music of pipes and lyres. This
passage proves that a form of the popular wedding song
existed in Homer's time. There is another reference
which is still more interesting because it may imply
that in Homer's time the poets had already begun to
compose wedding songs. In the twenty-fourth book
of the Iliad (57–63) Hera reminds Zeus that all the gods
attended the wedding of Peleus and Thetis, among
them Apollo with his lyre. Wilamowitz has suggested
that the statement implies the existence in Homer's
time of a narrative version of the wedding,[3] and we

may add that the mention of Apollo's lyre may not be merely ornamental; very possibly the god was made to sing the wedding song or to accompany others who sang it. Certainly Pindar knew a version of the story in which the song was uttered by the Muses and Apollo was present with his lyre.[4]

After Homer the next reference to a wedding song occurs in the *Shield of Hercules* (attributed to Hesiod), 273–280. The passage is much like the one in Homer: a wedding party depicted on the shield, only in this case the bride is riding in a car. Hesiod wrote a poem on the wedding of Peleus and Thetis of which a few lines survive.[5] According to Tzetzes these lines occurred in an epithalamium, but he may easily have been deceived by the direct address to Peleus which could have occurred in a narrative poem on the wedding as well as in an epithalamium.

The first certain traces of literary wedding songs are not earlier than the seventh century B.C. The lyric poet Alcman[6] at Sparta is said to have composed such songs, but no fragments have survived.

Not much later (*ca.* 600 B.C.) came Sappho, who was famous throughout antiquity as a composer of nuptial poetry. She employed various meters including the hexameter, and her poems in this field were extensive enough in the Alexandrian Age to form a book which is cited by later writers. Catullus admired Sappho, adapted in Latin one of her lyrics (the fifty-first poem), and there is no doubt that he knew her wedding poetry. Indeed he is supposed by many scholars to have imitated her so closely in his own epithalamia that his work has often been used to interpret and reconstruct the fragments of his supposed model. I shall say something about this problem later.[7] Meanwhile let us note that about a dozen and a half of short fragments have been assigned to Sappho's epithalamia.[8] A few of these fragments do not certainly belong to epithalamia, but if we exclude these we still have valuable information about Sappho's methods.

In the fifth and fourth centuries, apart from very brief fragments of Philoxenus and Telestes, the drama —both tragedy and comedy—contains specimens of wedding poetry, for example the *Trojan Women* (307–340) and a fragment of the *Phaethon* of Euripides,[9] and the *Birds* and *Peace* of Aristophanes. These passages are of less interest to us because they are not separate examples of the *genre*, but it may be noted that the end of the *Peace* seems to reflect rather closely the popular epithalamium while that at the end of the *Birds* is sung by the Fates as in Catullus (LXIV. 323–381).

The Greek sources on which Plautus modeled his *Casina*—a play of the New Comedy, perhaps with elements from some Greek farce (φλύαξ?)—contained a wedding procession and a song, cf. the *Casina*, 796 ff. The characters wear chaplets and there are torches, a piper, and the wedding cry, *Hymen hymenaee, o Hymen*.

In the Alexandrian Age the epithalamium was a favorite kind of poetry. In addition to Theocritus' *Helen*, Eratosthenes, Callimachus, and Parthenius wrote epithalamia, but only two or three lines have been preserved. Parthenius, as we have seen, was a younger contemporary of Catullus, and it is interesting to note that at the same period other Roman poets practiced this kind of poetry. Both Calvus and Ticidas are mentioned, but the fragments are limited to a very few lines.[10]

It is possible then to trace the existence of the wedding poem as a form of literature for more than five

centuries and a half before the time of Catullus and it
continued to thrive for six hundred years after his time.
The vitality of the *genre* was due not only to the fact
that it was always rooted in popular custom but also
that it was by its very nature festival poetry; the poets
were often called upon to write poems to honor the
weddings of friends or patrons.   Callimachus wrote an
epithalamium for the wedding of Ptolemy and Arsinoe[11]
just as Catullus wrote for Manlius and Vinia and Ovid
for the wedding of Fabius Maximus.   A variety of
this type was the narrative poem on the wedding of
mythological characters, Theocritus on the wedding
of Helen or Catullus on the wedding of Thetis.   Moreover the theme of marriage could be treated without
reference to individuals.   Catullus' sixty-second poem
illustrates this type; the poet seems to have no particular wedding in mind.   The poets ordinarily dealt with
a part or parts of the wedding ceremony, not the
whole. This is especially true of the sixty-second poem,
in which Catullus has in mind the time just after the
wedding feast.

The parts of the ceremony in fact gave rise to
special types of wedding poetry.   The earlier (and
always the common) general term for a wedding poem
was *hymenaeus* (ὑμέναιος)—a term which, like the name
of the god Hymen, probably originated in the wedding
cry *hymenaee*.   The word is applied by Homer to a
song uttered during the procession; it may have had
originally a special sense; later it became a general
term, and is so used by Catullus (LXII. 4, *iam dicetur
hymenaeus*).   In a fragment (43) of Aeschylus there is
probably reference to a "waking song."   In the third
century B.C. ἐπιθαλάμιος appears, which meant at first
a song at the wedding chamber, and this term, like

hymenaeus, was later generalized. Other terms appear such as ἀρμάτειον, "the car song" (we remember that in Hesiod the bride is in a car), κατακοιμητικόν, "retiring song," or κατευναστικόν, "sleeping song" (these seem to represent the same type as *epithalamium* in its strict sense), and ὄρθριον, "morning song," perhaps identical with the "waking song" (διεγερτικόν). We cannot now clearly differentiate these types, but the names bear witness to the variety of the wedding poem. The meter also varied within fairly wide limits but exact details cannot be given since the meter of a short fragment cannot always be exactly determined. There were, however, lyric meters, e.g., glyconics and anapaests, and the hexameter was always a favorite.

One of the most striking characteristics of the epithalamium is the persistence of certain topics—the prayer, the praise of the bride and groom, the contest, etc. Nothing proves more convincingly that the epithalamium was closely connected with actual customs. The fullest list of these topics may be gleaned from the rhetoricians, who in turn took them from the poets. Of course no real poet included them all in one poem. Nevertheless each poem known to us includes a surprising number of them. The poets vary them, each to suit the circumstances and his own taste, but in essence they remain the same and taken together they are a traditional feature of the wedding poem. The pseudo-Dionysius puts the point very well when he speaks περὶ τῶν εἰωθότων λέγεσθαι—"of the things customarily said" at weddings.

Thus the content of the wedding poem reflected to a very considerable extent actual wedding customs. In fact such a poem as a whole was the reflection of a wedding custom, the song. Each poet was familiar with the customs of his own land and period and after the earliest period each poet was also familiar with wedding poems in which the customs had been used as topics. In dealing with a given poem therefore—especially if the poem belongs to a period as late in the history of the *genre* as the first century B.C.—we must constantly bear in mind the possibility of two influences—the direct influence of the actual wedding customs of the day as observed by the poet himself and the indirect influence of customs, often the same customs, affecting the poet through the work of his predecessors. It is often impossible to separate these two elements, but not infrequently we can at least say that they represent a traditional feature of the *genre*, such as a prayer in some form, praise of the bride's beauty, etc.

If one would understand the wedding poems of Catullus, one must know not only the history of the *genre*, but also the wedding customs of the Greeks and Romans, since part of the task consists, so far as the content is concerned, in distinguishing the Greek from the Roman elements.[12] In this work a correct method is important for there is danger of reasoning in a circle. In the first place, despite the considerable body of evidence which we possess concerning ancient weddings, our knowledge of details and of differences in different lands and at different periods is very incomplete. Again, the Greeks and Italians were related peoples, offshoots of the same parent stock. It is not surprising therefore that the wedding, one of the oldest of human institutions, had in the customs of both races some identical or very similar features. And so when one finds in Catullus, for example, an allusion to a custom which was certainly Roman, it cannot be at once assumed without further investigation that this custom was not Greek or (from the literary point of view) that it is based on life and not upon some Greek poet. This suggests another point: the Greek and Roman wedding poems are themselves part of the evidence which must be used to reconstruct the Greek and Roman wedding. This is an important fact which the commentators and authors of handbooks on Greek and Roman life are prone to forget. Some of them assume, for example, that the sixty-second poem of Catullus is a pure Greek study, and they use its details as details of the Greek wedding, making no allowance for a possible admixture of Roman elements. Similarly many who have written on the content of Plautus have assumed that his references to law, for example, are to Roman law while others have assumed that the same references are to Greek law, not allowing for the proved fact that Plautus was often very free in altering his Greek models for production on the Roman stage.

It is clear that in a problem of this kind one must proceed with caution. Catullus is Romanizing a Greek *genre*. The first step is to establish what are the details of the wedding which Catullus himself presents. Then we must compare these details with the known evidence drawn from other sources both Greek and Roman. If a Catullian detail agrees exclusively with the evidence for the Greek wedding, or exclusively with the evidence for the Roman wedding, then presumably that detail is Greek or Roman, as the case may be. If the detail is found to be both Greek and Roman, as is sometimes the case, or uniquely Catullian, then no reliable conclusions can be drawn as to the source from which the poet obtained it. He knew both the Roman wedding customs and the Greek literature which embodied the Greek customs.

The three epithalamia of Catullus, including the
song of the Fates which is part of the sixty-fourth
poem, comprise about three hundred and fifty lines.
Since it is impossible to cover adequately so great an
amount of text in a brief lecture I have chosen to
devote most of my space to the sixty-first poem, which
is to me the most interesting of the three epithalamia
because it is a thorough-going effort to adapt the Greek
genre to Roman conditions.   As poetry the sixty-second
poem is more famous although it is not, in my opinion,
superior.   Even those who prefer the latter, however,
will admit that the sixty-first poem provides a much
better opportunity to study the poet's methods and
to study his methods is my chief object.

The sixty-first poem was written ostensibly to honor
the wedding of Manlius Torquatus with Vinia Aurunculeia and there is no reason to doubt the actual occasion.   The groom belonged to a famous old patrician
family several members of which were prominent in the
time of Catullus, but it is impossible to say with
certainty what Manlius is meant, although it is
tempting to identify him with the Manlius of the
sixty-eighth poem who was an intimate friend of
Catullus.   Nor can the bride be identified with any
individual known from other sources.[13]   Her double
name indicates that she was by birth an Aurunculeia—
this stock was of old plebeian origin—but that she
had passed by adoption into the Vinian family.   The
name Vinius was common enough at the time, but no
prominent member of the family is known.

A few verses are lost but the gaps do not obscure
the general run of the thought or the structure.   In
general the course of the poem reflects the actual
course of the wedding.   The poet represents himself as

the speaker and he assumes the rôle of a director of
ceremonies and chorus leader.[14]   There are three main
parts.   In the first part (1–113)[15] the poet with a throng
of youths and maidens stands before the house of the
bride waiting for her to come forth and join the procession to the groom's house.   There is a long invocation
to Hymen, the god of marriage, to come from his
home on Helicon clad in the marriage garb, to come
with dance and song, and attend the wedding of
Manlius and Vinia.   There is praise of the bride's
beauty, a call to the maidens to sing the wedding cry
and praise of Hymen as the god of marriage, without
whose aid neither family nor state can thrive.[16]   The
bride is weeping within the house.   She is encouraged
by further praise of her beauty, reminded that the
day is passing, that "the torches are shaking their
golden locks," and she is urged to come forth.

In this section the marriage cry (four times repeated)
is
> O Hymenaee Hymen
> Hymen O Hymenaee.

It is a static section.   The throng stands waiting for
the bride.

The second part (114–183) describes the procession
(*deductio*).   All is life and motion, and the marriage cry
changes to the more jubilant form,

> Io Hymen Hymenaee io
> io Hymen Hymenaee.

The torches are lifted as the bride appears.   The
abusive Fescennine verses are uttered against the
groom.   Both the groom and the bride are urged to
lifelong fidelity.   The bride is cautioned to step carefully over the threshold as she enters the groom's

house. The love of the pair is emphasized. The bride is led by the matrons to the marriage chamber. Here the jubilant marching cry ceases.

Now that the procession is ended, the third part (184–228), the scene of which is in the groom's house, is quieter, balancing the first section (before the bride's house) and contrasting with the second (the procession). The groom enters the chamber, the beauty of the pair is again praised, and the last lines (204–228) represent an epithalamium in the stricter sense—a song at the chamber. Here occurs one of the most beautiful passages in ancient poetry, the prayer for a son to perpetuate the old name of Torquatus.

Thus Catullus presents the main features of the wedding not as a narrative, but almost as a drama to which we could easily attach stage directions although no definite rôles. He represents himself as taking part in the various scenes. His poem reflects the progress of the ceremony step by step and the method which he adopts enables him to lead his reader into the midst of its life and color. This art is in reality a method of vivid narrative and description. From the point of view of poetic technique it is the most interesting feature of the poem, and I shall consider it presently in some detail. It will be better understood however if we first examine the content.

The poem follows the course of the wedding, but not the whole course. Catullus is a poet, not an antiquarian, and he selects those elements which are best adapted to his purpose. He omits the preliminary sacrifices and prayers, and begins just before the most picturesque feature, the procession. There are many other omissions, especially the wedding feast,[17] and yet a surprising number of the topics common in epitha-

lamia are included. The rhetoricians, as has been
already said, contain the most comprehensive list of
these topics, which they gathered for the most part
from the Greek poets of every period down to their
own time—from the seventh century B.C. to the sixth
century of our era. A brief comparison of these topics
—"the things customarily said at weddings"—with the
epithalamia of Catullus will illuminate the traditional
aspect of his work.[18] I shall consider, for the moment,
all his epithalamia.

There are first of all the nature and advantage of
marriage. Catullus employs several details of this
topic, all of which appear in the rhetoricians:[19] the
praise of Hymen as the greatest of gods (LXI. 46–50),
the emphasis on legal love and the necessity of aban-
doning illicit love (136),[20] the advantages of marriage
for the state (71–73), and for the family (204–208),
e.g., the salvation of the family; children necessary
to continue the family and to honor their parents.[21]
Even the passage in which Catullus compares the union
of the pair to the union of tree and vine (102–105, cf.
LXII. 49 ff.) is partly paralleled in the rhetoricians,
who recommend references to the unions of trees or
the use of myths on this subject.[22]

The functions and attributes of the god of marriage,
Hymen—or Gamos, as the rhetoricians call him—tally
very closely. In Catullus the god is the giver of the
bride to the groom, the uniter of the pair, the inspirer
of love. Personally he is young, and he is depicted as
wearing the veil and even possessing certain physical
attributes of a bride—the snow white foot (9), the
high, clear voice (13). All these characteristics—even
the curious conception of effeminacy—appear in
Menander.[23]

A second topic is the praise of bride and groom, especially the bride. Catullus praises her beauty, compares her to flowers—the hyacinth, the parthenice, the poppy, the myrtle. She is like Venus herself (16–25, 83–89, 186–189). She is tearful and modest, tender and loving. He has praise for the groom also, but he limits it, so far as physical charm goes, to the word *pulcer* (191). He refers however to the groom's wealth, his ancient lineage, and his honorable love. The rhetoricians recommend such praise: praise the beauty, wisdom, the families of the pair, says Menander.[24] The likening of personal beauty to that of trees and flowers is recommended by the rhetoricians, and the fragments of Sappho show that this was a very old detail of epithalamium. It is significant that Himerius declares that he must use the language of poets to describe the flower-like beauty of the bride's face (*Or.* I.19).

An exhortation to mutual conjugal love is recommended by the rhetoricians.[25] Catullus' word for this is *concordia* (LXIV. 336) and he touches on the topic in the sixty-first poem (139–146).

Another important topic is the prayer for children. This appears in Catullus (LXI. 204–223, cf. LXIV. 338 ff.) and in all the rhetoricians. Catullus prays that a son may be born who shall recall the features of both the groom and the bride, and he uses the mythological parallel of Telemachus and Penelope. Both these details appear in the rhetoricians, Menander and Dionysius.[26] In this connection the rhetoricians recommend the use of mythological parallels although the parallel employed by Catullus—Penelope and Telemachus—does not occur.

The wedding cry, the dance, the song, the flowers, and the general revelry were common features of the Greek and Roman wedding. Menander, for example, says: describe choruses of youths and maidens, wreath yourselves in roses and violets, hold the torch, dance and shout "Hymen." All these details are found in the sixty-first poem of Catullus. Many are repeated in the sixty-second and others are added, especially the importance of the evening star, Vesper or Hesperus.[27]

In the content of Catullus' epithalamia there is thus a large traditional element—all the main topics and many details connected with them. Catullus varies these topics a great deal—his invocation to Hymen, for example, is worked out (LXI. 1–45) in far greater detail than we find elsewhere—but in the main he holds to tradition.

Clearly in the sixty-first poem he is adapting a Greek *genre* to Roman conditions, retaining in the process many elements of content which are Greek. We must remember, however, that some of these elements were also Roman and that others, though not Roman, were thoroughly understood by the educated class for which Catullus wrote. In other words he is careful to introduce nothing so foreign as to injure the effect of the whole as a poem in honor of a Roman wedding.

Furthermore, to give the poem a Roman flavor, he includes a number of elements which are either exclusively or predominantly Roman. These are the *raptio*, the removal of the bride with simulated violence from her mother's arms (3, 56–58), a very old custom which appears among the Greeks only at Sparta;[28] the *pronubae* or matrons of honor (179–180), the boy called *praetextatus* (175) who conducted the bride,[29] the abusive Fescennine verses employed during the procession (119 ff.), the reference to the Roman marriage god Talasius (127), the reddish yellow color (*luteus*) of the bride's veil (*flammeum*), the scattering of nuts during the procession (124 ff.), the custom of assisting or lifting the bride over the threshold of the bridegroom's house. These things (and perhaps some others which I omit)[30] are, so far as our rather meager evidence indicates, Roman or at all events decidedly more Roman than Greek.

The most interesting of them all is the introduction of Fescennine verses.[31] The Romans, until they took over the Greek epithalamium, had never possessed any developed form of wedding poetry. From pre-literary times, however, they had employed certain rude abusive verses at weddings, the purpose of which was to avert the envy of the gods at a time of supreme human happiness. The abuse of the victorious general by his soldiers in the triumphal songs had a similar motive. Abuse, often scurrilous abuse, was also a custom of the Greek wedding, as we see in Sappho's gay abuse of the doorkeeper. But Catullus indicates by his use of the Italian term *Fescennina iocatio* that he has the native, not the Greek practice, in mind.

None of the popular Fescennine verses have survived, but there are at least a score of allusions to them in Latin literature[32] and it is certain that when they were used at weddings they were often exceedingly coarse. They were directed chiefly against the bridegroom but not even the ears of the bride were spared.[33] In verses 119–120 Catullus urges the youths to employ the "wanton Fescennine jest" and probably he means the real thing, but so far as he himself reflects the custom in the following verses he is rather mild. There is some

ragging of the groom and his favorite slave and a
warning to the bride. This restraint is due to the
fact that the poet is composing an epithalamium for
a wedding in high life. Furthermore the intrusion of
vulgar words would have violated the rather dignified
tone and style of the poem. Thus in that part of the
ceremony (the procession) in which the Greeks, according to the extant evidence, employed a song, Catullus
substitutes the native element of the Fescennine verses,
but in so doing he elevates this Roman element —
"epithalamizes" it, so to speak.

At the end of the poem he displays a similar restraint
in the lines which reflect the song at the chamber—the
real epithalamium (204–228). In the Greek and Roman
wedding this was the point at which the boisterousness
and scurrility of the guests probably reached their
height—with us a similar opportunity comes when
the bride and groom enter the motor or the train—
but Catullus merely refers to these things with the
innocuous phrase, *lusimus satis*.[34]

The Roman element, therefore, lies chiefly in the
content of the poem. But it is not certain that all the
customs mentioned were still in actual existence in the
time of Catullus. Some may have been already obso-
lete. The question cannot be settled with our inadequate evidence. But to a poet it mattered little whether
all the customs to which he alluded still existed or
not; they were all available for literary purposes, and
Catullus selected enough of them to enhance the Roman
coloring of his poem. The interesting thing is that he
did not select more. We hear nothing of the marriage
contract, of the preliminary sacrifices, of the dedication
by the bride of her playthings, of her peculiar *tunica
regilla*, of those six braids (*sex crines*) in which her

hair was arranged, of the parting of her hair with a spearpoint, a custom which caught Browning's fancy,

.... a Roman bride, when they'd dispart
Her unbound tresses with the Sabine dart,
Holding that famous rape in memory still,
Felt creep into her curls the iron chill,
And looked thus.[35]

Nothing is said of the adornment and anointing of the doorposts, or of many other things. We should rightly condemn a poet who attempted to introduce into such a poem as this every detail of the most elaborate form of Roman wedding. And yet it is plain that Catullus could easily have avoided such pedantry and yet could have made his work much more Roman than it is. The fact that he did not make it more Roman illustrates in striking fashion how strongly the Greek literary tradition influenced him.

To the traditional topics of the Greek epithalamium let us add, by way of illustration, other details of the sixty-first poem which are clearly Greek in origin.

In the long invocation after the style of a cletic hymn, with which the poem opens (1–45) the description of Hymen, whose name is Greek, has many Greek details. Some of these have already been mentioned. Here we may add that the god's home is said to be Helicon, which is described in terms of Greek topography (*Thespiae rupis Aonios specus, nympha ....* *Aganippe*), and his mother is the muse Urania (2).[36]

The myth of the judgment of Paris is used: Vinia is as lovely as was Venus when she came before her Phrygian judge (16–18). The comparison of the bride's beauty to the beauty of flowers was a very old detail of the epithalamium—probably as old as Sappho, although the famous lines on the hyacinth trodden

under foot are not certainly Sapphic.[37]   Some of the
names of flowers are Roman, e.g., *papaver* (188), but
most are Greek: *myrtus* (22), *flos hyacinthinus* (89),
parthenice (187).   Possibly these are merely Greek loan
words, but in certain cases in which there were Latin
names for the flowers, Catullus prefers the Greek, e.g.,
amaracus (7), Latin *matricaria*.

The groom's beauty also was praised.   Catullus
just touches on this topic (190-192), *nihilo minus pulcer
es*, *neque te Venus neglegit*—a passage which reminds
one of Sappho:[38] "Aphrodite has honored thee above
all," although Choricius testifies that these words were
addressed to the bride.

The Greek element appears most prominently, however, in matters of technique.   The most interesting
feature here is the mimetic-dramatic character of the
poem—the manner in which the poet represents himself
as taking part in the ceremony in the rôle of a master
of ceremonies and chorus leader.   It is the poet who
invokes Hymen, urges the girls to sing, addresses the
bride, apostrophizes the wedding couch, directs the boys
to lift their torches and sing, addresses the favorite slave,
the groom—all the persons in fact.[39] Sometimes he maintains his individuality as *At, marite, ita me iuvent* or *Torquatus volo parvulus*[40]; sometimes he associates himself
with the rest of the company, as *lusimus satis*.[41] This is
the device which more than anything else gives life to
the poem.   No other completely extant wedding poem is
composed in this way, but the same technique is employed in other forms of poetry, for example in some of
the *Hymns* of Callimachus (II,V,VI). *Hymn* V, *The Bath
of Pallas*, is a very good illustration.   The poet exhorts a
band of maidens to come prepared to escort Pallas to the
bath. He speaks in the first person, frequently addressing

the maidens; he exhorts the goddess to come forth[42]. And while the maidens await the goddess, he tells them the story of Teiresias. The story ended he announces that the goddess is coming. Even in detail this is clearly the technique employed by Catullus in the sixty-first poem. The same technique occurs in the third poem of Theocritus, the so-called *Serenade*. It is found in Augustan poetry, for example in Horace's *Odes* I. 27, *natis in usum*, etc., but the best parallel is Tibullus' account of the country festival (*Ambarvalia*) in which the poet takes the rôle of a householder and priest—a director of the festival on his own estate.[43]

There has been a tendency among scholars to attribute the invention of this quasi-dramatic method of presenting a ceremony or a series of events to Callimachus or to Theocritus.[44] In my opinion the credit should go to Sappho, who, as I believe, employed this method in her epithalamia.

Among the fragments of Sappho's epithalamia there are a number in which somebody addresses the groom and the bride:

Happy bridegroom, thy wedding has been accomplished as thou didst pray . . . .
To what, dear bridegroom, am I to liken thee . . . .
Farewell, bride, a hearty farewell, bridegroom . . . .

Somebody urges that the roof (or lintel?) be lifted high, the bridegroom is so tall.[45]

It is certain that Sappho made use of dialogue in her epithalamia. Demetrius quotes a passage in which the bride addresses Maidenhood and Maidenhood replies. Probably she used informal dialogue also, for the brief fragment,   'We will give,' says the father,

has been assigned with probability to an epithalamium.[46]

But fragments containing direct address and exhortation are certainly best interpreted as words of Sappho
herself in the rôle of poetess—choragus at some wedding—a rôle corresponding to that which Catullus
assumes in the sixty-first poem.[47] This view is supported by the fact that the rhetoricians, who derive
from poetry the principles which they recommend
for the wedding speech, say that the orator should
"exhort the groom and the bride," "utter the prayer,"
"urge on the youths; summon the hearers . . . . to escort
the pair to the wedding chamber."[48] The wedding
orator is thus advised to assume the very rôle that we
find in Catullus.[49] It might be said that since the
rhetoricians are later than Catullus they took their
idea from the Alexandrian writers, who certainly
employed it in other forms of poetry and so probably
in the epithalamium. But fortunately Himerius, who
often quotes and paraphrases Sappho—so closely indeed
that Edmonds and others attempt to reconstruct
Sappho's verse from Himerius' prose—is explicit.

In the preface to his first oration Himerius says that
in the style of the epithalamium the best principle is
to follow the poets. The actual oration begins with the
third section, which I paraphrase briefly: "They say
that Apollo sang a wedding song at the bridal chamber.
So it is fitting for me, youths, since I am devoting my
muse to nuptial dance and love, to drop my stricter
style in order that I may take part with maidens in
the dance in honor of Aphrodite.

"But[50] that it is difficult to invent a song tender
enough for the goddess we may learn from the poets
themselves who though skilful in matters of love . . . .
have left the rites of Aphrodite to Lesbian Sappho, the
singing to the accompaniment of the lyre and composing

the song at the chamber. She enters after the contest into the chamber, wreaths the doorposts, spreads the couch, urges the maidens into the house, brings Aphrodite on the car of the Graces and a band of Loves to join in the revels.[51] She binds with hyacinth the hair of the goddess except those tresses which she allows to play about her face or ripple in the breeze. She stations the Loves, their wings and locks adorned with gold, before the car, and as they escort the procession moving their torches on high she hastens them on. For me also this exhortation is necessary. . . . .

"If a song were needed, I would provide this: 'O bride exhaling roses and love! Go to the couch with tender play, sweet to the bridegroom! May Hesperus lead thee as thou dost go willingly, venerating silver-throned Hera of the wedding bond.' But where are my bands of youths and maidens? My speech yields the rest to you. Let someone seize a great torch: let another shout. Let song pervade all. . . . . I leave the dance to the dancers, but I will stand by the chamber and utter prayers to Fortune and Love and the gods of birth."

According to Himerius, then, the poets regarded Sappho as supreme in matters of love and especially in wedding poetry. In her poetry she acts; she exhorts; she enters the bridal chamber, puts up garlands, spreads the couch, urges on the maidens, brings Aphrodite, etc. Himerius himself resolves to follow her example and he does so—especially at the end of his speech: "let someone seize a torch, someone else raise a shout," and the rest.

Clearly Sappho, like Catullus, represented herself in her poetry as taking part in the ceremony; she invoked and described the gods, moved about, directed various

arrangements, urged on the youths and maidens.[52] To
her, not to the Alexandrian poets, we must assign the
earliest known application of this vivid literary method
to festival poetry.   It is essentially a lyric method.
Of its simpler form there are abundant traces in early
Greek lyric,[53] but a better idea of it can be obtained
from a complete poem.   Consider the twenty-seventh
poem of Catullus.   The poet wishes to present a picture
of himself enjoying the pleasures of wine.   "Boy, pour
me stronger cups," he cries.   "But you, water, ruination
of wine, away with you to the sober! Here we have the
pure liquid of the wine god!"   The poet is in the act
of drinking, he addresses and exhorts his slave, expresses
his opinion, etc.[54] Horace's *Persicos odi* (I. 38) is very
similar.   If we multiply the details of such a scene and
the persons taking part in it, the method becomes
somewhat more complicated as, for example, in Horace's
picture of a drinking bout (I. 27), for which I supply
stage directions:

(*The poet comes suddenly on a drinking party just as the
voices of the drinkers are being raised and an open quarrel is
imminent. Standing in the doorway he quiets them*):

Goblets were meant for pleasure. Only Thracians fight
with them. Away with such a barbarous custom. Do not
outrage revered Bacchus with bloody strife . . . . but cease
your impious din and stay quietly on your couches.
(*They subside, and the poet continues*)

Would you have me join you? Then let our young friend here
tell us who has smitten him with love.
(*A pause.*)

You hesitate? I'll drink on no other condition. You have
nothing to be ashamed of. Come! Drop your secret in this
safe ear of mine.
(*The youth whispers her name.*)

Poor fellow! in what a whirlpool you've been struggling!
What magic can ever extricate you from such a peril as *she* is!

Richard Heinze well characterizes this ode as a
scene from a symposium dramatically described in the
words of the poet who takes part in it, and he adds
that its technique—the representation of the progress
of an action during the course of the poem—is well
known from Hellenistic and Roman festival poems.

We may now add that the same technique was certainly employed by Sappho in her wedding poetry and
that many epithalamia—Catullus LXI is a good
example—were undoubtedly just as much festival
poems as Tibullus' description of the country festival
(II. 1) which Heinze cites.

Thus Sappho extended her lyric technique to subjects
involving a succession of scenes and a throng of persons.
In such poems the purity of her lyric power was of
necessity somewhat alloyed—the canvas was a bit too
large—but as a method of presenting such scenes this
technique was unexcelled. Contemporaries of Sappho
may have practiced it. In the Alexandrian Age at
least, when poetry was composed chiefly for recitation
and reading, it was eagerly imitated and it became, as
it is in Catullus and Tibullus, a literary device for the
purpose of vivid description. Catullus must have known
many more examples belonging to various periods of
Greek poetry than we have today, but the use of it by
so ardent an admirer of Sappho in epithalamium, a
genre in which she was supreme, may safely be attributed to Sapphic influence.

The dramatic and realistic quality of this art is
obvious and this feature more than anything else has
led many scholars to the belief that the sixty-first
poem was intended to be sung in parts which could be

assigned, like the parts of a drama, to definite singers. But such poems are never dramatic in so formal a sense. Stage directions may indeed be supplied for them, characters may be addressed or quoted, but unlike the sixty-second poem or the *Carmen saeculare* of Horace, they contain no clear hints of the assignment of parts.[55] The assignment of parts however is only one element in the problem. Any poem can be sung whether the author intended it for song or not. Others, if not the author, may set a poem to music and have it sung—a procedure which was particularly easy in antiquity since there were no copyright laws. Sometimes poems which seem to us ill adapted to music were presented with musical accompaniment. Ovid for example informs us that his poetry—apparently parts of the *Heroides* and *Ars amatoria*—was presented with dancing and music on the stage.[56] Certain poems of Calvus and Catullus were sung in the time of Horace,[57] and it is probable that such performances occurred while the two poets were still living. But for their period and indeed for generations before and after it, when poetry was composed chiefly for reading and recitation, one cannot assume without explicit evidence that a given piece was ever sung or accompanied by music. Such evidence exists for Andronicus' hymn and for Horace's *Carmen saeculare*, but for Catullus it is entirely lacking. Singing a poem was the exception; reading it aloud to oneself, to one's friends, or to a larger audience (recitation) was the rule. Even the lyric, unless there is explicit evidence to the contrary, must be regarded as conforming to the rule. It is therefore wrong to cite the *Carmen saeculare* (an exception) to prove that the thirty-fourth poem of Catullus, since like the *Carmen saeculare* it is a hymn, was sung.

The hymn and other so-called lyrics had become literary forms. They were often written as if for song, but as a rule the poet's use of lyric meters, his references to singing and music, the assignment of parts to various singers were then as now conventions. The fact that a poem is composed as if for song shows merely that it could have been sung, not that it was actually sung. The poets wished to produce the semblance of song; their purpose was as a rule artistic, not practical. But the methods characteristic of the artistic purpose are often identical with those which would have been employed if the purpose had been practical, and so wherever the semblance of song is best maintained, as in hymns or wedding poems, it has often been wrongly assumed that these pieces were composed for actual song. The evidence in Catullus and in most other poets is wholly contained in the poems themselves[58] and in view of the general practice it concerns at the utmost the extent to which the poet intended to approximate the conditions of actual musical presentation. The approximation may be almost perfect, as in the thirty-fourth or the sixty-second poem, but (to repeat) this fact does not prove that the poet intended such poems to be sung, much less that they were sung.[59] We should start with the assumption that a poet is following the normal practice.

In certain cases an examination of the poet's intention strengthens this assumption. The sixty-first poem is an example. This poem was written for a definite occasion and has so many of the characteristics of song that attempts have often been made to determine just how it was sung. Various arrangements have been suggested for a soloist and a chorus or perhaps two choruses, and the fact that scholars have come to no

agreement proves at least that Catullus has given no
precise information. But it is unnecessary to discuss
these suggestions since they start from the questionable
premise that the poet intended this poem for song. If
on the other hand we consider the poem as a poem
and ask how the poetic intention agrees with the theory
that Catullus had song also in mind, we shall be
convinced, I think, that the two purposes clash.

We have seen that the poet depicts himself as present
at the ceremony as a sort of director and thus causes
certain parts of it to take place, as it were, before our
very eyes. We have seen furthermore that this realistic
technique was not new and that it was commonly used
both before and after the time of Catullus in poems
which were not intended to be sung. It was a method
of describing a scene or a series of scenes with special
vividness. In the sixty-first poem then the poetical
intention was to describe the wedding by picturing in
succession certain parts of the ceremony. Each part
seems to be sung as the corresponding action occurs
and the parts seem to progress swiftly and without a
break to the close. All this is certainly literary art.
Is it anything more? If we assume for the moment
that Catullus had song also in mind, the only clear
indication of the method of presentation is that the
song should be synchronized with those parts of the
ceremony which he depicts. But this could not have
been done without distressing repetitions and pauses
since many necessary parts of the actual ceremony are
omitted in the poem.[60] Moreover the time required to
sing the lines in which the selected scenes are covered
could hardly have been made to agree everywhere
with the time necessary for these scenes in the actual
wedding—unless we allow for repetitions and pauses.

The scene before the bride's house (1–113) would indeed have caused no difficulty, but the actual procession could hardly have taken place in the short time required to sing vv. 114–158, and the same conclusion holds for the scenes at the groom's house (vv. 159–228) where also several details occurred which are not mentioned in the poem. We must conclude that the only method of musical presentation for which there is any possible evidence would have destroyed the impression of swift and unbroken progress which it was clearly the poet's intention to produce. In fact his purpose was literary, not musical.

There is then no evidence that the sixty-first poem was intended for anything more than reading and declamation. It was probably sent as a compliment to Manlius and Vinia, just as the sixty-eighth was sent to a Manlius, perhaps this same Manlius, and the sixty-fifth and sixty-sixth to Hortensius. Whether the poem, after it left Catullus' hand, was made public at the wedding we have no means of knowing. Certainly if it was presented at all, we should like to believe that the poet's friends respected his art and had the poem presented as a unit—a single, beautiful feature of the occasion.[61]

The meter of the sixty-first poem, a Glyconic-Pherecratic stanza, is taken over from the Greek.[62] Whether the Greeks used it for wedding poetry or not cannot be certainly determined. Sappho employed various lyric verses for this purpose and it is not improbable that the Glyconic—probably not in the precise stanza form which we find in Catullus—was among them. The details of the verse as it appears in Catullus seem to indicate that he followed a late rather than an early Greek form. But we can compare only lines, not the whole stanza, with Greek work (or, it may be added, with Horace) for no stanzas earlier than Catullus survive. Some of the characteristics of the Catullian form may be survivals of the early Greek technique: the freedom of the first foot (– ◡, – –, or ◡ –),[63] the substitution (only once) of a spondee (– –) for a dactyl in the second foot, the regularity of the position of word-ends. But the almost universal fixed quantity of the last three syllables and the strict observance of synapheia point on the whole to a rather conventional form which was, as in other meters, characteristic of a late period. This conclusion is still more probable if Wilamowitz and his school are right in assuming that in the early period the Glyconic had great variety,[64] for in that case the Catullian forms must be the result of selection and refinement.

The wedding cry was used as a refrain by Sappho[65] and was a traditional feature of wedding poetry, but there are no exact parallels in Greek for the complete forms which Catullus employs in the sixty-first and sixty-second poems. The cry is Greek, but it was intelligible to the Romans more than a hundred years before the time of Catullus, for Plautus uses it in one of his comedies (*Casina* 799–800, 808). It must have been thoroughly Romanized, and the poets gave it various forms to suit the convenience of various meters. Catullus interjects a Latin word into it in the sixty-second poem, where indeed he treats it as something more than a cry: *Hymen, ades, o Hymenaee.* It is possible that he does the same in the sixty-first poem where, as the procession begins, he substitutes *io* (yo) for *o*:

Io Hymen Hymenaee io
io Hymen Hymenaee.

For *io* may be Latin. I am inclined to think it is Latin, but it must be admitted that the word may represent the Greek ἰώ.[66]

The other refrains—*quis huic deo compararier ausit, prodeas nova nupta, concubine nuces da,* and the recurrent line in the epithalamium uttered by the Fates, *currite ducentes subtegmina, currite, fusi,* are certainly in the Alexandrian style.[67]

Kroll remarks that in the invocation to Hymen (1–75) Catullus employs the technique of the Greek cletic hymn: the summons to the god, the god's name, birth, and dwelling place, together with several minor details.[68] No other extant epithalamium has this trait. Perhaps it is Catullus' own idea, but again we are hampered by lack of material with which to compare him.

In the details of phraseology and ornament the sixty-first poem has many Greek touches, but it is noticeable that these are relatively fewer than they are in the sixty-fourth, the short epic, in which the atmosphere is wholly Greek and the style much more elevated. The best commentaries are filled with Greek parallels, but here also, as in the sixty-fourth poem, one can rarely say that Catullus is translating a definite passage of a definite extant Greek poem; he is Romanizing types of Greek phenomena, as when he speaks of the Hamadryads (23–25) nursing the flowering branches of the myrtle for their plaything: *ludicrum* (ἄθυρμα, παίγνιον); or when the "torches shake their gleaming (or golden) locks" (78, 95), or when *Aonius* is used meaning Boeotian (28). Greek also are *vaga nox,* "fleeting night" (110); cf. θοὴ νύξ, the "white-footed couch" (κλίνη ἐλεφαντόπους or the like), the "polished doorway," *rasilem—forem* (161), cf. ξεστός, εὔξεστος, the "hyacinth flower," *flos hyacinthinus* (89), cf. Homer's ὑακίνθινον ἄνθος. Ellis calls this last "an exact translation," and so it may be, but it is questionable whether Catullus had the particular passage (*Od.* VI. 231) cited by Ellis in mind. And granting that he wished to use the Greek word for the flower, how else would he have said in Latin "flower of the hyacinth?"

There are a few touches of obvious rhetoric, for example the sands and stars representing an indefinite large number (199–200). If we could discover a source for the following phrase, *vostri—multa milia ludi* (202–203), we should probably find it in a single passage, for it is certainly an oddity. One may suspect Callimachus since the only fairly close parallel occurs in Catullus' translation of the *Coma Berenices* (LXVI. 78 *milia multa*, sc. *unguenti*).

The sixty-first poem is, then, a very interesting combination of Greek and Roman elements. The Roman element is found chiefly in the content, but it is fused with the traditionally Greek topics of the wedding poetry. The Greek element predominates in the form and technique. Not all the important features, to say nothing of all the details, can be tested by comparison with Greek productions of the same sort.

In general however the evidence is quite sufficient to demonstrate that Catullus attempted to adapt a Greek *genre* to Roman conditions and to carry out his purpose chiefly by methods which he had learned from the Greek poets. The result, the sixty-first poem, is an excellent illustration of a method which in a broad sense is characteristic of Roman poetry. Catullus wished to Romanize this kind of Greek poetry; at the same time he wished to continue the Greek tradition, not to break with it. If he had wished to make his poem as completely Roman as possible he could very

easily have done so. He could have omitted Hymen,
the Greek geography, the Greek myths, and substituted
Talasius and more of the Fescennine element. He could
have introduced more of the Roman customs. In
many other ways he could have Romanized his poem.
But he did not choose to do this. A more Roman
composition would probably have excelled, from our
point of view, the poem which Catullus actually composed; we should regard such a poem as more original.
But the ancient conception of originality differed
essentially from ours; the poets held much more closely
to tradition, and the power of tradition over one of the
greatest of ancient poets is nowhere better illustrated
than in the sixty-first poem of Catullus.

The sixty-second poem is an epithalamium of a
very different type. Like the sixty-first it is a Graeco-
Roman product but the Roman elements are so un-
obtrusive that it may fairly be described in Robinson
Ellis' phrase as "almost a Greek study."

The setting is Greek. In some place from which
Olympus and Oeta[69] can be seen, a company of youths
and maidens are still at the tables on which the feast
has been served. The bride has left them to prepare
herself for the coming procession to the groom's house.[70]
Suddenly the evening star is seen hanging low in the
west, the signal for the procession and for the contest
of song (*hymenaeus*, 4)[71] which all have been expecting.
The companies of youths and maidens, each under the
direction of a chorus leader, face each other, feminine
earnestness and worry on the one side, masculine con-
fidence, masked by the assumption of carelessness and
defeat, on the other. (The contrast of the feminine and
the masculine, which the poet presents with fine
humor in this passage (6–19), presages the character

and result of the coming struggle.)   Now comes the
contest.[72]   Using Hesperus as a symbol the maidens
complain in general terms of the cruelty of marriage,
for it violates virginity.   The youths counter by emphasizing the rightness and the happiness of marriage.
The maidens, becoming specific, accuse Hesperus of
stealing one of their companions: in effect marriage
is thievery.   The youths contradict: Hesperus is no
thief, on the contrary he detects thieves (a humorous
shift of meaning); but in reality the maidens are
insincere; they are attacking something which they
secretly long for (an *argumentum ad feminam*).

The maidens come to their chief point: the virgin
is like a flower growing in a walled garden—beautiful
and loved by all as long as she is a virgin, but as
the flower withers when it is picked, so the girl becomes unlovely and unloved as soon as she has lost
her virginity.   No, answer the youths, the virgin
is like an untrained vine, producing nothing, winning
no devotion, growing old in neglect, but once she is
wedded she is no longer a burden on her father and she
has the love of many and especially of her husband.
(Here ends the strictly amoebaean and more general part
of the song.)   The youths proceed to clinch their argument in a direct address to the bride (who is assumed to
have entered when the real song began, v. 20): it is not
right for her to resist her husband; her parents, whom
she is bound to obey, have given her to him, and besides
to struggle would be hopeless, for her virginity is only
one-third her own; two-thirds belong to her parents who
have surrendered their rights to their son-in-law.

Let us not pause to refute some parts of this masculine argument since the general point of view at least
is correct and the victory of the youths is a foregone

conclusion. The central theme of the poem is the age-old contrast between virginity and wedlock: each has its beauties and its peculiar happiness, and the maidens (so they say!) hate to leave the one for the other, but the claims of wedlock are superior—and right. In short, marriage is the proper state of man.

In spite of realistic details the poem deals with certain ideas concerning marriage as a human institu-tion—with wedlock, not with a wedding. It is an ideal poem, and the general, rather philosophical point of view is characteristic of a time when men had begun to theorize about marriage—a time not earlier than the fourth century B.C. and perhaps much later. The reflective undercurrent recalls the passage with which Catullus closes the sixty-fourth poem (384–408) and for this Catullus himself may be responsible. At any rate one cannot imagine Sappho persisting for many lines in such a point of view; if it is Greek, it must be late Greek.[73]

Kroll asserts that there is nothing in the references to wedding customs which does not conform with Greek usage. If we are very strict, this statement is true. And yet there are things which, if we may trust the meager evidence, are more Roman than Greek. The seizure of the bride with simulated violence can be proved to have occurred in Greece only among the Spartans;[74] among the Romans it was a prominent custom. The insistence on law and rights—the bride's duty and the parents' authority (60–65), the "equal" marriage (57)—seems Roman.[75]

In the technique the Greek elements are obvious: the contest (ἄγων), the refrain, the amoebaean element, the symmetry. And again, the character of these phenomena shows that they came to Catullus from later Greek poetry. The refrain recurs at regular intervals; Catullus even interjects a Latin word. The detailed responsion and the careful symmetry are characteristics of the age of Theocritus. Sappho employed the refrain, the dialogue, the contest, and probably choruses,[76] but in Catullus these elements have become artificialized. Sappho could not have composed in this manner. She compared the bride. to an apple, the groom to a sapling, and she knew the regret for lost virginity,[77] but it may be doubted whether she worked out her comparisons with the fulness of detail which we find in vv. 39–58. The central idea of the first comparison—the unwedded girl is like a flower in a walled garden—may easily be Sapphic, but for the second—the unwedded girl is like an untrained vine—this conclusion is much less probable.[78] Sappho also referred to the vine trained upon a tree,[79] but the custom of training vines upon trees suits Italian conditions far better than Greek. Moreover the idea of "marrying" the vine to the tree, so common in Roman poetry, does not seem to occur among the Greeks although both their myths and their poetry bear witness to the thought that there may be love between tree and tree.[80] When we observe that Catullus' comparisons are pervaded with the tendency (noted above) to generalize, that at bottom they deal, not with individuals, but with the states of virginity and wedlock, and that in technique they are carefully balanced to the smallest detail, it becomes probable that whatever Sapphic elements they may contain have been much altered and it is certain that they are presented in a very un-Sapphic manner.

To explain these modifications of elements which may be traced back ultimately to Sappho we do not need to assume that Catullus is following, perhaps translating, some Hellenistic imitation of Sappho[81] or even, in accordance with Kroll's somewhat hesitating suggestion, that he himself had a single poem of Sappho before him to which he applied his own methods.[82] The Sapphic motives, the Roman touches, the later Greek technique (which Catullus had mastered) taken together with the poet's admiration of Sappho point to the conclusion that the sixty-second poem is a free composition by Catullus himself. There is much that is Sapphic but there is also much that comes from later modes of thinking, and the art in general is certainly not Sappho's.

There is no hint in the poem that it was written for a definite wedding. The fact that, like the sixty-first, it is composed as if for song affords no proof that it was sung. The utmost that can be said in either case is that both poems could have been sung. And yet it is a curious fact that the very qualities which produce the impression that the sixty-second is an ideal poem give it a certain universality which adapts it for singing on special occasions. The meager references to Greek geography would have been no hindrance and no changes of detail would have been necessary if some Roman grandee had desired to use it to enhance the splendor of a wedding in high life. But there is no evidence that it was ever actually used in this way. As in the sixty-first poem we have only the poet's intention as a guide, and his intention, in the absence of external testimony to the contrary, must be assumed to have been literary, not musical. The whole is a poem, not a song, but it is throughout a well-nigh perfect reflection of song and the view that the first nineteen verses were intended to be spoken and the rest to be sung must be rejected.[83]

CHAPTER VIII

THE SHORT POEMS

Following the line of increasing resistance I come finally to the consideration of the short poems including those gems which have won for Catullus the major part of his fame. The difficulties of making a just estimate of his position are greatest in this part of his work because here there is the greatest dearth of Greek poetry of the same or closely similar type. The Greek epigram is sufficiently well preserved but the lyric, from the earliest period to the time of Catullus, is in a deplorable condition. As we search for analogies we may in many cases ransack all the extant remains of Greek lyric and epigram only to find little or nothing which illumines Catullus. But when Greek analogies are lacking, we must not jump at once to the conclusion that Catullus is wholly original, for sometimes a single brief fragment shows that a Greek poet had preceded him in composing the same type of poem, and whether Catullus had that poem definitely in mind or not, the fact of its existence proves that he was not first in the field and so limits the degree of his originality.

On the other hand, when good Greek parallels to certain details of a Catullian poem exist, we must not jump to the conclusion that Catullus had in mind a single Greek poem (now lost) very much like his own. It is true that no assumption concerning the unknown is more probable than that he had at his disposal a much greater body than we know of Greek poetry of the same general type as his short poems. But a survey of all the facts gives warning that we should always allow for a widely varying amount of Greek material and Greek suggestion as well as for originality in the strictest sense of the word. In short we must base our conclusions on known material, and despite the intentionally conservative remarks which I have just made considerable material exists. With a great many of the little poems we can do little or nothing,[1] with others we can do much, and from the latter class chiefly I shall select my illustrations.

In every kind of poetry hitherto examined, we have seen that Catullus was strongly influenced by tradition, most strongly in his miniature epic, much less strongly in the elegies and in the first wedding poem (LXI). We have seen that his poetry reflects both life and literature; that it is not only the product of his own experience and observation but also of his reading, his study, his discussions with his contemporaries. We have now come to that part of his work in which life plays its most important part. Nevertheless the literary influence, the influence of tradition, persists; in a good many of the short poems it is obvious, in many others it approaches or seems to approach the vanishing point. The evidence of it is just the same in character as in the longer poems: the identities and resemblances between the work of Catullus and that of Greek and Roman poets. But the great general difference between the long and the short poems from this point of view is that in the latter there is a much smaller number of resemblances and a much greater fluctuation in their amount. For this reason such resemblances as exist assume relatively greater importance and there is great danger of inferring too much from them. As I have already suggested in the lecture

on the short epic, it is advisable to study them as far
as possible in classes. Reasonable inferences can be
made only from groups of similar or related phenomena,
not from an isolated instance.

Studying similar phenomena means in the first place
comparing single poems or groups of poems with their
Greek counterparts, if any such exist. It has already
been argued that in composing a large group of varied
short poems Catullus was following the practice of the
later Greek poets and that his attitude toward this
group as a whole was much the same as theirs. It has
been noted also that within this large group, although
by no means all its members can be classified, there
are nevertheless a number of clearly marked types.
Fortunately some of these types can be followed back
into Greek poetry and wherever this is possible we
shall learn much about the nature of Catullus' work in
the field of the short poem. Both within and apart
from these types there is a mass of details of the varieties with which we have already become familiar:
translations of Greek words, Greek figures, and the like.
With these, except when they occur in the poems which
I shall proceed to discuss, we need not deal at present.
Let us begin with the larger entities.

Among the Greeks and Romans the custom of composing poems or bits of prose to accompany a book of
poems (sometimes a single poem) or a prose work was
well established and was practiced in considerable
variety. The dedication, the preface, the introduction,
the epilogue, the program poem may all be grouped
together as varieties of one general type. We are at
present concerned with poetry alone and for the most
part with single poems. There are in Catullus four
pieces, one of which is a mere fragment, belonging to

this group: the first poem, which is almost purely a
dedication, the fragment numbered XIV*b*, which
certainly possesses elements of a preface or an epilogue,
the sixty-fifth poem, which was composed to accompany the translation from Callimachus (LXVI), and
the first part of the sixty-eighth (LXVIII*a*), which was
intended to perform the same function for the rest of
that poem (LXVIII*b*). It is a characteristic of the
group that a reader or readers are addressed, often by
name, and the four poems of Catullus illustrate both
forms: three are addressed to individuals by name, the
fourth (XIV*b*) to readers, although names may have
occurred in that part of the poem which is lost. Any
one of the elements which I have indicated as characteristic of the group may occur in combination with others.
For example, the first poem of Catullus is chiefly
dedicatory but it has a prefatory element. So the
first ode of Horace is at once dedicatory and prefatory.
Again the dedication may be expressed in a word or
two which are part of a poem whose main content and
purpose are not dedicatory, as in the first satire of
Horace or the first elegy of Tibullus in which the
addresses to Maecenas and Messalla respectively serve
as dedications. In Catullus there is no dedication of
this last variety, but the sixty-fifth poem is similar;
the introductory purpose of the poem is indicated in
two lines (15–16):

> sed tamen in tantis maeroribus, Ortale, mitto
> haec expressa tibi carmina Battiadae.

The first poem best reveals the general method of
Catullus in composing poems of this general type. The
poem is intended as a dedication to Cornelius Nepos
of a book (*libellus*) of the poet's trifles (*nugae*). The

poet touches modestly on the character of the book
not only by calling the poems "trifles" but also in the
phrases *quidquid hoc libelli*, "this bit of a book," and
qualecumque, "however poor it may be."

The opening words imply that Catullus is following
a custom: "To whom am I to dedicate my pretty new
book?" The question in his mind is not "shall I
dedicate?" but "to whom am I to dedicate?" And in
fact the dedicatory poem was a well recognized Greek
type of which we get the first hint as early as the fifth
century B.C. in Dionysius Chalcus (fr. 1 [Diehl]),
Ὦ Θεόδωρε, δεχοῦ τήνδε προπινομένην τὴν ἀπ' ἐμοῦ ποίησιν,
etc.[2] By 200 B.C. the custom was well established
and the earliest extant dedication of a collection of
short poems is the poem in which Meleager dedicates
his *Garland* of so-called epigrams to Diocles.[3] This
poem, unlike the first poem of Catullus, is both a
dedication and an introduction or proem to the collection which is dedicated. The character of the collection, upon which Catullus touches so lightly, is for
Meleager the chief element and he gives in poetic
form a veritable table of contents. This is due chiefly
to the fact that Meleager was dedicating an anthology
containing the work of many poets in addition to his
own, whereas Catullus was dedicating exclusively his
own work. Nevertheless there are some similarities
of detail. Catullus opens with a question: "to whom
am I to dedicate?" and later addresses (probably) the
Muse. Meleager illustrates both these points, but he
combines them in his opening sentence: "Dear Muse,
for whom dost thou bring (φέρεις, cf. *dono*) these richly
varied songs?" Another detail which is the same in
both poems is the compliment paid to the friend—a
single adjective in Meleager (ἀριζάλῳ . . . . Διοκλεῖ),

in Catullus three lines of praise for Cornelius Nepos'
historical work, the *Chronica*.

The only other Greek details occur in the last two
lines:
                                        o patrona virgo
            plus uno maneat perenne saeclo.

For the idea that poets are clients of the Muses and the
prayer to the Muses that a literary work may have
long life the editors quote several parallels.[4]

In content then the first poem is almost wholly
Catullian. The Greek influence appears first of all in
the type which Catullus here follows or (better) continues, and in several details of the technique. All
these things had become as traditional as the sonnet
form is with us and there is no evidence that Catullus
had in mind any definite Greek poem or passage. In
short Catullus here accepts a traditional Greek type
together with a few of its details and expresses in it his
own thoughts in a charming, intimate way which was
attained nowhere else, so far as we know, in ancient
literature. The choice of the meter also may have been
his own idea. Other Romans must have preceded him
in the composition of such poems and many followed
his example, notably Martial, who often has the first
poem in mind.[5]

Some poems of the erotic group supply good illustrations of Catullus' methods. The sparrow poems
must be placed at the head of the list because in connection with them there is the richest Greek material—
nearly thirty poems in the *Greek Anthology*[6]—so that
we know very well how the Greeks composed little
poems on birds, dogs, even insects and fish! More
than half of these, including the best examples, are the
work of contemporaries or predecessors of Catullus—

Anyte and Simias of the fourth and third centuries, Tymnes, Meleager, and Archias (Cicero's friend) of the second and early first centuries. All are written in elegiac couplets, and Catullus' use of hendecasyllables may be one of the novelties which he introduced.

The Greeks then had long been accustomed to write little poems of this type, chiefly playful and pathetic variations on the sepulchral epigram, for most of them, like Catullus' third poem, deal with the death of a pet or some wild creature. But Catullus' poems are something more than examples of this simple type; they present not merely a picture of the pet in life or in death, they reflect also the mutual love of Lesbia and Catullus. The simple type has been developed into a subjective-erotic poem. In the second poem Lesbia plays with her sparrow to quiet the pangs of her love and the poet wishes that he might do likewise. In the third she weeps over the death of her dear pet and the poet identifies her grief with his own. But his pity for the sparrow is mingled with chiding because the pet has made his sweetheart's eyes so red! in one breath "poor little sparrow!", in the next "It's all your doing now that my sweetheart's eyes are swollen and red with weeping!" These are the touches which change the type into love poetry.

But here too one of the Greeks, Meleager, had pointed the way. On this account Meleager's two poems (*A. P.* VII. 195, 196) are the only good Greek parallels. The first is addressed to a locust, a creature whose note gave much pleasure to the Greeks,[7] and runs in part as follows:

Locust, beguiler of my passion, comforting me to sleep, thou natural mimic of the lyre, sing me a lay of love . . . . that thou mayst free me from the pangs of sleepless care, uttering a note that driveth love away. . . . .

Thus the little poem, ostensibly on a locust, becomes infused with personal erotic and the locust, like the sparrow in the second poem of Catullus, becomes a comfort to the lover; cf. *solaciolum sui doloris—ut—acquiescat ardor* (of Lesbia), and *tristis animi levare curas* (of Catullus). The simple original type is Greek and its application to the poet's own love is also Greek, but Meleager, unlike Catullus, does not address the pet of her whom he loves; the touch of Catullus is more tender, more intimate.

The third poem illustrates the same process; it combines the elements of the Greek sepulchral epigram and the epicede. As a whole it is a miniature epicede infused with the poet's own love.

Many of the details of the two poems are Greek, but they are commonplaces, not imitations of definite passages. Lesbia loved the sparrow "more than her very eyes." This comparison appears first in Greek, but as Kroll says, it had long been naturalized in Rome.[8] In my opinion it is one of the numerous expressions which demonstrate that the Greeks and Romans, related peoples, often had the same point of view; the idea was as much Roman as it was Greek.

The sparrow "passes along the shadowed path to that place from which they say no one returns" (III. 11–12), and Catullus curses the shades of Orcus which "devour all pretty things" (14). These ideas are Greek, cf. for the first Simias, Archias, Philetas, Theocritus; for the second (the curse) Crinagoras and certain anonymous epigrams; for the third (Hades devouring beauty) Bion.[9] By the time of Catullus these things had become commonplaces of poetry.

In the two sparrow poems Catullus has taken Greek types at their best and adapted them to his own

purposes. Of all the earlier or later poems of the same
type known to us (Greek or Roman) his are by far
the best. It would be interesting, if there were time,
to follow the type down through the centuries. We
should find that the later Roman poets turn for inspiration to Catullus, not to the Greeks, and of all their
efforts I like best an anonymous poem, an inscription
of the second century A.D., which was discovered
in France in 1865. The subject is a pet dog Fly
(*Myia*).[10] The poem is printed by Ellis in his large
text (p. 306) together with a fine translation by
Shadworth Hodgson:

> Quam dulcis fuit ista, quam benigna,
> Quae cum viverat in sinu iacebat
> Somni conscia semper et cubilis.
> O factum male, Myia, quod peristi!
> Latrares modo si quis adcubaret
> Rivalis dominae licentiosa.
> O factum male, Myia, quod peristi!
> Altum iam tenet insciam sepulcrum
> Nec sevire potes nec insilire
> Nec blandis mihi morsibus renides.

> The pet so dainty and so gentle dead!
> Nursed in her mistress' lap, and in her bed
> Nightly partaker of her sleep. O Fly,
> 'Twas wrong, 'twas very wrong of you to die!
> A rival for your lady's favour too,
> For did one sit a little closer, you
> Would bark, a graceless libertine! O Fly,
> 'Twas wrong, 'twas very wrong of you to die!
> Now all unwitting you lie buried deep,
> Nor can show fight, nor on the knee can leap,
> No more you gleam on me with teeth that bite
> In gentle snatches, half of play, half spite.

The sixth poem deserves a word or two because Friedrich Leo and Felix Jacoby have shown that it contains one or two Greek motives.[11] Catullus infers from the appearance of his friend Flavius and from the presence of perfumes and flowers in his apartment that he is in love but is ashamed to confess. He urges him to confess, asserting that he wishes to extol him and his inamorata in verse. Various details of this situation are so widespread in Greek and Roman poetry both before and after Catullus that there can be little doubt of the influence of tradition.

The idea that the lover's appearance betrays him is reflected in literature as early as the fourth century B.C.[12] The exhortation by the poet to a friend to confess his love does not appear earlier but it is common later among Greeks and Romans who had read the erotic literature which was familiar to Catullus. We may safely assume that this idea also occurred in Alexandrian poetry. It is employed by Propertius (I. 9), Tibullus (I. 8), Horace (*Odes* I. 27), and Maecius, a Greek epigrammatist of Tiberius' time. It appears sometimes with the addition of the principle that confession to a friend is a good thing for the lover—a principle which Catullus expresses in another poem (LV. 18–20).

It is quite possible of course that Catullus discovered these not very subtle things for himself, but it is more probable that he got the suggestions from some part of the Greek erotic literature which is now lost to us. At any rate he makes the theme wholly his own and works it into a poem which is utterly devoid of Greek ornament.

The eighth poem has always been a puzzle to scholars. The difficulty lies in the apparent contradiction between the first and the second halves of the poem. The first lines (1–11) have seemed to most readers to be very pathetic. To take an extreme case, Lord Macaulay could not read them without being moved to tears.[13] The second part (12–19) is anything but pathetic. A brief paraphrase:

(1) Wretched Catullus, cease to play the fool; accept your loss. Once you were happy with her whom you loved as you will never love another. But now she casts you off. Do not pursue one who shuns you; do not live in wretchedness. Persist in your purpose; harden your heart.

(2) Farewell, sweetheart. Catullus is now firm in his purpose. He will seek you no longer. But you will suffer. Wretched girl! What a life is in store for you! Who will seek you? Who will think you pretty? To whom will they say that you belong? Whom will you kiss? Whose lips will you bite? . . . .

But you, Catullus, with firm purpose harden your heart.

Scholars have generally taken this to be a serious poem written after a quarrel with Lesbia: they are suited to a girl of the lower classes, a *libertina*, and neither the tone nor the language are those of a man who is shaken to the depths of his being. And if the second part is not deeply serious, the (supposed) seriousness of the first part is brought into question.

In 1909 Professor E. P. Morris published an interpretation of this poem which is to my mind the only satisfactory one. I present the main outlines of this interpretation here because it has remained unknown to most students of Catullus.[14] None of the commentators appear to know anything about it. Moreover if Professor Morris' interpretation is correct, Catullus here utilizes his knowledge of Greek literature in a manner which has hardly been suspected, and so the poem is an important illustration of my theme.[15]

In Professor Morris' view the poem is not serious. It is "a light and humorous presentation of a lover— Catullus himself playing the part—trying to move the heart of the inconstant girl by appeals and pathos and sternness and threats." Catullus is writing a certain type of poem, modifying it to suit his own relations with Lesbia. In particular he tones down some of the more extreme features of the type, but he accepts others which by their very inapplicability to Lesbia show that "it is all a jest" and that "he is still her lover." Lesbia was witty, as we know from a number of the Lesbia poems; she and Catullus often jested together,[16] and so when Catullus "paid (her) the compliment of admitting her dominion over him by a humorous portrayal of himself in the character of a lover trying to touch her heart by the vain threat of leaving her, (she) certainly . . . . appreciated both the humor and the compliment."

The type which Catullus has in mind appears first in Greek literature and Professor Morris supplies the evidence. The motive of the lover apparently resolved to break away from the girl but secretly hoping a reconciliation and so trying to browbeat or wheedle her into it appeared in the Greek New Comedy. No close parallel from the original Greek has happened to survive,[17] but the frequent recurrence of the motive in both Roman comedy and Roman elegy prove beyond a doubt that it occurred in the Greek comedy. Professor Morris cites numerous parallels from Plautus and Terence, who were adapting plays of the New Comedy. The best of these is the *Truculentus* of Plautus (759–769) where the picture of the lover is the same: he is resolved to break away, threatens the girl, but is conscious of his own weakness; cf. also the *Bacchides* (500–525).

The same motive appears twice in Propertius (II. 5, III. 25—this last passage not mentioned by Morris), once in Ovid (*Am*. III. 11*a*, *b*), once in Horace (*Epode* XV). All three poets, like Catullus, adapt the motive to their own cases.[18]

Professor Morris declares that "there is not a single poem in the Palatine Anthology which can be used as a parallel." There is however at least one poem (V. 107) in which Philodemus, a contemporary of Catullus, chiding a girl after a break, implies the existence of the same type:[19] "I warned you but you did not listen . . . . so now you are sobbing while I rest on Nais' breast." Here we have a later stage of the same general situation: the threat has been carried out.

The eighth poem then is an excellent illustration of one of the methods of Catullus: it combines elements from both life—his own life—and literature. He takes a typical situation from Greek erotic and applies it with imagination and with humor to his own case. He modifies it so little that the bookish, the traditional elements are still clear. Who can say whether the idea of writing such a poem first came to him from some experience of his own—some insignificant tiff with Lesbia[20]—or from his reading? If the latter is true, the tiff is purely imaginary. At any rate both elements, life and literature, are there in the poem. It is impossible to say where Catullus got the bookish elements, but it is worth noting that the great storehouse of such motives was the New Comedy and that Menander was better known at Rome than any other Greek poet except Homer.

The seventieth poem illustrates the same general method, only in this case we have some positive imitation:

My lady says she prefers as a husband no one to me, not if Jupiter himself should woo her. She says so, but what a woman says to her eager lover should be written on the winds and the swift flowing water.

Catullus here takes up a gay remark of Lesbia's—she would prefer not even Jupiter to Catullus—and works it into a humorous poem the main purpose of which is to characterize lovers' oaths. The unreliability of woman's oaths had become proverbial as early as the time of Sophocles (fr. 741): "woman's oaths I write on water." Probably the apothegm was older still but it is quite enough for us to be able to trace it as far as the fifth century B.C.[21]

In composing his own poem however Catullus had in mind not only this misogynistic sentiment but also a definite poem of Callimachus (*A. P.* V. 6):[22]

Callignotus swore to Ionis that she would ever be dearer to him than any man or woman. He swore it; but 'tis a true saying that lover's oaths do not enter the ears of the gods. Now he burns with love for another, etc.

Catullus secures his emphasis by repeating *dicit— dicit—dicit*, as Callimachus repeats ὤμοσε . . . . ὤμοσεν, and in both poets the second occurrence is placed first in the line.[23]

Again Catullus mingles the stuff of life and literature, and again we cannot say with certainty from which source the original suggestion came. Lesbia's words about the rivalry of Jupiter show that she too was familiar with a commonplace of Greek erotic,[24] and perhaps they reminded Catullus of the epigram of Callimachus. On the other hand, if the poet began with Callimachus, he worked out his own epigram as a whole in very different fashion. The whole poem is certainly not modeled throughout on Callimachus.[25]

In the group of invitations and greetings the thirteenth poem has a special interest:

My dear Fabullus, you'll have a fine dinner at my house
if you bring it with you, for I am absolutely broke (*plenus
sacculus est aranearum*). I'll supply only one thing: the
perfume which the Venuses and Cupids gave to my sweetheart. When you smell that, you'll ask the gods, Fabullus,
to make you all nose!

Catullus is here practicing a familiar type of Greek
poem.[26] Some scholars however assert that he had a
definite model in Philodemus' invitation to his patron
Piso (*A.P.*XI.44).[27] Let us see. The poem of Philodemus is written in elegiac couplets and runs as follows:[28]

Tomorrow, dearest Piso, your friend, beloved by the
Muses, who keeps our annual feast of the twentieth[29] invites
you to come after the ninth hour to his simple cottage. If
you miss udders and draughts of Chian wine, you will see at
least sincere friends and you will hear of things far sweeter
than the land of the Phaeacians. But if you ever cast your
eyes on me, Piso, we shall celebrate the twentieth richly
instead of simply.

The poem resembles that of Catullus in being an
invitation to dinner, in suggesting that the fare will be
simple (in Catullus nothing, unless the friend brings
the dinner), and in offering a substitute for the fare
(Philodemus offers friends and good talk, or verse;
Catullus the perfume). If we could interpret the final
sentence of Philodemus as a hint that Piso should give
this particular dinner,[30] we should have a more striking
and peculiar resemblance. But Philodemus, as his
last phrase shows, is hinting that Piso should give
another dinner in the future on the same anniversary
—"your turn next, Piso!" He is inviting a patron and
his poem more closely resembles Horace's ode (I. 20)

written in expectation of a visit from Maecenas than the invitation which Catullus extends to a friend of his own class. Hence Philodemus is more conventional, Catullus is absolutely outspoken. The mention of simple fare in such invitations was as much of a convention in antiquity as it is with us, and the good talk and verse—if Philodemus means verse—were both conventions of Roman dinners.[31] These conventions are all that Catullus needed to produce the gaily exaggerated variation of the type which is represented by the thirteenth poem, and it is very improbable that he had a definite poem as a model.[32]

I lay no stress on the fact that the poem of Catullus contains three other details which are certainly, or probably, Greek but are not found in the epigram of Philodemus. These are the use of cobwebs to denote emptiness,[33] the idea of a perfume so fine that it must have been a gift of the gods,[34] and the expression "to make one all nose." The last phrase cannot be exactly paralleled in Greek, but it is of the same type as "all ears and tongue" (Herondas) and "all face" (Aelian).[35]

The twenty-sixth poem was written for the sake of the play on *opponere* in the sense of "expose to" and "pledge" or "mortgage":

Furius, your little villa is not indeed exposed to the draught of the winds, but to the much worse draft of 15,200 sesterces, a terribly noisome draught! This represents Ellis' effort to render the pun in English by shifting it to a noun. Perhaps I may be allowed to suggest: "Your villa is not indeed exposed to winds, but to foreclosure." This is tame but it has at least the merit of confining the pun to the word in which it lies, *opposita est*. (Too bad that in English these things so often need a diagram!)

The precise application of the joke would not be perfectly clear even if we knew certainly whose villa is meant, the villa of Furius, as I have taken it, or the villa of Catullus. Shall we read *vostra* or *nostra* in the first line? Both have excellent support in the manuscripts and both make good sense. The point illustrates better than any other with which I am acquainted how the change of a single letter may alter our understanding of an entire poem.[36] Our uncertainty about this point, however, does not alter the probable Greek element—the pun and the figure in the last line, "a hurricane of debt." There is evidence that both of these had appeared in Greek, although no poem exists in which they are combined as in Catullus. The idea that a house may be so situated as to be exposed to debt appears in Pherecrates and the figure, "great storms of debt," in an epigram of Callimachus, although the poem as a whole is very different from that of Catullus.[37] If we should remove these two things, there would be nothing left of Catullus' poem. Again he utilizes his reading to give point to one of his own experiences.

The little drinking song (XXVII) represents a type practiced from time immemorial by the Greeks, a favorite type with Horace. The major part of the content also is traditional. The piece embodies, as Kroll says, a drinker's principle (*Trinkspruch*), and (we may add) a hard drinker's principle, for reduced to its lowest terms it means simply: Give me stronger drink, boy. Water ruins wine. Old Trimalchio expresses the idea as a principle in four words: *aquam foras, vinum intro*! ("Out with the water, in with the wine!") undoubtedly a popular maxim.[38] In Greek both the situation—the poet addressing the slave who serves him—and the principle which he utters can be traced back to the fourth century B.C. The best parallel is Diphilus: "Stronger stuff, by Zeus, boy! For everything watery is an evil for the soul!"[39] By the time of Catullus the thing was sheer tradition and it would be absurd to assign it to any definite literary source. On the other hand it is not certain that the poem was suggested to him by any definite occasion in his own life although he so represents it, and for this reason he mentions an Italian wine (Falernian) and a Roman *magistra bibendi* ("mistress of the drinking"), Postumia, who may have been a real person. His final word, however, is Greek and very peculiarly Greek: *hic merus est Thyonianus*. Thyonianus, an adjective from Thyoneus (Dionysus) occurs nowhere else in this sense —as if "Thyonian," like "Falernian," were a sort of wine. Indeed Catullus seems to have the Greek οἶνος in mind, as the gender of the adjective shows.

In the twenty-seventh poem then Catullus continues an ancient type, best represented for us by the Greek sympotic epigrams; he accepts a traditional situation, a traditional content, and touches up the whole with Roman and Greek details to suit his own purpose. The method is characteristic.

The foregoing illustrations have been purposely chosen from a group of poems each of which contains a considerable number of Greek elements. The list might be somewhat extended but at best it would include only about twenty poems, for such fairly good illustrations are not the rule; they represent the most favorable side of the general problem. The unfavorable side is represented by a group of some fourteen others for which, apart from the general Greek types to which they belong, it is impossible to quote any really significant Greek material. With these last we can do little in detail except from the metrical point of view.

The great mass of the short poems—the poems which represent the rule—fall between the two extremes. Each of them has one or two demonstrably Greek details, not enough to indicate a single Greek model or even the general use of Greek material. Nevertheless when grouped together these scattered parallels are instructive, for they reveal the poet's normal procedure. They are of much the same kinds as those which have already been noted in the discussion of the sixty-fourth poem, but naturally they occur less frequently because in the short poems Catullus is working more independently and because the style is for the most part simple and colloquial—appropriate to the themes—and has much less ornament. As briefly as possible I shall set down some illustrations with the purpose of indicating at least the range of these Greek details. And first the content:

In XLI a lady who thinks herself so fine is advised to consult her mirror, cf. Lucilius, *A. P.* XI. 266; Alciphron, I. 33. 4.[40] The thought of snatching kisses that are sweeter than ambrosia (XCIX. 2), appears in Meleager, *A. P.* XII. 68. The lover's compact (*foedus*) is mentioned several times (CIX, LXXXVII, LXXVI), cf. Plautus, *Asin.* 746 ff. (the *syngraphum*), i.e., the Greek New Comedy.[41] In XLV meeting a lion is chosen as a type of danger, cf. Simonides of Amorgos, fr. 12 (Diehl). In LXXXV (LXXV, LXXII, LXXVI) hate and love battle for the mastery, cf. Theognis 1091 ff.; Terence, *Eun.* 72 (i.e., the New Comedy); Anacreon, fr. 79 D.[42] Greek myths are occasionally employed: II*b* (Atalanta and the golden apples), LV (Talos, Hercules, Pegasus, Rhesus). The theme of the advantages of poverty (XXIII) is paralleled many times in Greek, e.g., Alexis, fr. 174 (Kock); Antiphanes, fr. 226 K. The inability of men to see their own faults (XXII. 18–21) appears in Euripides, fr. 1042 and in Menander, fr. 631 K. The shortness of life (V) and the road to death over which none return (III) are very old themes, cf. *A. P.* XII.50, VII. 203; Anacreon, fr. 44 D. Some of the comparisons have a proverbial ring: dearer than gold (CVII), cf. Sappho, fr. 138 D.; bitterer than hellebore (XCIX), cf. *A. P.* V.29; nothing sillier than a silly laugh (XXXIX. 16), cf. Menander, *monost.* 88, 108. Harpocrates is the type of silence (LXXIV), cf. Plutarch, *De Is.* p. 378c.

Some of these things probably came to Catullus through his rhetorical training, not directly from his reading. This is certainly the case with his use of the sands and stars for an indefinitely large number (VII), the winds carrying away empty words (XXX), cruelty expressed by comparisons to a lionness or to Scylla (LX).[43]

Greek technique may be illustrated by many of the figures, e.g., eyes drunk with love (XLV), love a disease (LXXVI. 25), Tethys for the sea (LXXXVIII). We may add such phenomena as the use of hymn style (XXXVI. 11 ff.), of refrains (XLV, LII, LVII), of dialogue even in short poems (X, XLV), and of course many a detail of vocabulary (loan words and translations of Greek words) and meter.

But I fear lest this catalogue grow wearisome. Excluding details of meter and prosody I have collected from the commentators (supplemented by my own reading) almost two hundred parallels of the foregoing and still other varieties. Obviously in the time of Catullus a large number of them belonged to the common stock which any poet could use; they were not merely traditional, they were conventional. The impressive fact, however, is that so long a list of phenomena had occurred in Greek poetry. One may explain some of them away as accidental coincidences, others as due to the fact that the Greeks and Romans often had the same point of view, but a great many remain which resist such explanations; the proof of Greek influence is cumulative.

Sometimes Catullus himself was probably unconscious of this influence, but in most cases he certainly knew what he was doing—when, for example, he made use of Greek myths, Greek figures, hymn style, etc. Yet it is rarely possible to say that he was imitating a definite Greek passage. Even Ellis, who wrote his commentary at a time (before 1889) when excessive credulity prevailed concerning the imitation of definite passages, asserts imitation of the Greek or regards it as probable only some fifteen times in the short poems (in addition to LI).[44] The conservative critic of today will reduce Ellis' cases of imitation almost to the vanishing point.

Among the Latinizations of single Greek words or very brief phrases a few are so unusual that we may infer the use of definite passages. For example when Catullus humorously renders σιλφιοφόρος by *laserpicifer* (VII. 4) he must have had a passage of Callimachus (let us say) in mind, and one may suspect the same method in the cases of *tardipes* (XXXVI. 7), *pinnipes* and *plumipes* (LV.3a,5a). On the other hand, the phrase *longe resonante* (XI. 3) suggests the Homeric πολυφλοίσβοιο, though not a particular passage of Homer.

When we study longer passages we find (in addition to a large part of the fifty-first poem) only four probable

or possible cases of imitation.   Two of these—the
"storm of debt" (XXVI) and a part of the treatment
of lovers' vows (LXX)—were probably taken from
Callimachus.[45] Others occur in the fortieth and fifty-
sixth poems, in both cases perhaps derived from
Archilochus.

On the fortieth poem Ellis cites two fragments of
Archilochus which begin, as Catullus' poem begins,
with indignant questions addressed to the individuals
whom he attacks.   This is a bit of the invective technique which Catullus need not have learned from these
particular lines.   But the references in both poets to the
madness of the person addressed and to the anger of
some deity which he has aroused against himself render
imitation on the part of Catullus possible.[46]

The opening of the fifty-sixth poem (in which
Catullus recounts to a friend an amusing incident)
closely resembles still another fragment of Archilochus:
"Charilaus, I'll tell you a laughable incident and you'll
be amused when you hear it."   This technique clearly
goes back to Archilochus whom Catullus may quite
possibly have had in mind, but the Greek epigrammatists also had made use of it, as Kroll shows, so that
the relation of Catullus to Archilochus may here be
indirect.[47]

In short poems Catullus was continuing and practicing freely in Latin a large number of Greek types
which we still find in the *Greek Anthology* and in the
remains of early Greek lyric.   The surviving Greek
examples, however, are rarely earlier than the fourth
century B.C.—a condition due in part to the loss of
most of the early Greek poetry of this sort.   Under these
general types it is possible to classify nearly all the
short poems.[48]

I have already indicated these general categories: the invective or satiric poem, the erotic, the poem of invitation and greeting, the votive poem, the anecdote, the dedication, etc., etc. Within these general types there are often sub-types or varieties. These last also quite often have Greek prototypes.

In his short poems Catullus was not breaking absolutely new ground; he was not, in Horace's phrase, composing a kind of poetry untouched by the Greeks; rather he was continuing in Latin the same kinds and types of poetry that the Greeks had composed. In general he was working very freely, but the degree of his independence varies greatly in different cases. He never followed a single Greek model throughout one of his own poems. This is the conclusion to be drawn from the extant evidence and it is supported by everything we know of the poet's methods. Even the fifty-first poem is not wholly based on Sappho, and among the short poems the fifty-first is the extreme case.[49] If there is any other, either the Greek model is lost to us or Catullus has successfully concealed the fact of his dependence. The single example in all his work of thorough-going dependence on one Greek poem is the avowed translation, LXVI.

The result of this study of the short poems has been to reduce translation and imitation of definite Greek poems or passages to a minimum. The Greek element, which is very much less in amount than we found it to be in the longer and more elaborate poems, is almost entirely of a traditional character—traditional content, traditional technique—but at the same time it is used more independently than is the case with the longer poems because here tradition was less binding than it was, for example, in epic or in elegy. But the traditional element is there: in the idea of composing such a group, in the general types, in the meters, in the rhetorical touches, in a considerable number of miscellaneous details. Yet the content is to a very large extent Roman, often Catullian. The impulses which suggested these little poems are usually easy to discern; they sprang mostly from personal experiences or observations of the poet. Those which have no basis in reality, the ideal or purely fanciful poems, such as the hymn to Diana, Septimius and Acme, perhaps the Juventius cycle, do not on the most liberal estimate exceed twenty, and this total includes at least a dozen which are doubtful because we do not really know what suggested them. Catullus drew most of the material for his short poems from life itself, but their art could not have been what it was unless he had been thoroughly familiar with Greek poetry and its methods.

LIST OF ABBREVIATIONS OF TITLES OF BOOKS, PERIODICALS, ETC.

ABBREVIATIONS	TITLES
A. J. P.	*American Journal of Philology.*
A. L. L.	*Archiv für lateinische Lexikographie und Grammatik mit Einschluss des älteren Mittellateins.*
A. L. W.	Arthur Leslie Wheeler.
A. P.	*Anthologia Palatina.*
Abh. bayer. Akad.	*Abhandlungen der philosophisch-philologischen Klasse der bayerischen Akademie der Wissenschaften.* Munich.
Abh. Göttingen	*Abhandlungen der Gesellschaft der Wissenschaften zu Göttingen, philologisch-historische Klasse.* Berlin.
Acta Soc. Scient. Fennicae	*Acta Societatis Scientiarum Fennicae.* Helsingfors.
Anth. Plan.	*Anthologia Planudea.*
Anthol. lyr.	Diehl, E., editor. *Anthologia lyrica,* Leipzig, 1922-1924. 6 vols.
Athenaeum	*Athenaeum, Studii Periodici di Letteratura e Storia dell' Antichità.* Pavia.
B. sächs. Gesellsch.	*Berichte über die Verhandlungen der sächsischen Gesellschaft der Wissenschaften zu Leipzig.*
Baehrens	Baehrens, Emil, editor. *Catulli Veronensis Liber.* Leipzig, 1876 and 1885. 2 vols.
Benecke, *Antimachus of Colophon*	Benecke, E. F. M. *Antimachus of Colophon and the Position of Women in Greek Poetry.* London, 1896.
Bernhardy	Bernhardy, G., editor. *Dionysius Periegetes Graece et Latine, cum vetustis commentariis et interpretationibus.* Leipzig, 1829. 2 vols. (= *Geographi Graeci Minores.* Vols. I and II.)
Birt, *Das antike Buchwesen*	Birt, Theodor. *Das antike Buchwesen in seinem Verhältniss zur Litteratur, mit Beiträgen zur Textgeschichte des Theokrit, Catull, Properz und anderer Autoren.* Berlin, 1882.
Blümner, *Röm. Privataltertümer*	Blümner, H. *Die römische Privataltertümer,* ed. 3. Munich, 1911.
Bolaffi, *De scuti Herculis descriptione,* etc.	Bolaffi, A. *De scuti Herculis descriptione in eo carmine quod* 'Ασπὶς 'Ηρακλέους *inscribitur. Accedunt duae aliae disputatiunculae.* Pesaro, 1919.

Büttner, *Porcius Licinus,* etc.   Büttner, R. *Porcius Licinus und der litterarische Kreis des Q. Lutatius Catulus. Ein Beitrag zur Geschichte der römischen Litteratur.* Leipzig, 1893.

C. I. L.   *Corpus Inscriptionum Latinarum.*

C. Lat. epig.   Buecheler, F., editor. *Carmina Latina epigraphica.* (=*Anthologia Latina,* pars posterior fasc. 1.) Leipzig, 1895.

Χάριτες   Χάριτες *Friedrich Leo zum 60. Geburtstag dargebracht.* Berlin, 1911.

Class. Phil.   *Classical Philology.*

Class. Rev.   *Classical Review.*

De Gubernatis, ed. 1928   De Gubernatis, M. Lechantin, editor. *Il libro di Catullo Veronese, testo e commento.* Torino, 1928.

Diehl   Diehl, E., editor. *Poetarum Romanorum veterum reliquiae.* (*Kleine Texte für theologische und philologische Vorlesungen und Ubungen* 69.) Bonn, 1911.

Diehl, *Anthol. lyr.*   See *Anthol. lyr.*

Drachmann, *Catuls Digtning*   Drachmann, A. B. *Catuls Digtning, belyst i forhold til den tidligere Graeske og Latinske litteratur.* Copenhagen, 1887.

Dübner, Himerius   Dübner, F., editor. *Himerii Declamationum quae supersunt. In* Westerman, A., *Philostratorum et Callistrati Opera.* Paris, 1849.

Dziatzko   Dziatzko, K. *Untersuchungen über ausgewählte Kapitel des antiken Buchwesens, mit Text, Ubersetzung und Erklärung von Plinius, Nat. hist.,* XIII: 68–89. Leipzig, 1900.

Edmonds, *Lyra Graeca*   Edmonds, J. M., editor and translator. *Lyra Graeca, with an English Translation.* Loeb Classical Library. London and New York, 1922-1927. 3 vols.

Einl. Alt.   *Einleitung in die Altertumswissenschaft;* ed. 2, I,

Einl. in die Alt.   Leipzig, 1912; ed. 3, I, Leipzig, 1927; ed. 3, II, Leipzig, 1922.

Ellis, 1878   Ellis, Robinson, editor. *Catulli Veronensis Liber,* ed. 2. Oxford, 1878.

Ellis, 1904   Ellis, Robinson, editor. *Catulli Carmina.* Oxford, 1904.

Ellis' Oxford text (1904)

Ellis, *Commentary*   Ellis, Robinson. *A Commentary on Catullus,* ed. 2. Oxford, 1889.

F. H. G.	Muller, C. and T., editors. *Fragmenta histori-corum Graecorum*. Paris, 1841, and reprinted. 5 vols.
F. P. L.	Morel, W., editor. *Fragmenta poetarum Latin-orum epicorum et lyricorum, praeter Ennium et Lucilium, post Aemilium Baehrens iterum edidit*. Leipzig, 1927.
Farrington, *Primum Graius homo*	Farrington, B. *Primum Graius homo, an An-thology of Latin Translations from the Greek, from Ennius to Livy, with an introductory Essay and running Commentary*. Cambridge University Press, 1927.
Festschrift für Hirschfeld	*Beiträge zur alten Geschichte und griechisch-römi-schen Alterthumskunde. Festschrift zu Otto Hirschfelds 60. Geburtstage*. Berlin, 1903.
Foerster, Libanius	Foerster, R., editor. *Libanii Opera*. Leipzig, 1903-1927. 12 vols.
Foerster-Richtsteig, Choricius	Foerster, R., and Richtsteig, E., editors. *Choricii Gazaei Opera*. Leipzig, 1929.
Frank, *Catullus*	Frank, Tenney. *Catullus and Horace, two Poets in their environment*. New York, 1928.
Frank, *Catullus and Horace*	
Friedrich	Friedrich, G., editor. *Catulli Veronensis Liber*. Leipzig, 1908.
Friedrich, *Kommentar*	
Gimm, *De Vergilii stilo bucolico*	Gimm, R. *De Vergilii stilo bucolico quaestiones selectae*. Leipzig Diss. Weida, 1910.
Gummere, *Handbook of Poetics*[3]	Gummere, F. B. *A Handbook of Poetics for Students of English Verse*, ed. 3. Boston, 1890.
Hampel, *De apostrophae . . . usu*	Hampel, E. *De apostrophae apud Romanorum poetas usu*. Jena, 1908.
Haupt, *Opusc.*	Haupt, M. *Opuscula*. Leipzig, 1875 and 1876. 3 vols.
Heinze, *Virg. Ep. Tech.*	Heinze, R. *Virgils epische Technik*, ed. 3. Leipzig, 1915.
Heinze on Horace's Odes	See Kiessling's Horace.
Helbig, *Wandgem.*	Helbig, W. *Wandgemälde der vom Vesuv ver-schütteten Städte Campaniens; nebst einer Ab-handlung über die antiken Wandmalereien in technischer Beziehung*, von Otto Donner. Leip-zig, 1868.
Holder, *Altcelt. Sprach-satz*	Holder, A. *Alt-celtischer Sprachsatz*. Leipzig, 1896 and 1904. 2 vols.
J. K. P.	*Jahrbücher für klassische Philologie*.
Jour. Phil.	*Journal of Philology*.

Kiessling's Horace	Kiessling, A. *Q. Horatius Flaccus, Oden und Epoden;* ed. 7 revised by R. Heinze. Berlin, 1930.
Kroll	Kroll, W., editor. *C. Valerius Catullus,* ed. 2.
Kroll, *Catull*	Leipzig, 1929.
Kroll, *Stud.* (or *Studien*)	Kroll, W. *Studien zum Verständniss der römischen Literatur.* Stuttgart, 1924.
Lafaye, *Catulle*	Lafaye, G. *Catulle et ses Modèles.* Paris, 1894.
Leo, *Lit.*	Leo, F. *Geschichte der römischen Literatur.* Berlin, 1913.
Leo, *Pl. F.*²	Leo, F. *Plautinische Forschungen zur Kritik und Geschichte der Komödie,* ed. 2. Berlin, 1912.
Leo, *Plaut. Forsch.*²	
Lindsay, Paul. Fest.	Lindsay, W. M., editor. *Sexti Pompei Festi de verborum significatu quae supersunt cum Pauli epitome, Thewrewkianis copiis usus edidit.* Leipzig, 1913.
Mair, *Callimachus*	Mair, A. W., editor and translator. *Callimachus and Lycophron, with an English Translation.* Loeb Classical Library. London and New York, 1921.
Marx's *Lucilius*	Marx, F., editor. *C. Lucilius, Carminum reliquiae.* Leipzig, 1904 and 1905. 2 vols.
Mélanges Weil	*Mélanges Henri Weil; recueil de mémoires concernant l'histoire et la littérature grecques dédié à Henri Weil à l'occasion de son 80ᵉ anniversaire.* Paris, 1897.
Merrill, E. T.	Merrill, E. T., editor. *C. Plini Caecili Secundi Epistularum Libri Decem.* Leipzig, 1921.
Mnemos.	*Mnemosyne.*
Morel, *F. P. L.*	See *F. P. L.*
Mueller, *Griech. Privataltertümer*²	Mueller, I. von. *Die griechischen Privataltertümer,* ed. 2. Munich, 1893. (1st part of I. von Mueller and A. Bauer's *Die griechischen Privat- und Kriegsaltertümer.*)
Mueller's *Handbuch*	Mueller, I. von, editor. *Handbuch der klassischen Altertumswissenschaft.* Munich.
Munro	Munro, H. A. J. *Criticisms and Elucidations of Catullus,* ed. 2. Cambridge and London, 1905.
Munro, *Criticisms and Elucidations*	
N. Jhb.	See *Neue Jahrb.*
Naber, Marcus. Aurel.	Naber, S. A., editor. *M. Cornelii Frontonis et M. Aurelii Imperatoris Epistulae.* Leipzig, 1867.
Neue Jahrb.	*Neue Jahrbücher für das klassische Altertum, Geschichte und deutsche Literatur.*

Nicholson, *Keltic Researches* — Nicholson, E. W. B. *Keltic Researches. Studies in the History and Distribution of the Ancient Goidelic Language and Peoples.* London and New York, 1904.

Norden, *Aen. VI* — Norden, E. P. *Vergilius Maro Aeneis Buch VI,* ed. 3. Leipzig, 1926.

Ox. Pap. — *Oxyrhyncus Papyri.* Hunt, A. S., editor. London, 1910. Vol. VII.

P. G. — See *Patrolog. Gr.*

P.-W. — Pauly-Wissowa, *Realenzyklopädie der klassischen Altertumswissenschaft.*

Palaeog. of Greek Papyri — Kenyon, F. G. *The Palaeography of Greek Papyri.* Oxford, 1899.

Pasquali, *Quaestt. Callim.* — Pasquali, G. *Quaestiones Callimacheae.* Göttingen, 1913.

Paton, *Greek Anthology* — Paton, W. R., editor and translator. *The Greek Anthology, with an English Translation.* Loeb Classical Library. London and New York, 1918. 5 vols.

Patrolog. Gr. — Migne, J. P., editor. *Patrologia Graeca.* Paris, 1857–1899. 161 vols.

Patrolog. Latina — Migne, J. P., editor. *Patrologia Latina.* Paris, 1844–1902. 221 vols.

Pernice, *Hochzeit,* etc. — Pernice, E. *Griechisches und römisches Privatleben.* Leipzig, 1922.

Ph. V. B. 1915 — *Jahresberichte des philologischen Vereins zu Berlin* XLI (1915); published with *Sokrates, Zeitschrift für das Gymnasialwesen* III (LXIX) [1915].

Philol. — *Philologus.*

Phil. U. — *Philologische Untersuchungen.*

Powell, *Collectanea Alex.* — Powell, J. U., editor. *Collectanea Alexandrina; reliquiae minores poetarum Graecorum aetatis Ptolemaicae 323-146 a.C., epicorum, elegiacorum, lyricorum, ethicorum; cum epimetris et indice nominum.* Oxford, 1925.

Preller — Preller, L. *Griechische Mythologie;* ed. 4, revised by C. Robert. Berlin, 1894. 2 vols.

Prescott, *Development of Virgil's Art* — Prescott, H. W. *The Development of Virgil's Art.* Chicago, 1927.

Prosopog. Imperii Romani — Rohden, P. de, and Dessau, H., editors. *Prosopographia Imperii Romani.* Berlin, 1898. Vol. III.

Rabe, *Aphthonius* — Rabe, H., editor. *Aphthonii Progymnasmata.* Leipzig, 1926. (=*Rhetores Graeci,* Vol. X.)

Reitzenstein, *Hellen. Wundererzähl.*	Reitzenstein, R. *Hellenistische Wundererzählungen.* Leipzig, 1906.
Rev. des Études lat.	*Revue des Études latines.*
Rev. de Phil.	*Revue de Philologie, de Littérature et d'Histoire Anciennes.*
Rh. M.	*Rheinisches Museum.*
Riv. di fil.	*Rivista di filologia e di istruzione classica.*
Riv. fil.	
Rohde, *Griech. Roman*	Rohde, E. *Der griechische Roman und seine Vorläufer,* ed. 3. Leipzig, 1914.
Roscher	Roscher, W. H., editor. *Ausführliches Lexikon der griechischen und römischen Mythologie.* Leipzig, 1884-1924. 5 vols.
Rothstein, Propertius	Rothstein, M., editor. *Die Elegien des Sextus Propertius erklärt,* ed. 2. Berlin, 1920. 2 vols.
S. B. Heidelberg	*Sitzungsberichte der Heidelberger Akademie.*
S. B. Wien	*Sitzungsberichte der Akademie der Wissenschaften in Wien.*
S. B. Berlin	*Sitzungsberichte der preussischen Akademie der*
S. Ber. Berlin	*Wissenschaften zu Berlin.*
Samter, *Geburt, Hochzeit u. Tod*	Samter, E. *Geburt, Hochzeit und Tod; Beiträge zur vergleichenden Volkskunde.* Leipzig, 1911.
Schanz	Schanz, M. *Geschichte der römischen Literatur bis zum Gesetzgebungswerk des Kaisers Justinian;* ed. 4 newly revised by C. Hosius. Munich, 1927. Vol. I.
Scheer, *Lycophronis Alexandra*	Scheer, E., editor. *Lycophronis Alexandra.* Berlin, 1908. 2 vols.
Schmidt, B.	Schmidt, B., editor. *C. Valeri Catulli Veronensis Carmina.* Leipzig, 1887.
Schulze, *Beiträge,* etc.	Schulze, K. P. *Beiträge zur Erklärung der römischen Elegiker.* (I) Programm No. 55, 1893, des Friedrich-Werderschen Gymnasiums zu Berlin. Berlin, 1893.
Schulze, *Röm. Elegiker*	Schulze, K. P. *Römische Elegiker. Eine Auswahl aus Catull, Tibull, Properz und Ovid,* ed. 3. Berlin, 1890.
Schwabe (ed. 1886)	Schwabe, L., editor. *Catulli Veronensis Liber, ad optimos codices denuo collatos.* Berlin, 1886.
Schwabe, *Quaestt.*	Schwabe, L. *Quaestionum Catullianarum Liber Primus.* (=G. *Valeri Catulli Liber,* Ludovicus Schwabius *recognovit et enarravit; Voluminis prioris pars prior.*) Giessen, 1862.

Sidgwick, Aeschylus	Sidgwick, A., editor. *Aeschyli Tragoediae, cum fabularum deperditarum fragmentis poetae vita et operum catologo.* Oxford, 1902.
Smith, Tibullus	Smith, Kirby Flower, editor. *The Elegies of Albius Tibullus, the Corpus Tibullianum, edited with introduction and notes on Books I, II, and IV, 2-14.* New York, 1913.
Stangl, Asconius	Stangl, T., editor. *Ciceronis Orationum Scholiastae.* Vienna and Leipzig, 1912. Vol. II.
Studi ital. di fil.	*Studi italiani di filologia classica.*
Studi ital. fil. class.	
Studj di fil romanza	*Studj di filologia romanza.*
Tom Jones	Fielding, Henry. *The History of Tom Jones.* Everyman's Library. London. 2 vols.
Trevelyan's Life	Trevelyan, G. O. *The Life and Letters of Lord Macaulay, by his Nephew.* London, 1876. 2 vols.
Univ. Calif. Publ. in Class. Phil.	*University of California Publications in Classical Philology.*
Usener, *Kl. Schr.*	Usener, H. *Kleine Schriften.* Leipzig, 1912–1914. 4 vols.
Usener-Radermacher, *Dionysius*	Usener, H., and Radermacher, L. *Dionysii Halicarnasei Opuscula.* Leipzig, 1899-1929. 2 vols.
W. St.	*Wiener Studien.*
Walde, *Lat. Etymol. Wörterbuch*[2]	Walde, A. *Lateinisches etymologisches Wörterbuch,* ed. 2. Heidelberg, 1910.
Westphal, *Catull's Gedichte*[2]	Westphal, R. *Catull's Gedichte in ihrem geschichtlichen Zusammenhange, übersetzt und erläutert,* ed. 2. Breslau, 1870.
Wilamowitz, *Gr. Versk.* Wilamowitz, *Griech. Versk.* Wilamowitz, *Griech. Verskunst*	Wilamowitz-Moellendorf, U. von. *Griechische Verskunst.* Berlin, 1921.
Wilamowitz, *H. D.*	Wilamowitz-Moellendorf, U. von. *Hellenistische Dichtung in der Zeit des Kallimachos.* Berlin, 1924. 2 vols.
Wilamowitz' second edition	Wilamowitz-Moellendorf, U. von, editor. *Callimachi Hymni et Epigrammata,* ed. 2. Berlin, 1897.
Wright, *Feminism*	Wright, F. A. *Feminism in Greek Literature from Homer to Aristotle.* London, 1928.
Zell, *Ferienschriften*	Zell, K. *Ferienschriften.* Freiburg im Breisgau, 1826-1833. 3 vols.

NOTES FOR CHAPTER I

1. Catullus, 2284 lines: *Aeneid*, i-iii, 2278 lines. But in Vergil the lines are on the average of greater length.

2. I use the term in the general sense of the wedding poem.

3. I follow here the traditional numbering. It should be remembered that the pieces formerly numbered XVIII–XX are now not included in the body of the text, but the old numbering has been retained so that in the standard texts XVII is immediately followed by XXI.

4. Vahlen has been the leading champion; cf. *S. Ber. d. k. preuss. Akad. d. Wiss. zu Berlin*, 1904, XXXVIII: 1067–1078. H. A. J. Munro assumed the same view in his article, "Catullus' 29th Poem" (*Jour. Phil.* II [1869]: 4), but in a footnote (p. 71) in *Criticisms and Elucidations of Catullus* (Cambridge and London, 1878; ed. 2, 1905) he shows that, before that article was reprinted in the book, he had changed his mind. There have been many other discussions of the problem; cf. Schanz, *Geschichte der römischen Literatur*, I[4] (ed. C. Hosius [Munich, 1927]): 294–295, for bibliography, and add G. B. Pighi in *Raccolta di scritti in onore di Felice Ramorino (Pubbl. dell' Univ. cattol. del Sacro Cuore*, ser. 4: scienze filol., VII [Milan, 1927]): 361–377; K. Barwick, *Hermes*, LXIII (1928): 66–80; cf. Kroll, *C. Valerius Catullus*[2] (Leipzig, 1929): ix-x, and Frank, *Catullus and Horace* (New York, 1928), especially pp. 96–98. There is much disagreement in detail among those who oppose the view of Vahlen.

5. On the chronology see pp. 91 ff.

6. Ellis doubted whether V was discovered in Verona. Recently Frank suggested Padua as the place of its discovery; cf. *A. J. P.* XLVIII (1927): 273–275. The exact date of the discovery of V has not been determined, but the manuscript was probably known to Hieremias de Montagnone late in the thirteenth century. Rajna (*Studj di fil. romanza*, V [1891]: 201) suggested that Hieremias' *Compendium* was published *ca.* 1290–1300. Ellis (*Catullus in the XIVth Century*,[3] [London, 1910]: 9) doubted this. Ullman (*Class. Phil.* V [1910]: 66 ff.) accepts a date somewhere between 1300 and 1310.

7. Hale in 1908 stated the number then known as 120 (*Class. Phil.* III [1903]: 235). Before his death Hale expressed the wish that Ullman should finish the comprehensive work which he had planned on the manuscripts. On the basis of our present knowledge I hold (with Schulze, Ellis, and others) that there are traces in our manuscripts of more than two copies of the *Veronensis*.

8. The uncial fragment containing CIV–CVI published by A. Malein and A. Truchanov (*Comptes rendus de l'Académie des Sciences de l'U. R. S. S.* [Leningrad, 1928]) seems to be a forgery. Cf. Ullman, *Class. Phil.* XXIV (1929): 294–297. Kroll also is skeptical (*Catull*, 295).

9. *Patrolog. Latina,* ed. Migne, CXXXVI: 752: Catullum nunquam antea lectum.

10. Cf. de Campesani's epigram (Ellis, 1878, *Prolegomena,* xii):

> Ad patriam venio longis de finibus exul,
> causa mei reditus compatriota fuit,
> Scilicet a calamis tribuit cui Francia nomen,
> quique notat turbae praetereuntis iter.
> quo licet ingenio vestrum celebrate Catullum,
> cuius sub modio clausa papyrus erat.

Haupt pointed out the scriptural reference in *sub modio* (*Opusc.* I.5). The third and fourth lines conceal the name and occupation of the discoverer, but no convincing interpretation has been made; cf. Frank, *A. J. P.* XLVIII (1927): 273–275, for the latest discussion.

11. Schwabe (ed. 1886: xiii-xiv) prints some half-dozen references (not counting T and Rather) which fall between Isidore and De Campesani, but even when the citations are not made from some intermediate source, they do not indicate a text different from that of our single tradition.

I am now convinced that my theory of the existence of a manuscript arranged on a metrical basis (*A. J. P.* XXIX [1908]: 186–200) is not supported by the citations of Hieremias de Montagnone; cf. Ullman, *Class. Phil.* V (1910): 66 ff.

12. E. W. B. Nicholson, *Keltic Researches,* 152 (see Ellis [1904] on *fr.* 7) refers to A. Holder, *Altcelt. Sprachschatz,* II: 137, who quotes Martial, xiv.100:

> Panaca
> Si non ignota est docti tibi terra Catulli,
> potasti testa Raetica vina mea.

The word *panaca* is Celtic, as Holder shows, and we may add that the authenticity of *fr.* 7 is made probable by the fact that Martial connects with the homeland of Catullus not only this Celtic drinking vessel but also Raetian wine, both products of the region about Verona.

13. Pliny, *N. H.* xxviii. 2(4). 19 (on charms and incantations): hinc Theocriti apud Graecos, Catulli [Catuli V] apud nos proximeque Vergilii incantamentorum amatoria imitatio. Wilamowitz ("Textgesch. Bukol." in *Phil. U.* XVIII [1906]: 112) thought that Pliny meant an imitation of Theocritus' *Pharmakeutriai* by Catullus. It is possible that Catullus may have imitated the *Pharmakeutriai,* but Pliny does not say so; he is merely giving three illustrations of *incantamenta* reflected in amatory poetry: Theocritus ii, Vergil, *Ecl.* viii, and some poem (now lost) of Catullus.

14. Cf. Kroll on *fr.* 1.

15. Eduardus a Brunér, "De ordine et temporibus carminum Valerii Catulli," *Acta Soc. Scient. Fennicae,* VII (Helsingfors, 1863): 599–657 (the paper was actually presented Nov. 4, 1861). Brunér was the first to publish a

thorough discussion which anticipated a very large part of the later work such as Birt's (1882), B. Schmidt's (1887), Ellis' (1889), etc. Unfortunately the *Acta* of the Finnish Society are not easily accessible and Brunér's essay, which deals with other Catullian problems also, should be reprinted in separate form.

16. Theodor Birt, *Das antike Buchwesen*, 286 ff.

17. Ellis, *Commentary*, I, note 2, estimates 2480 lines, Birt at least 2400.

18. Cf. Propert. iii. 3. 19–20:

> Ut tuus in scamno iactetur saepe libellus
> quem legat expectans sola puella virum.

19. No extant roll is quite complete; cf. W. Schubart, *Das Buch bei den Griechen und Römern* (ed. 2; Berlin and Leipzig, Walter de Gruyter & Co., 1921): 52.

20. *Palaeog. of Greek Papyri* (1899): 17; cf. also W. Schubart, *loc. cit.*: whenever the length of a papyrus roll (containing literature) can be estimated with some degree of accuracy an average of from seven to ten meters is rarely exceeded. (Schubart is including prose, and we know that books of poetry were shorter.)

21. Cf. Ovid, *Tristia* ii. 261 with S. G. Owen's note, *P. Ovidi Nasonis Tristium Liber Secundus* (Oxford, Clarendon Press, 1924).

22. The terms *liber* and *libellus* were not always distinguished as clearly as Birt would have us believe. In *Tr.* i. 1. 1 Ovid uses *liber* and *ibid.* i. 11. 1 *libellus*, both referring to Book I; cf. also F. Barta's program (cited below, note 26): 13–16 and Vahlen, *op. cit.* 1072. But we should note that in Catullus I *libellus* occurs, not alone, but in conjunction with *nugae*.

23. See p. 53 f.

24. Brunér, *op. cit.*, traces this suggestion to Ludovico Carrio (1547–1595); cf. the beginning of Martial's ninth book to which Martial prefixes an epigram which, as he says in the prose preface immediately following, is *extra ordinem paginarum*. After the prose stands the poem which is numbered I.

25. Vahlen (*op. cit.* 1074) gives the references. Goethe was preparing an edition of all his works in eight volumes. In a letter (Aug. 28, 1787) he says: "Meine Sächelchen—denn sie kommen mir sehr im Diminutiv vor—muss ich wenigstens mit Sammlung und Freudigkeit enden."

26. A useful collection of the terms which the Romans applied to poetry or a single poem may be found in F. Barta, *Ueber die auf die Dichtkunst bezüglichen Ausdrücke bei den römischen Dichtern* (Linz, 1889–1890 [Gymn. Progr.]). For *nugae*, cf. the second part (1890): 28–29, where more than twenty cases are cited, the majority from Martial. A similar collection for Greek poetry (not so full as Barta's) is G. Kuhlmann's *De poetae et poematis Graecorum appellationibus* (Diss.; Marburg, 1906).

27. J. W. Beck, *Mnemos.* XLI (1913): 302 ff.

28. Cf. K. Dziatzko, *Untersuchungen über ausgewählte Kapitel des antiken Buchwesens* (Leipzig, Teubner, 1900), Chap. VI.

29. Cf. also XLVIII and Frank, *Catullus*, 84.

30. As late as the Augustan Age Crinagoras sent a copy of the *Hecale* to Marcellus; cf. *A. P.* IX. 545. In XCV Catullus alludes to the publication of Cinna's *Zmyrna*.

31. Ovid, *Ex P.* iii. 9. 51–56.

32. But see pp. 28 ff., 39 f.

33. E.g., Beck. See above, note 27.

34. Cf. I. 3–7; LXVIII. 15–18, 34–35.

35. Note also that XIV*b*, whether it is part of a proem or program or an epilogue, is out of place; that LX looks like a rhetorical sketch (more fully worked out in LXIV. 154 ff.) attached to other short poems; cf. also LVIII*b*, which may be a substitute variant (for LV. 3–12) found among Catullus' papers and included among the poems by his friends; cf. K. Barwick, *Hermes*, LXIII (1928): 66–80; Frank, *Catullus*, 97–98.

36. *Sappho und Simonides* (Berlin, Weidmann, 1913): 292 ff.

37. Cf. the *Theognidea* and Sappho's book of epithalamia (at least in the form arranged by the Alexandrians).

38. Ellis, *Commentary*, l. Westphal's discussion (1870) well illustrates the artificial arguments which were once customary in dealing with this question; cf. his *Catulls Gedichte*[2] (Breslau, F. E. C. Leuckart, 1870): 1–32.

39. About the second part (LXI–LXIV) one must be very skeptical. Wilamowitz (and earlier, Westphal) argued that the two wedding poems were intentionally placed together by Catullus, LXI first to continue the lyric meters of I–LX. Perhaps also the two hexameter poems, LXII and LXIV, are intentionally separated, and Kroll (*Catull*, x) sees purpose (certainly not Catullus' purpose) in the placing of LXIV as a sort of culmination of the first half of the poems. But the dangers of allowing free play to the imagination here are obvious. There are only four poems in this group and it is safe to say that any other order, if sanctioned by the manuscripts, would have seemed just as "intentional" as the one we have. The only points which seem to be reasonably certain are that these four poems were grouped because they are *long* poems, with LXI–LXII side by side because they are of the same *kind*, but it is not probable that Catullus is responsible for this arrangement. Certainly he published LXIV separately.

40. Servius on Vergil (*Ecl.* vii. 1) recognizes the principle and illustrates it by means of the *Eclogues*.

41. Other cases of grouping together are: LXXV–LXXVI, XCVII–XCVIII, CX–CXI, CXIV–CXV, and possibly LXI–LXII. Cases of separation (*variatio*): XVI–XXI (XXI, if consecutively numbered, would be XVIII), XXI–XXIII, XXXVII–XXXIX, XLI–XLIII, LXIX–LXXI, LXX–LXXII, LXXXV–LXXXVII, CVII–CIX, and quite possibly II–III

(if II*b* is part of another poem). With the three cases cited above the total is only seventeen.

42. The general question of arrangement in books containing numbers of separate poems has been discussed by Kroll, *Studien*, Chap. X. Cf. also *Neue Jahrb.* XXXVII (1916): 93 ff., where he includes Horace, and *Catull, Einl.*: ix-x. Certain books of Augustan poetry (Vergil's *Eclogues*, Horace's *Odes, Epodes, Satires*, Tibullus, Ovid's *Amores*) have been well discussed by W. Port, "Die Anordnung in Gedichtbüchern augusteischer Zeit," *Philol.* LXXXI (1925–1926): 280 ff., 427 ff. Port discusses Theocritus also, and although the evidence is not at all points clear, it is sufficient to reveal the beginnings at least of artistic arrangement in the collection made by Artemidorus.

43. Cf. pp. 252, nn. 39 and 41, 253, nn. 42 and 46, 254, n. 10.

44. Counting II*b*, XIV*b*, LVIII*b* as remnants of separate poems.

45. See pp. 19–21.

46. Or what seems to us to be planlessness. But probably more cases of the original order exist in our collection than we can detect. I would not attribute to Catullus an arrangement which verged on the artificial, and if we could see one of the books which he published I think we should find that he did not at every opportunity resort to forms of *variatio*. There would probably be groupings in which we could discern no particular purpose. But we must deal with the rather obvious phenomena which we can detect, and originally these must have been considerably more numerous.

47. Some poems were overlooked or purposely omitted by the editors; cf. the fragments.

48. Compare with this conception of the history of Catullus' poems Dziatzko's general statement (*op. cit.* 177) that most of the ancient authors have come down to us in editions made after their deaths by friends or grammarians and kept up in the book trade; in most cases these editions were based on collections made by the author.

49. His poems contained too much erotic; cf. Quintilian, i. 8. 6–7.

50. Admiration for Catullus appears first in Cornelius Nepos, metrical interest first in Caesius Bassus; cf. Schwabe's *testimonia*, and my article on Hieremias, *A. J. P.* XXIX (1908): 193 ff.

51. See pp. 40, 47–49.

NOTES FOR CHAPTER II

1. F. Jacoby, *Rh. M.* LX (1905): 84.

2. On the history of the ancient epigram, cf. especially R. Reitzenstein, *P.-W. s. v. Epigramm*; Wilamowitz, *H. D.* I (1924): 120 ff.; J. W. Mackail, *Select Epigrams from the Greek Anthology* (new ed., London, Longmans, Green and Co., 1906), Introduction.

3. Mackail's figures (*op. cit.* 11). A good many of the poems (or parts of poems) included are not epigrams in any sense of the term.

4. But in its original form Meleager's *Garland* contained a larger proportion of non-elegiac pieces; see below pp. 38 ff.

5. *A. P.* IV. 1.

6. J. W. Mackail's statement is not strong enough: "It is difficult to avoid the inference that he [Meleager] included other kinds of minor poetry as well."—*Op. cit.* 15.

7. I.e., the *Anthology* proper: Books V–VII, IX–XI.

8. Mackail gives the total of elegiac pieces as 2539, non-elegiac (all other meters), 274.—*Op. cit.* 7.

9. Wilamowitz (*H. D.* I: 149 ff.) notes the prevalence of the small poem in distichs, called "epigram," in the late fourth and in the third centuries.

10. If Catullus himself published some of the elegiac pieces together (see p. 24) they were afterward disarranged and augmented by the process I am here suggesting. One is reminded also of the *Codex Bernensis*, of Horace, in which a metrical grouping has been attempted.

11. Wilamowitz (*H. D.* I: 112) conjectures that Simias may have been the first to use lyric forms for recitation poetry, witness his pattern poems; cf. *ibid.* 149.

12. Strato, *A. P.* XII. 258, applies the term to the epigram in distichs.

13. Wilamowitz, *H. D.* I: 149 ff.

14. See pp. 205–213 (on LXI).

15. Kroll (*Stud.* 225) thinks that the iambics included trimeters, choliambics, trochaic tetrameters, etc., and suggests that a practical reason for making collections of varied small poems was the danger that they might be lost; cf. A.W. Mair, *Callimachus*, 270. H. von Arnim thought it improbable that the trochaics formed part of the book of *Iambi* (*S. B. Wien*, CLXIV [1910], *Abh.* IV: 10 f.).

16. On Horace, *Odes*, iii. 1. 2.

17. Laevius is cited by name, by meter (once), by name and title of poem, and by numbered books (6 are known) of *Erotopaegnia*. The last method does not appear, however, until Nonius. Probably the book numbers were made not earlier than the second century. Kroll (*Stud.* 225, n. 2) suggests that Simias may have collected his mixed poems into four books and

was in this imitated by Laevius. Laevius was certainly familiar with Simias; cf. Morel, *F. P. L.*, Laevius, *fr.* 22 with the *testimonium*.

18. *Sappho und Simonides*, 292.

19. Other types: introductory, prefatory, dedicatory (I, LXV); cf. XIV*b*.

20. Cf. A. Kurfess, "Die Anfänge der Invektive in Rom," *Ph. V. B.* (1915), and the continuation in the same author's program, *Die Invektivenpoesie der sullanish-cäsarischen, augusteischen und nachaugusteischen Zeit* (Wohlau, 1915).

21. Suetonius, *Julius*, c. 73.

22. Translated by Cornelia Catlin Coulter, Professor of Latin, Mount Holyoke College.

23. The best interpretation of this poem was suggested by E. P. Morris. See pp. 227–230.

24. Cf. also the original form of Meleager's *Garland* (see p. 38). Furthermore, the fact that the poems which can be certainly dated about 55–54 B.C. display metrical variety agrees with the view here expressed: XI (sapphics), XLV, LV (hendecasyllables), CXIII (elegiacs). These poems belong to one and the same narrowly restricted period, and if they had been published by Catullus they would have been included in the same *libellus*.

25. According to Kroll (*Stud.* 228), Martial (who uses elegiacs most commonly) inserts the other meters so as to obtain variety. With reference to theme the poems are now paired, now separated by a single piece on some other theme.

26. A. L. W., "Satura as a Generic Term," *Class. Phil.* VII (1912): 457–477.

27. About 43 hendecasyllabics, 46 elegiacs (excluding LXV–LXVIII and LXXVI).

28. E. T. Merrill's edition (Leipzig, Teubner, 1921), IV. 14, V. 3, VII. 4 and 9, IX. 25.

29. Probably suggested by Catullus' title *Passer*.

30. The books of Martial provide illustrations; see p. 19.

31. Propertius, ii. 34. 85. Once *epyllion* is termed a *lusus* (*Ciris*, 19) but only in contrast with some grand philosophical work which the author had in mind.

32. E.g., in Martial, i. 1. 2 and 4; cf. *parve liber* (i. 3. 2).

33. *Libellus* cannot always be distinguished from *liber*; see p. 19.

34. See pp. 227–230.

35. Kroll, *Stud.* 225 ff. Cf. his article, "Hellen.-röm. Gedichtbücher," *Neue Jahrb.* XXXVII (1916): 93–106.

36. For example Sappho, iv and Alcaeus, i.

1. See p. 78 for the quotation.

2. There is probably a hint of his attitude in XIV. 5–12. Calvus' gift of bad poetry might have come, Catullus suggests, from a Roman schoolmaster (*litterator*), a man who admired the worthless old Roman stuff; cf. B. Schmidt's suggestion (*Prolegom.* lxix) that Caesius, Aquinus, and Suffenus—the bad poets whom Catullus proposes to send back to Calvus— were disliked by Catullus particularly on account of their archaistic tendencies. Furthermore, the attraction which Memmius at first had for Catullus and Helvius Cinna must have been his complete, indeed exaggerated, devotion to Greek literature and probably his contempt for those Roman poets who were not devoted to the Greek. Cicero calls Memmius perfectus litteris, sed Graecis, fastidiosus sane Latinarum (*Brutus*, 247).

3. Long after I had written this paragraph I came upon the sentence of P. de Nolhac which is quoted in the Preface.

4. For the fragments of early Latin verse (apart from the drama) see *F. P. L.*; cf. E. Diehl's *Poetarum Romanorum veterum reliquiae* (Bonn, Marcus and Weber, 1911).

5. Catullus was not then directly influenced by Ennius and other early Roman poets although he profited indirectly by their contributions to poetic technique. As Skutsch says (*P.-W. s. v. Ennius*, 2615), it was impossible for a later poet to avoid the influence (i.e., the indirect influence) of Ennius. Formulae such as *Iuppiter omnipotens* or *pater divum*, compounds such as *caelicola* or *magnanimus* so pervaded Roman poetry that their Ennian origin was forgotten. I do not therefore regard the parallels between Ennius and Catullus collected by the editors and by J. Froebel (*Ennio quid debuerit Catullus* [Weida, 1910]) as evidence of direct imitation of Ennius by Catullus. Indeed, Froebel ventures to assert direct imitation in only a dozen cases. But not one of these is convincing, e.g., effudit voces proprio cum pectore sancto (Enn., *Ann.* 540) and Catullus LXIV. 125, clarisonas imo fudisse e pectore voces; cf. 202. The expression is as commonplace as the English "to pour forth words from the heart." Ennius first used it (so far as we can say) in a form convenient for dactylic verse and it became part of the common stock available to all poets. See pp. 114–117 on imitation.

6. LXV. 5–14, LXVIII. 20–24, 92–97, CI. On the *nenia* cf. H. de la Ville de Mirmont, *Rev. de Phil.* XXVI (1902): 263–271, 335–348.

7. Cf. LXVIII. 15–17 and see pp. 91 ff.

8. See Chap. II.

9. Pliny (*Ep.* v. 3. 6) includes Ennius and Accius among those who composed this type of small poem, but there are no fragments although (for

Accius) there is a reference to *versus Sotadici*, *F. P. L.*, p. 38. Lucilius wrote a book entitled *Collyra* (so Porphyrio), but Marx considers this to be the title of a single poem; cf. Marx's *Lucilius*, Book xvi. Books vii–viii also contained erotic poetry.

10. *Ad fam.* xvi. 21. 3.

11. Hosius' text, xix. 9. 7.

12. Plato, *Phaedr.* 237 A.

13. For the text of these poems see *F. P. L.* 42 ff.; Diehl, 148–149.

14. A lover passing along the street at night addresses his slave.

15. Cf. Marcus Aurel. to Fronto, i. 2 (Naber): Et ego ubi animus meus sit nescio: nisi hoc scio, illo nescio quo ad te profectum eum esse.

16. Cf. Cicero, *De n. d.* i. 79; Diehl, 149. Cicero (through his character Aurelius Cotta) is discussing the fact that the blemishes of loved ones often delight the lover, e.g., the mole on the boy's joint delighted Alcaeus; Roscius, though *perversissimis oculis*, seemed to Catulus *deo pulchrior*; cf. the well-known passages in Lucretius, iv. 1160 ff. and Horace, *Sat.* i. 3. 38–40.

17. C. Cichorius with characteristic ingenuity fixed the date of Lutatius Catulus' admiration for Roscius *ca.* 120–115 B.C.; cf. his *Untersuchungen zu Lucilius* (Berlin, Weidmann, 1908): 291. Unfortunately neither the date of Roscius' birth nor that of Lutatius Catulus can be determined very precisely. Groag conjectures *ca.* 150 B.C. for the birth of Catulus (*P.-W. s. v. Lutatius*, 2072) although Cichorius (*op. cit.* 151) prefers a date several years earlier. He could hardly have been more than (say) twenty-five when he wrote his verses on Roscius.

18. *Apolog.* 9.

19. Suggested by H. Usener, *Kl. Schr.* II: 65; cf. Leo, *Lit.* 438–439.

20. For criticism see R. Büttner, *Porcius Licinus*, etc. (1893): 103 ff., F. Leo, *Lit.* (1913): 433 ff., and A. L. W., *A. J. P.* XXXVI (1915): 164–165.

21. *A. P.* XII. 73 (No. 41, Wilamowitz' second edition).

22. *C. Lat. epig.* 48; cf. *A. P.* IX. 15 and XVI (=*Anth. Plan.* IV), 209— both anonymous.

23. Leo, *Lit.* 439.

24. Theocritus, xviii. 27 (Helen compared with the dawn).

25. Reitzenstein (*P.-W. s. v. Epigramm*, 96) asserts that although these Roman epigrammatists resembled Meleager they were not influenced by him.

26. *Casina*, prologue.

27. F. Marx, *B. sächs. Gesellsch.* (*Philol.-hist. Kl.*) LXIII (1911): 39–82; Frank, *A. J. P.* XLVIII (1927): 105–110. Marx takes *fato* as the utterance of an oracle, Frank as equivalent to *fortuito*.

28. *Sat.* ii. 1. 80–83.

29. *De l. l.* vii. 28.

30. Pompilius (Diehl, *op. cit.* 149). But see Leo, *Lit.* 406 and *F. P. L.* 42.

31. *F. P. L.* fr. 12 (p. 50).

32. It has been suggested that IV is related to the dedicatory epigram (Birt, *Philol.* LXIII [1904] : 453 ff. and Kroll, 7) and that CI represents, as Reitzenstein puts it, the freest development of the grave epigram; cf. *P.-W. s. v. Epigramm*, 101. There are elements of truth in both suggestions, but in neither case do the early Roman epigrams throw light on Catullus. See pp. 62–66, 69–72.

33. Diehl, 48, No. 392.

34. Diehl, 149.

35. Suetonius, *De gram.* 3. On Laevius and the other poets of this period, cf. Leo, "Die röm. Poesie in der sullan. Zeit," *Hermes*, XLIX (1914): 161-195.

36. Porphyrio on Horace, *Odes*, iii. 1. 2 (carmina non prius audita): Romanis utique non prius audita, quamvis Laevius lyrica ante Horatium scripserit. Sed videntur illa non Graecorum lege ad lyricum characterem exacta; cf. Schanz, I: 270.

37. Charisius, 204, ed. Keil (*Grammatici Latini*, I [Leipzig, 1857]).

38. xix. 7.

39. This sesquipedalian compound, "naggers with lifted brows," is at once a contemptuous reference to his critics and an exaggerated example of one of the points for which he was criticized. He stuck to his guns.

40. There is no evidence that he practiced the long epic or the didactic poem, but he may have composed some pieces as long as Catullus LXIV.

41. *Frs.* 4 and 11.

42. *Frs.* 10, 23, 24, 27, 28.

43. On the other hand Gellius (xix. 9. 9) implies that Laevius somewhere in his poetry played the lover: audite ac discite nostros quoque antiquiores ante eos, quos nominastis, poetas amasios ac venerios fuisse. Among those who had been named (§7) was Laevius.

44. *Frs.* 7, 13, 25, and Gellius, xix. 9.

45. Also Furius Bibaculus, if he was the Furius whose style is ridiculed by Horace (*Sat.* ii. 5. 41; cf. i. 10. 36).

46. Cicero's scores of quotations from and references to Ennius (see Vahlen's Ennius, 244-245) begin with the *De inventione* (two quotations), which he wrote when he was almost a boy (*De or.* i. 2. 5).

47. Another characteristic of Euphorion was distasteful to Cicero—his excessive obscurity; cf. *De div.* ii. 64. 133: ille vero nimis etiam obscurus Euphorion. The phraseology shows that the view was a current one. Cicero was here opposed once more to Catullus, for the latter, although not often obscure himself, admired (XCV) the *Zmyrna* of Helvius Cinna, which was probably obscure in the same way that Euphorion was obscure.

48. CXVI. 8, tu dabi' supplicium.

49. B. Schmidt, *Prolegom.* lxvi. The poem shows clearly that Gellius was threatening Catullus. He had probably used the phrase *dabi' supplicium* and Catullus in his rejoinder says, mocking him, "Not I, but you (*tu*) shall suffer." Leo's view (*Plaut. Forsch.*[2] 255) that CXVI is the earliest poem

since it contains the only example of this usage in Catullus seems to me to be untenable. R. Heinze (*A. L. L.* XV [1906–1908]: 99) thinks *dabis supplicium* an archaic formula. This view can be combined with Schmidt's, i.e., Gellius quoted (in verse) the formula.

50. Athenaeus, iii. 72 A, reports this as follows: ὅτι Καλλίμαχος . . . . τὸ μέγα βιβλίον ἴσον ἔλεγεν εἶναι τῷ μεγάλῳ κακῷ. Certainly this phrase did not refer to the size of the roll only. See A. W. Mair, *Callimachus*, 4.

51. Probably also the *Magna Mater* of Catullus' friend Caecilius; cf. XXXV.

52. Cf. Ticidas (*F. P. L., fr.* 2, p. 91) on the *Lydia* of Val. Cato: Lydia doctorum maxima cura liber. The Greek epyllia required commentaries and Cato made his *Lydia* of the same character. A commentary on the *Zmyrna* was written by Lucius Crassicius.

53. The *Lydia* which has survived is hardly his; it is not *doctorum maxima cura* in the sense intended by Ticidas.

54. On Memmius see p. 256, n. 2. On Varro of Atax, cf. Else Hofmann, "Die lit. Persönlichkeit des P. Terentius Varro Atacinus," *W. St.* XLVI (1928): 159–176. Frank identifies Ticidas (which has a pseudonym) with Clodius Aesopus, son of the actor (*Class. Rev.* XXXIV [1920]: 91–93), and suggests that Cornificius (whom he identifies with the Codrus of Vergil) succeeded Calvus as the leader of the neoteric school (*ibid.* 49–51).

55. XCV. 9. The best conjecture for this broken line is *sodalis* (Ald. 1).

56. Cf. the offensive characterization of Volusius' *Annals*, XXXVI. 1 and 20.

57. *A. P.* XII. 43: ἐχθαίρω τὸ ποίημα τὸ κυκλικόν . . . . σικχαίνω πάντα τὰ δημόσια.

58. Schol. Dionys. Perieget, *Life of Dionysius*, p. 317 (Bernhardy); cf. *ibid.*, p. 977, on v. 21. See A. W. Mair, *Callimachus*, 236.

59. Cf. CXVI and see pp. 112–114.

60. Kirby Flower Smith on Tibullus, iv. 6. 2.

NOTES FOR CHAPTER IV

1. See *testimonia* in Schwabe (ed. 1886): vii ff.
2. Schwabe, *Quaestt.* (1862): 15–16.
3. Münzer (*P.-W. s. v. Caelius*, 1266) remains undecided between 88 and 85 B.C. as the year of Caelius' birth.
4. Cf. Ellis' notes on LII. The earlier scholars took LII at its face value and dated the poem 47 B.C. when Vatinius was consul for a few days (December); cf. H. Paldamus, *Römische Erotik* (Greifswald, Koch, 1833): 27–28.
5. Catullus calls himself the "master," "owner" (XXXI. 12), but the word *ero* should not be interpreted to mean that the villa was his own personal property.
6. XLIV.
7. Schwabe, *Quaestt.* 55.
8. *Philol.* LXXVIII (1923): 1–30; cf. also G. Giri, *Athenaeum*, VI (1928): 215–219 and K. Riedel's dissertation *Untersuchungen zur Dichtung Catulls* (Frankfurt am Main, 1924), of which only a brief abstract has been published. Riedel argues for the old view (that of Paldamus, *op. cit.* 30–31, who refers in turn to K. Zell's *Ferienschriften*) that Lesbia was merely an *amica* of the same type as the Cynthia of Propertius. I have been unable to find Zell's book even in the Bodleian, but it is easy for anybody who examines the (later) inscriptions at Verona where the names Clodia and Clodius occur (not to mention Caelius, Egnatius, etc.) to shift the Lesbia affair to Verona and identify her with some provincial Clodia. But the evidence does not permit us to class Lesbia with Ameana, or Ipsithilla, or even Cynthia.
9. Rothstein, following Riese (*J. K. P.* CV [1872]: 747 ff.), takes *vir* (LXVIII. 146, LXXXIII. 1) as meaning "lover," but he cites no parallel earlier than the Augustan Age; cf. R. Pichon, *De sermone amatorio apud Latinos elegiarum scriptores* (Paris, Hachette, 1902). The erotic vocabulary developed gradually and we are not justified in assuming that Catullus used *vir* in this erotic sense.
10. LXVIII. 51–72.
11. LXVIII. 11–26, 91–100, written about the same time as LXV; cf. v. 5 *nuper*.
12. Wilamowitz, *H. D.* II: 308; F. Arnaldi, *Riv. di fil.* LV (1927): 350–356; cf. Rothstein, *Philol.* LXXXI (1925–1926): 472–473.
13. Caelius in Quintilian, viii. 6. 53; Cicero, *Pro Caelio*, 62.
14. Rothstein reduces the number to twenty-three. Apart from those poems in which the name Lesbia occurs scholars will always differ as to the exact number of Lesbia poems.

15. Translated by Cornelia C. Coulter. Miss Coulter has kindly permitted me to make use of this fine translation hitherto unpublished.

16. See also p. 83.

17. The date is based on Catullus. Memmius' tenure of office must have terminated sometime in 56 B.C. since C. Caecilius Cornutus took over the office in that year. See the commentators.

18. *The Poems of Catullus*, translated by Theodore Martin (Edinburgh and London, William Blackwood and Sons [1875]): 152.

19. Cf. Ellis and Kroll on CI.

20. *Catullus, the Complete Poems*, translated and edited by F. A. Wright (London, George Routledge & Sons, Ltd., and New York, E. P. Dutton & Co., no date): 167.

21. Cinna, *fr.* 11, *F. P. L.* 89.

22. Friedrich, 99.

23. Translated by J. H. Frere; cf. Wright, *op. cit.* 169–170.

24. H. Nissen, *Italische Landeskunde*, I (Berlin, 1883): 190.

25. The regional map *Provincia di Verona*, pub. by F. Zappi (1923), gives the elevation of the lake as 65 m., of the Mincio marshes near Mantua as 18 m. The river therefore falls about 47 m. or 154.1 feet, and the descent seems to be pretty gradual. Cichorius (see p. 101) has shown that the ancient *phaselus* was a small craft designed to navigate shallow waters although such boats were also used on the sea. The ancient skippers watched the weather and hugged the shore wherever it was possible.

26. See G. G. Orti, Conte di Manara, *La penisola di Sirmione* (Verona, G. Antonelli, 1856): 24–25. The suggestion was made by Count Bennasù Montanari. Richard Bagot also asserts (*The Lakes of Northern Italy*[2] [London, 1913]: 238), that "Under the Romans, Peschiera was known as Arilica, and had direct communication by water with the Adriatic," but he neither describes this water route nor cites any authority for his statement here.

27. See the geological map in W. Deecke's *Italy* (Eng. transl. London, Macmillan, 1904): 89.

28. In 1439 the Venetians took a fleet of war galleys up the Adige above Mori and thence over the mountains into Lake Garda at Torbole; cf. Assmann's letter to K. P. Schulze in the latter's *Beiträge zur Erklärung röm. Elegiker* (1893): 5. Bagot also describes this expedition (*op. cit.* 248–251).

29. C. Cichorius, *Festschrift für Hirschfeld*, 467–483.

30. Wilamowitz, *H. D.* II: 298.

31. E.g., the Serenus of the Bernese *scholium*; cf. Baehrens' notes on IV and Wilamowitz, *H. D.* II: 297.

32. In this case we should expect *phaselus hic*, not *ille*, but cf. Birt, *Philol.* LXIII (1904): 453 ff.

33. Theodore Martin, *op cit.* 54.

34. Perhaps with Julius Caesar. They had been in Spain together *ca.*
61–60 B.C. (IX, XII, XIII) while Catullus' love for Lesbia was still happy
(XIII). No provincial governor's name is mentioned in these poems and
Pollio (XII. 9) is called a *puer*—he was born 76 B.C. They had made
another provincial venture with Piso (XXVIII, XLVII—no province is
mentioned in these poems). Everything points to L. Calpurnius Piso
Caesoninus and to Macedonia as the province, since they certainly returned
about the time when Catullus returned from Bithynia (56 B.C.); cf. also
Frank, *Catullus*, 28–29.

35. XXVIII, XLVII, and (for Catullus' opinion of Memmius) X.

36. Both men fostered poetry. Philodemus was a client of Piso's and his
pretty little dinner invitation to his patron (*A. P.* XI. 44) reminds one of
Horace's tone to Maecenas; cf., e.g., *Odes* i. 20. It is tempting (with Friedrich, 228, and Frank, *op. cit.* 83) to identify Socration, the "petty Socrates,"
with Philodemus.

37. F. A. Wright, *op. cit.* 120.

38. Theodore Martin, *op. cit.* 66.

39. G. Lafaye on XXXVI and XLV (*Catulle*, 123–124, 130–131).

40. Cf. Horace's remark about Lucilius (*Sat.* ii. 1. 32–34) which, as I
now see, is adapted to Catullus by Kroll (p. vii): patet omnis votiva veluti
descripta tabella vita adulescentis.

41. As E. P. Morris says, "This collection of poems and verses is not a
methodical record of a life. Catullus was a poet, not a diarist, and the
interpretation of his writings must be founded upon the motives, the traditions, and the ideals of a poet. This is particularly true of the Lesbia
poems" (*Transactions of the Connecticut Academy of Arts and Sciences*, XV
[1909]: 151). A. Couat's chapter on the poet's youth at Verona though occasionally suggestive is very fanciful; cf. *Étude sur Catulle* (Paris, Thorin,
1874): 20–34.

42. Kornemann, *P.-W. s. v. Colonia*, 517; cf. Asconius on Cic. *In Pisonem*,
p. 12, ll. 13 ff. (ed. Stangl, 1912); Caesar, *B. C.* iii. 87.

43. H. Nissen, *op. cit.* II. 1 (1902): 198; cf. I. 164.

44. A. L. W., "Topics from the Life of Ovid," *A. J. P.* XLVI (1925): 28.

45. But Valerii Catulli are comparatively rare. There is one from the
region of Susa (*C. I. L.* V. 7239), another from Brixia (*ibid.* 4484), and we
note that Catullus speaks of Brixia as the "mother of Verona" (LXVII. 34
Brixia Veronae mater amata meae—the words of the Veronese door).
Perhaps the Valerii Catulli of Verona came originally from Brixia. Kroll
(p. vi) cites from a coin inscription (*Prosopog. Imperii Romani* III. 354, no.
38; H. A. Grueber, *Coins of the Roman Republic in the British Museum*, II
[London, 1910]: 111) a L. Valerius Catullus who, he suggests, may have been
descended from the poet's brother. A. Holder (*Altcelt. Sprachschatz*, I [1896]:
858, *s. v. Catullos*) adds *C. I. L.* XIV. 2095 (Lavinia), 2466 (near Marino),
XV. 416 (Rome).

46. "Zur Geschichte lateinischer Eigennamen," *Abh. Göttingen*, 1904: 106.

47. Volesius occurs on a Verona inscr. (*C. I. L.* V. 3844), Valesius at Perugia (*C. I. L.* XI. 2081).

48. Vergil, *Aen.* x. 752; Ovid, *Ex P.* iii. 2. 105; cf. Silius Italicus, ii. 8.

49. C. Cichorius, *Untersuchungen zu Lucilius*, 151.

50. If Catullus is a diminutive (which is not certain), we must assume a form (*catu* ?) from which the diminutive was derived. The play on Cato Catullum (LVI. 3) may indicate that Catullus believed his name to be the diminutive of Cato.

51. According to W. Schulze (*op. cit.* 321) the Etruscans laid stress on *cognomina* or second *gentilicia*.

52. *Op. cit.* 55 and 407 Anm. 8; cf. Wilamowitz in *Mélanges Weil*, 449; *Reden und Vorträge*, I (Berlin, Weidemann, 1925): 218; F. Leo in *Die Kultur der Gegenwart* (Berlin-Leipzig, Teubner, 1905) I, Abteil. viii: 330. A. Holder, *Altcelt. Sprachschatz*, I: 847 f., 853, derives *Catullo-s* from Celtic *catu*, "Kampf" ("fight"), and gives a long list of Celtic names into which the word enters: *Catuodus, Catulaunos, Lovocatus*, etc.

53. *N. H.* iii. 19 (23). 130. Cf. Nissen, *op. cit.* I: 477, 479 ff.; II: 196 ff. Nissen guesses that the Celts began to occupy Po Valley *ca.* 600 B.C.

54. Nissen, *op. cit.* II: 204. Nissen remarks that only seven leagues northwest of Verona lies the famous wine-growing district of the Val Policella, in which the Octavii once had estates, and that probably Augustus' favorite Raetian wine came from this place. We remember that a remark on Raetian wine is attributed to Catullus by Servius (cf. *fr.* 7 [see p. 11]), and if we were following a method not unknown to philology, we might suggest that Catullus' father had served Raetian wine to Caesar (when he visited Verona) and that Caesar passed on his knowledge of it to the Octavii!

55. Strabo (v. 213) calls Verona "large"; Tac. (*H.* iii. 8) "rich," cf. Martial, i. 61, xiv. 195.

56. *Prolegom.* vi.

57. On Latin translations from the Greek cf. Leo, *Lit.* 59 ff. (on Livius Andronicus); Kroll, *Stud.* 11 f.; A. B. Drachmann, *Catuls Digtning* (Copenhagen, Jorgenson & Co., 1887), Chap. IV. B. Farrington, *Primum Graius homo* (Cambridge University Press, 1927) has made an interesting collection.

58. For this principle of imitation see p. 116.

59. Plautus, *Asin.*, prologue 11, Maccus vortit barbare; Terence, *Adel.*, prologue 10–11, locum . . . . verbum de verbo expressum, but the passage (from Diphilus) was inserted into a play based on Menander and so changes were necessary. The Latin could not have been in our sense a "word-for-word" translation.

60. Stemplinger (*op. cit.*—see below, note 63) with the passages from Cicero there quoted at p. 210.

61. G. Vitelli, *Studi ital. di fil.* N. S. VII (1929): 3 ff., with aid in deciphering the papyrus from Medea Norsa; cf. also E. Fraenkel, *Gnomon*, V (1929): 265–268; H. W. Prescott, *Class. Phil.* XXIV (1929): 290–292. Vitelli's publication had not appeared at the time these lectures were delivered (Spring, 1928) and I welcome this opportunity to expand what was then said on Catullus as a translator. The view which I expressed (in which probably most scholars believed) was that LXVI was as close a translation as one poet translating another could be expected to make. This view, based upon the scanty fragments of the Greek which were known before 1929, is now confirmed.

62. Fraenkel, *loc. cit.*

63. From the many discussions of *imitatio* I select the following: E. Stemplinger, *Das Plagiat in der griechischen Literatur* (Leipzig, 1912 [this contains most of the direct Greek and Latin statements about imitation]); G. C. Fiske, *Lucilius and Horace* (Madison, *Univ. of Wisconsin Studies* [1920]), Chap. I (contains a good bibliog.); E. Norden, *Aen. VI* (ed. 3), 365 ff.; Mlle A. de Guillemin, *Rev. des études lat.* II (1924): 35–57.

64. This principle is clearly recognized as especially Vergilian by the elder Pliny, who was a stickler for naming his own sources (*N. H., praefat.* 22): scito enim conferentem auctores me deprehendisse a iuratissimis et [ex *May-hoff*] proximis veteres transcriptos ad verbum neque nominatos, non illa Vergiliana virtute, ut certarent. When (according to Pliny) Vergil transcribed closely, he made artistic changes so as to rival (*certarent*) his model.

65. Seneca the Elder reports Gallio as saying that, when Ovid borrowed the phrase *plena deo*, fecisse illum quod in multis aliis versibus Vergilii fecerat, non subripiendi causa, sed palam mutuandi, hoc animo ut vellet agnosci; cf. *Suasor.* iii. 7. Apparently such borrowings were always brief; cf. Macrobius (*Sat.* vi. 1. 7), who says that Vergil took *vel ex dimidio sui versus vel paene solidos.*

66. Stemplinger, *op. cit.* 196 ff.

67. *Tom Jones* (*Everyman's Library;* London), II: 100.

68. Afranius, *fr.* 17 R.

69. Suetonius, p. 66 R.

70 See p. 139.

71. C. Pascal, *Poeti e personaggi catulliani* (Catania, Battiato, 1916): App. I: "Elementi rettorici nella poesia catulliana" (reprint of a paper published 1915). Pascal does not pretend to treat the subject completely, and he exaggerates the admitted rarity of rhetorical influence on the short erotic poems.

72. A. Couat, *Étude sur Catulle*, 20–24.

NOTES FOR CHAPTER V

1. On the epyllion, cf. J. Heumann, *De epyllio Alexandrino* (Koenigsee, 1904); G. Lafaye, *Catulle*, Chap. IV; Schanz, I: 285 f., 295–298. Athenaeus was apparently the only ancient to use ἐπύλλιον as a literary term (ii. 65 A, cf. xiv. 639A), τὸ εἰς Ὅμηρον ἀναφερόμενον ἐπύλλιον, but not in the modern sense.

2. See pp. 127, 177.

3. The details and variations of the stories may be found fully presented in the mythological lexicons of Preller (*ss. vv. Peleus* and *Achilles*) and Roscher, III. 2: 1827 ff. (by L. Bloch). Cf. also R. Reitzenstein, *Hermes*, XXXV (1900): 73–105. On Ariadne, in addition to Preller (*op. cit.* I: 679 ff.) and Roscher, cf. Wagner in *P.-W. s. v. Ariadne*.

4. Vv. 265–266 are transitional.

5. Cf. in general E. Rohde, *Griech. Roman* (ed. 3), 112.

6. The adjective is here not merely conventional, for Hera mentions her act as a service to Thetis.

7. *F. H. G.*, Pherecydes, *fr.* 16; cf. Euripides, *Andromache*, 16 ff.

8. ἀμάρτυρον οὐδὲν ἀείδω (*fr.* 125, A. W. Mair, *Callimachus*).

9. Friedrich, *Kommentar*, 323.

10. *Kommentar*, 336.

11. Cf. *Auct. ad Herenn.* iv. 28. 39: poema loquens pictura <pictura>, tacitum poema debet esse.

12. On the technique of description in epic and especially the expression of the poet's interest, cf. Norden, *Aen. VI* (ed. 3), 120 ff. The ancient commentators noticed the latter point; cf. *Schol. Daniel.* on *Aen.* ix. 399 (cf. 426), mire adfectum suum poeta interposuit. See also Heinze, *Virg. ep. Tech.* (ed. 3), 396 ff., and Prescott, *Development of Virgil's Art*, especially p. 265 ff.

13. Catullus practices the technique of insertion in LXV and (an extreme form) in LXVIII, but in both cases the themes are organically connected. On the history and probable genesis (the Homeric digression?) of this device, cf. the author's article, "Catullus as an Elegist," *A. J. P.* XXXVI (1915): 155 ff., and the remarks of Norden, *Einl. Alt.* I²: 451, although the latter seems wrong in accepting the results of E. Bethe's article, "Ovid und Nikander," *Hermes*, XXXIX (1904): 1 ff. It is to be noted that parts of Catullus LXIV as well as the whole display the same method, but always with organic connection between the sections, e.g., (A) Ariadne on the shore (52–70), (B) Her love and flight (71–123), (A) Ariadne on the shore (124–131), cf. vv. 202–248: (A) Ariadne's curse and the forgetfulness of Theseus (202–211), (B) story of Aegeus' directions (212–237), (A) forgetfulness and punishment of Theseus (238–248). Thus the narration ever recoils upon itself before passing to a new part.

14. The *Shield* was part of the *Eoiai* and so not Hesiodic and not originally a separate poem. When the lines on the shield (57–480) were to be delivered by a rhapsode as part of the *Eoiai* the text was doctored in such a way that the description came in naturally; or the description could be omitted.

The structure of the whole (in the extant text) is the same as Catullus LXIV: (A) preparation for the conflict between Hercules-Iolaus and Ares-Cycnus, (B) the Shield, (A) the conflict. There is also an introduction (1–56), but this belongs properly to the *Eoiai* so that the *Shield* itself consists of 57–480; cf. Wilamowitz, *Hermes*, XL (1905): 116–124; A. Bolaffi, *De scuti Herculis descriptione*, etc. (Pesaro, 1919).

15. In epigram there are passages which may indicate the germs from which the technique of Catullus springs. In *A. P.* XI. 38 (attributed to Polemo), a relief (a jar, loaf, chaplet, skull) speaks: ' πῖνε ', λέγει τὸ γλύμμα, 'καὶ ἔσθιε', etc.; cf. *ibid.* IX. 687, in which possibly the portrait speaks the last line.

16. The poem comprises over 400 lines about half of which have been provided with one or more Greek parallels, and yet my collection is incomplete. It is impossible to present all this material here; I have limited myself to a few illustrations representing some of the different classes into which the parallels naturally fall: passages of considerable extent (a line or more), e.g., the comparisons, and single words or short phrases, e.g., epithets, figurative expressions, compounds, various phenomena of vocabulary and syntax, etc. The parallels from Greek verse range in date all the way from Homer to Nonnus and some are cited from Greek prose as well. Certain Greek authors are cited most often on certain sections of the poem, e.g., Homer on the comparisons and on the song of the Parcae, Hesiod on the close (384 ff.), Euripides on the opening lines and on the description of Bacchus and his followers (251 ff.), Apollonius and Euripides on Ariadne's lament (132–201), etc., etc. The resemblances in authors *later* than Catullus (Nonnus, etc.) are often used by scholars to show that both Catullus and the Greek author cited have imitated some lost source earlier than Catullus or at least that Catullus is influenced by Greek modes of expression which are not available for us until after his time.

17. For example, Donatus on Terence's relations to the Greek plays or Macrobius on Vergil's borrowings. In modern times Tennyson, for example, sometimes revealed his use of sources which without his testimony could not be detected; cf. W. P. Mustard, *Classical Echoes in Tennyson* (New York, 1904), esp. Appendix C.

18. See pp. 115–117 on imitation.

19. See pp. 117, 139.

20. See p. 117 f.

21. Cf. Apollon. Rhod. iii. 1128 f. (Jason to Medea).

22. E. Maass, *Hermes*, XXIV (1889): 528.

23. *Studi ital. fil. class.* XII (1904): 219–227, controverted by M. Valgimigli, *Giornale storico e letterario della Liguria*, VII (1906): 401–428.

24. Many scholars of the first group believe that though Catullus is in general following one or two Greek poems, he imitates here and there still others or even Roman poets, e.g., Ennius, but not to such an extent as to obscure the work of his chief sources.

25. *Opusc.* II. 67–81.

26. This view crops up wherever a pictorial passage occurs in ancient literature. Peleus and Thetis and Ariadne were favorite subjects of ancient artists—Helbig, for example, enumerates 30 representations of Ariadne at Pompeii and Herculaneum (*Wandgem.* 253–262); but in the absence of clear hints from a poet it is very difficult to prove that his chief stimulus is painting or sculpture, especially any particular work of art. Cf. A. Morpurgo (*Riv. fil.* LV [1927]: 331 ff.), a critique of G. Pasquali (*Studi ital. fil. class.* N. S. I [1920]: 1 ff.), who tried to show that Catullus is exactly describing "modelli figurati," and G. Ramain (*Rev. de phil.* XLVI [1922]: 135 ff.). On the contrary, the frequent occurrence of such passages suggests that they were a part of the poet's technique; the poets strove to approximate, so far as their medium allowed, the effect of painting and sculpture. Catullus paints his own pictures.

27. Cf. O. Jahn, *Archäologische Beiträge* (Berlin, 1847): 251–299.

28. Apart from the question of models several scholars have found more or less allegory in the poem: the woes of Ariadne deserted by Theseus represent the sorrows of Catullus abandoned by Lesbia, etc. I pass over these attempts, the most thoroughgoing of which are L. L. Sell's dissertation, *De Catulli carmine LXIV quaestiones diversae* (New York, 1918) and A. Morpurgo's article in *Riv. fil.* LV (1927); Morpurgo does not mention Sell. But Catullus is not the poet to resort to allegory without some clearer hint than can be found in LXIV. Even if we could date the poem after the Lesbia affair, we should need to seek no other explanation of the sympathetic treatment of Ariadne than the art of a great poet who had himself experienced the anguish of love.

29. Cf. LXII, in which the slight Roman touches do not mar the Greek atmosphere. In LXIV. 47–48 the wedding couch stands *sedibus in mediis* and Catullus seems to have in mind the Roman custom of keeping the couch in the *atrium* (Kroll), but at a royal wedding among the Greeks, when the people were invited to view the splendors of the palace, it is by no means certain that the wedding couch and its fittings were not so displayed. So at the end of the poem (397–406), in which Drachmann and others have seen a reference to Roman degeneracy (Catiline, etc.) the basis is certainly Greek— the contrast of the iron present with the golden past.

30. A device which began in Homer but was especially convenient for the brief poems of the Alexandrians; cf. Heinze, *Virg. ep. Tech.* (ed. 3), 394 ff.

31. On apostrophe, cf. E. Hampel, *De apostrophae ap. Rom. poetas usu* (Jena, 1908), who does not go far enough. Apostrophe of characters, not common in Homer, was highly developed as a device of style and metrical technique by the more subjective Alexandrian and Roman narrators.

32. Cf. the long fragment (Pap. Parthen. Ἐρωτ. παθ. xiv). For the *Cydippe* (*Ox. Pap.* VII, 1011) and the new fragment of the *Coma Berenices*, see pp. 113, 177.

NOTES FOR CHAPTER VI

1. F. Plessis, *Études critiques sur Properce* (Paris, 1884): 275 ff.

2. *Encycl. Britann.* (ed. 14), *s. v. Elegy.* F. B. Gummere, *Handbook of Poetics,*³ 50.

3. *Grammatici Latini,* I: 484, 17–20.

4. See pp. 34 ff.

5. Cf. *Alfred Lord Tennyson: A Memoir by his Son* (London, 1898), II: 11–12, 500.

6. See the dedicatory letter of the Ἐρωτικὰ παθήματα in *Mythographi graeci,* II. 1, ed. E. Martin (Leipzig, 1902).

7. Cf. Quintilian, x. 1. 93 and i. 8. 6. Ovid also implies that elegy is erotic (*Rem. Amor.* 361–396) and that the meter is suited to such a content; cf. Horace, *Odes,* i. 33, addressed to an Albius (probably Tibullus) who was writing erotic elegy.

8. Cf. F. Plessis (*op. cit.* 252 ff.) quoting the Abbé Fraguier. I have modified the attempts of these two scholars.

9. E. F. M. Benecke, *Antimachus of Colophon* (London, 1896) and F. A. Wright, *Feminism in Greek Literature* (London, 1923). Both these authors are full of exaggerations, but they have done a service in emphasizing what Wright calls "the low ideal of womanhood" among the Greeks.

10. *Epigramm und Skolion* (Giessen, 1893): 47.

11. *The Elegies of Albius Tibullus* (New York, 1913): 27–28.

12. See above pp. 111–114.

13. For a more extended account of the question see my articles, "Erotic Teaching in Roman Elegy," *Class. Phil.* V (1910): 440–450, and VI (1911): 56–77. Add now Wilamowitz, *H. D.* I: 229–241.

14. ii. 34. 87.

15. A. L. W., "Topics from the Life of Ovid," *A. J. P.* XLVI (1925): 1–28.

16. For example O. Crusius, *P.-W. s. v. Elegie.* Fuller details on Catullus as an elegist may be found in my article, *A. J. P.* XXXVI (1915): 155–184.

17. Tibullus, i. 3. 55–56; Lygdamus, 2. 29–30.

18. Wilamowitz (*H. D.* I: 234) asserts that brevity alone distinguished such "epigrams" as CI, XCIX, from elegy.

19. Cf. the elaborate study of O. Weinreich, *Die Distichen des Catull* (Tübingen, 1926).

20. Propertius, iii. 17; Ovid, *A.* iii. 11.

21. See A. L. W., *A. J. P.* XXXVI (1915): 173–180.

22. Propertius, i. 10.

23. i. 19. 7–10.

24. Von Mess (*Rh. M.* LXIII [1908]: 488 ff.) goes much too far.

25. LXXII.

26. Cf. Reitzenstein, "Zur Sprache der lateinischen Erotik," *S. B. Heidelberg* (1912): 12.

27. On elegiac style, cf. A. L. W. *Proceedings of the Classical Association* (British), XVIII (1921): 132–150. (At p. 150 read "content" for "context").

28. The *Coma*, which gave the origin of the most recent constellation, was an etiological elegy, and although it was one of the latest poems of Callimachus (not earlier than *ca.* 246–245 B.C.: cf. Ellis, *Commentary*, 357–361), it may well have been included in the fourth book of the *Aitia*, perhaps in a second edition. This view is now supported by the recent suggestion of G. Coppola (*Riv. di fil.* LVIII [1930]: 273–291) that the queen referred to at the end of the *Aitia* is Berenice, not Arsinoë.

29. *The Bath of Pallas* (*Hymn* V) is a hymn in elegiac verse—a type not closely connected with Roman elegy.

30. On some details of the translation, see p. 113 f.

31. Edited by A. S. Hunt, *Ox. Pap.* VII, 1011.

32. Clement of Alexandria, *Stromata*, v. 676 P. Clement thus characterizes Euphorion and Lycophron's *Alexandra* as well as the *Ibis* and the *Aitia* of Callimachus. Fortunately the new fragment clears up one of the puzzles —the *unigena* (v. 53)—and in this case we now absolve Callimachus, for Catullus has rendered him inadequately; cf. p. 114.

33. iv. 3.

34. *Anthol. lyr.* ed. E. Diehl, II: 227–229; cf. A. L. W., "Elegiac Style" 149–150. See note 27.

35. *Anthol. lyr.* ed. E. Diehl, I: 39 ff.

36. *Anthol. lyr.* ed. E. Diehl, I: 86 ff.

37. See p. 84.

38. See the two epigrams, i. 27, 28 of Mackail's *Select Epigrams*, p. 107 (=*A. P.* V. 150, 164), and cf. Benecke, *op. cit.* 72 ff., who gives more, some of them παιδικά. The latter are excluded from my discussion.

39. And the social backgrounds of the Greek and Roman poets differed; cf. Wilamowitz, *H. D.* I: 234–237. Wilamowitz does not develop his suggestion; cf. (above) p. 160.

NOTES FOR CHAPTER VII

1. The song of the Parcae is a prophecy, cf. *veridicos . . . cantus* (306), *talia . . . . . fata*, etc. (321), *talia felicia carmina* (382–383), and (in the song itself) *veridicum oraclum* (326), but at the same time it is a wedding song and contains many of the same topics as LXI and LII. It represents in fact the tradition that the Parcae sang the hymeneal at this particular wedding; cf. the François Vase on which the Parcae are depicted as present in person.

2. On the history of the *genre*, cf. R. Reitzenstein, "Die Hochzeit d. Peleus u. Thetis," *Hermes*, XXXV (1900): 73–105; E. Mangelsdorff, *Das lyrische Hochzeitsgedicht bei den Griechen und Römern* (Hamburg, 1913); E. Maass, *P.-W. s. v. Hymenaios;* C. Morelli, "L'epitalamio nella tarda poesia latina," *Studi ital. fil. class.* XVIII (1910): 319–432; Wilamowitz, *Gr. Versk.* 254.

3. *Hermes*, XIV (1879): 201.

4. *Nem.* v. 41 ff. Cf. Aeschylus, *fr.* 350 (Sidgwick), and Plato, *Repub.* 383B: οὐδὲ Αἰσχύλου (sc. ἐπαινεσόμεθα), ὅταν φῇ ἡ Θέτις τὸν Ἀπόλλω ἐν τοῖς αὑτῆς γάμοις ᾄδοντα ἐνδατεῖσθαι τὰς ἑὰς εὐπαιδίας, etc.

5. Cf. Tzetzes, εἰς τὸν Λυκόφρονα Σχόλια *Lycophronis Alexandra* (ed. E. Scheer, II: 4), who cites these lines and attributes them to Hesiod:

τρὶς μάκαρ Αἰακίδη καὶ τετράκις, ὄλβιε Πηλεῦ,
ὃς τοῖσδ' ἐν μεγάροις ἱερὸν λέχος εἰσαναβαίνεις.

Reitzenstein cites thirteen broken lines of this poem from two papyrus fragments and thinks that *fr.* 38 Rz. and 216 Rz. belong to the same poem; cf. Reitzenstein, *op. cit.* (see above, note 2) 79–81, 85, note 1.

6. Cf. Leonidas, *A. P.* VII. 19, ὑμνητῆρ' ὑμεναίων.

7 See pp. 201 ff., 215 ff.

8. Diehl's revision of Bergk's *Anthol. lyrica*. E. Lobel, ΣΑΠΦΟΥΣ ΜΕΛΗ (Oxford, 1925).

9. *Fr.* 781 N.

10. *F. P. L.* pp. 84–85, 90.

11. *Fr.* 55 (A. W. Mair, *Callimachus*).

12. On the Greek and Roman wedding in general see (in Mueller's *Handbuch der klass. Alt.*): I. von Mueller, *Griech. Privatertümer²;* H. Blümner, *Röm. Privatertümer* (1911); cf. also E. Pernice, *Hochzeit*, etc., in *Einl. in die Alt.* II³ (1922): 51 ff.; E. Samter, *Geburt, Hochzeit u. Tod.*, 1911.

13. Schwabe, *Quaestt.* 332–344.

14. See pp. 200–202.

15. The lines are numbered as in Ellis' Oxford text (1904).

16. Attributes rather of Gamos than of Hymen; cf. Wilamowitz, *H. D.* II: 282.

17. The feast normally occurred, both among the Greeks and among the Romans, in the bride's house (as in LXII) and the probable assumption is that the poet omits the feast entirely since he begins while the bride is preparing for the *deductio*.

In exceptional circumstances, however—if, for example, the bride's family was too poor to furnish an entertainment,—the feast occurred in the groom's house, and some scholars have interpreted vv. 164 ff. as a reference to it: as the bride enters she beholds the groom *accubans . . . . Tyrio in toro.* Ellis says that "the *cena nuptialis* is here in the bridegroom's house," and that *torus* means a "banqueting couch." But the groom was certainly understood to be present during much of the *deductio* unless we assume that the address to him (134 ff.) was made *in absentia*. Only shortly before the end of the *deductio* could he have entered the house. Moreover the bride was usually present at the *cena*. Kroll's interpretation is therefore better: the groom is seen reclining on the *lectus genialis* in the *atrium*. Kroll shows that *accubare* at the time was used only of reclining on a dining couch. But the word could hardly have been so strictly limited. Probably the groom entered the house before the bride and reclined on the *lectus genialis* in order to receive her symbolically as master of the house and as husband (as De Gubernatis *ad loc.* suggests) to put her in communion with fire and water as indicated by Paul. Fest. 3 (Lindsay): *aqua et igni tam interdici solet damnatis quam accipiunt nuptae videlicet quia hae duae res humanam vitam maxime continent.* Then the couch was moved to the marriage chamber, the *collocatio* occurred, and the groom was summoned (179–198). Thus there is no need of the lacuna assumed by Ellis after 173, and indeed a lacuna is improbable since one of the boys who had assisted the bride over the threshold (159–161) still holds her arm at 174.

18. For a more complete discussion, see my article, "Tradition in the Epithalamium," *A. J. P.* LI (1930): 205–223.

19. References are to the following editions: Dionysius or pseudo-Dionysius, ed. Usener-Radermacher (1904); Menander, ed. C. Bursian (*Abh. bayer. Akad.* XVI [1882]); Himerius, *Orations* i, Dübner's ed. (1849); Choricius, *Orationes nuptial.* v-vi in the ed. of Foerster-Richtsteig (1929); Gregory of Nazianzus, ed. Migne, *Patrolog. Gr.* XXXVII: 521–573; cf. Aphthonius in *Rhetores Graeci*, X, ed. H. Rabe, and Libanius VIII, ed. R. Foerster.

20. Dionysius, *op. cit.* I. ii. 3–4.

21. *Ibid.*, I. ii. 6; Menander, *op. cit.* xiv. 11 and 25; Gregory Naz., *loc. cit.* 531.

22. Menander, *ibid.* xiv. 12 and 15.

23. Menander, *ibid.* xiii. 23. To Catullus Hymen is a god who represents the duties and responsibilities as well as the pleasures of marriage—a sort of combination of the attributes which the Greeks associated with Gamos and Hymen, cf. Wilamowitz, *H. D.* II: 282; cf. A. L. W., *A. J. P.* LI (1930): 210–211, note 15.

24. Menander, *op. cit.* 13–20; Dionys., *ibid.* I. ii. 6–7; Himerius, *op. cit.* i. 13–15, cf. 19–20; Choricius, *op. cit.* v. 19 praises the bride.

25. Dionys., *ibid.* I. iv. 3; Menander, *ibid.* xiv. 25; Choricius, *ibid.* vi. 40 (ὁμόνοια).

26. Menander, *ibid.* xiii. 22, says παῖδας ὑμῖν τε ὁμοίους; cf. Dionysius, *ibid.* I. ii. 6, I. iv. 3; and Choricius, *ibid.* vi. 51.

27. Menander, *ibid.* xiv. 5. 16 and 22.

28. Plutarch, *Lycurg.* 15.

29. Cf. Ellis, *Commentary*, 210, on the general importance of boys in the ceremony.

30. Cf. the reference to *manus* (56); the *collocatio* (181); the statement that without marriage no land could guard its boundaries (72), which may allude to the old Roman custom of excluding illegitimate sons from the army; the assignment of a Roman veil to Hymen. Cf. Wilamowitz, *H. D.* II: 282.

31. Cf. Jacoby, *Rh. M.* LXV (1910): 50.

32. C. Kühn, *De priscorum Romanorum poesi populari* (Diss.; Halle, 1882), collects the passages.

33. Cf. Varro, *Sat. Menipp., fr.* 10 (Buecheler), *pueri obscenis verbis novae nuptulae aures returant.*

34. Cf. ludite ut lubet (204), munere, etc. (227–228). Menander (*ibid.* xiv. 3) advises that the speaker should keep to what is honorable and dignified and not descend to what is unseemly.

35. *The Complete Works of Robert Browning* (Fireside ed., (1) [Boston and New York, 1909]: 220 [Sordello]).

36. Wilamowitz (*H. D.* II: 283) considers these details Hellenistic since Hymen is son of Urania only in Nonnus 33. 67 and in this passage of Catullus.

37. *Fr.* 117 Diehl. See p. 211 f.

38. *Fr.* 128 Diehl.

39. Read consecutively vv. 6, 9, 12, 14; 39; 82, 91, 106, 113, 145, 161; 107; 114, 116; 125, 132; 135.

40. 189, 209.

41. 225.

42. Read vv. 3, 55, 56; 4, 13, 17, 29, 31; 33, 43; 137.

43. Tibullus, ii. 1; cf. also ii. 2 and 5, and see R. Reitzenstein, *Hellen. Wundererzähl.* (1906): 159 ff.; G. Pasquali, *Quaestt. Callim.*, 148 ff.; L. Deubner, *N. Jhb.* XLVII (1921): 361–378; Wilamowitz, *H. D.* II (1924): 282 ff.; R. Heinze on Horace's *Odes*, i. 27 (ed. 7, 1930); E. Stemplinger, "Der Mimus in der horazischen Lyrik," *Philol.* LXXV (1919): 466–469.

Wilamowitz thinks that the speaker in LXI is impersonal, in Tibull. ii. 1 Tibullus himself. I can see no difference.

44. Cf. Pasquali, Deubner, and Wilamowitz.

45. *Frs.* 127, 128; cf. 123, 129, 130 Diehl.

46. *Frs.* 122, 131 D.

47. Cf. also XLII, but not LXII, which is really dramatic in form and can be divided among speakers (singers).

48. Cf. Menander, *ibid.* xiv 1. 21, 22; Himerius, *Orat.* i, *passim.*

49. Presumably the wedding orations were delivered at the ceremonies, whereas the sixty-first poem was probably *not actually* sung; cf. p. 209. But the poem is composed *as if* it were to be sung and the literary method is the same in both cases.

50. From this point (§4) I translate freely.

51. The text of this passage is broken but the general connection is clear.

52. Note that Himerius has been speaking of Sappho's poetry, not about real actions of Sappho in person, and that some of the acts mentioned must be figurative, e.g., bringing Aphrodite and the Loves. Clearly all the actions are taken from Sappho's poetry.

53. Cf. Alcaeus, *fr.* 90 D., together with Horace's imitation, *Odes*, i. 9, *vides ut alta,* etc.

54. Kiessling's Horace, ed. 7 revised by R. Heinze (1930), on *Odes*, i. 27. Heinze repeats Porphyrio's note, *cuius sensus sumptus est ab Anacreonte ex libro tertio,* and considers Anacreon (*fr.* 43 D.) to be probably a part of the original: ἄγε δή, φέρ' ἡμῖν, ὦ παῖ, etc.; cf. Edmonds' trans. (*Lyra graeca* [1924], II: 177): "Come bring me a jar, lad; I want my first drink; ten ladles of water to five of wine, for I would e'en play the Bacchanal in decent wise. . . . . Come let us give up this Scythian drinking with uproar and din over our cups, and drink moderately between pretty songs of praise."

It is quite possible that Horace had this passage in mind when he wrote vv. 1–8. Certainly he made use of the same technique. Perhaps Anacreon, like Horace (9 ff.), passed to an erotic theme. For Anacreon's address to the slave who serves the wine, cf. Catull. XXVII and Horace, *Odes*, i. 38.

55. Except possibly the refrains *O Hymenaee Hymen*, etc. (39–40), *Io Hymen*, etc. (117), but these passages are probably deceptive. Equally deceptive is the possible assignment of vv. 1–114 to a chorus. If we survey the whole poem, it is clear that there is one speaker, the poet, who represents himself as a master of ceremonies. The use of the first person singular (115, 189, 209), or plural (94, 126[?], 139, 225), the frequent exhortations, etc., are all manifestations of this one device.

56. *Tr.* ii. 519 f. (with Owen's note), *ibid.* v. 7, 25; cf. *Rem. Amor.* 753.

57. *Sat.* i. 10. 18-19, *simius iste* . . . . *Calvum et doctus cantare Catullum.* It would be interesting to know what poems of the two friends were sung.

58. This point by no means disproves a musical rendering. The precise indication of parts, etc., may have been wholly outside the text or they may have been lost from our manuscripts, just as almost all the musical annotation has disappeared from the manuscripts of Plautus. Moreover scholars do not agree as to the precise manner in which the *Carmen saeculare* was rendered, and yet we know that it was sung. But the problem in Catullus

is radically different since we have no external testimony, for nobody will trace back to an ancient source the assignments of the stanzas of LXII to *puellae* or *iuvenes* (as the case may be) in the MSS *G. R. B. Ven.*; cf. A. Morgenthaler, *De Catulli codicibus* (Strassburg, 1909): 19–20 (on the metrical notes found in the same MSS).

59. Kroll remarks (*Stud.* 202) that the wedding *song*, as distinct from wedding poetry, had disappeared. The evidence for this statement is Philodemus, *De musica*, 68 K., who uses the phrase νῦν δ[ὲ] δὴ σχεδὸν καὶ παντάπ[α]σι καταλελυμένων τῶ[ν] ἐπιθαλαμ[ί]ων.

60. The prayers, anointing of doorposts, etc.

61. The objection raised by Wilamowitz (*H. D.* II: 282) and repeated by De Gubernatis, ed. 1928, p. 105—that the lines on the *concubinus* would have been displeasing to Manlius if the poem had been sung or declaimed at the wedding—is not valid. The passage would have been hardly less objectionable on this score if the poem was intended merely for reading.

62. Cf. L. J. Richardson, *Univ. Calif. Publ. in Class. Phil.* II (1915): 257–265; W. Schubart, *S. Ber. Berlin Akad.* (1902): 204–205; Wilamowitz, *Griech. Verskunst* (1921): 245 ff.; W. J.W. Koster,"De Glyconei et Pherecratei origine,"*Philol.* LXXX (1925): 353–365. De Gubernatis, ed. 1928: 106 cites Sappho,*fr.* 100 D., ἀλλ᾽ ἔων φίλος ἄμμιν—apparently not an epithalamium. Koster and Wilamowitz (?) believe that the Glyconic was originally an Aeolic form. Schubart cites from a papyrus*fr.* (which he assigns to Book v) stanzas consisting of two glyconics and an Aeolic dactylic line:

$$- \; \bar{\cup} \; - \cup \cup \; - \cup \; \bar{\cup}$$
$$- \; \bar{\cup} \; - \cup \cup \; - \cup \; \bar{\cup}$$
$$- \; \bar{\cup} \; - \cup \cup \; - \cup \; \cup \; - \cup \bar{\cup}$$

63. Not in LXI, but cf. XXXIV. 1 (Dianae).

64. Cf. E. Bickel in *Einl. Alt.* I² (1912): 604 f.; Wilamowitz, *Griech. Versk.* (1921): 128, Anm. 1, regards the form of the stanza in the sixty-first poem as probably Hellenistic.

65. *Fr.* 123 D.

66. *Io* is occasionally monosyllabic, but apparently ἰώ is not. Walde, *Lat. etymol. Wörterbuch*, thinks io probably borrowed from ἰώ.

67. LXIV. 327, 333; LXI. 65, 70, 75, 92, 96, 106, 113, 128, 133.

68. Cf. Kroll, p. 107, who refers to Wünsch, *P.-W.* IX: 142.

69. *Olympo* (1) and *Oetaeos* (7) are often taken figuratively, but Catullus in this part of the poem is as concrete as possible.

70. The assertion of Kroll (based on C. Robert, *Hermes*, XXXV [1900]: 658 f.) that the bride does not take part in the feast is not certain. Robert, interpreting the Aldobrandini wedding scenes, one of which (he thinks) depicts the bride preparing in her own room for the procession, cites Catullus LXII. 4, *iam veniet virgo*, to show that among the *Greeks* the bride did not ordinarily take part in the feast, but he admits exceptions.

71. Cf. 4, *iam dicetur hymenaeus*, and the corresponding verse 9, *canent*, etc.; cf. also 16, 18. The *hymenaeus* and the *certamen* are identical.

72. The first three sections (1–19) are introductory to the *certamen* proper (20–66), of which the last section (59–66) serves also as a close for the whole poem. The strictly amoebaean portion consists of vv. 20–58 and here exact symmetry is indicated, the youths in each case balancing and refuting the words of the maidens. I assume therefore (with Ellis) a lacuna of 9 lines, including the refrain, after v. 32, i.e., the section beginning with v. 32 originally had 8 lines and was balanced by an equal section extending through v. 38. Furthermore, Hermann was probably right in assuming the loss of a line after v. 41 and the refrain after v. 58 so that these two sections had 11 lines each. On the other hand, there is no need of marking a lacuna of one line in the close (e.g., after 61) so as to make this section equal to vv. 11–19. Both these sections are outside the strictly amoebaean part.

73. One would in this case assign it to the period in which love became a theme of philosophic discussion; cf. M. Pohlenz, "Die hellenistische Poesie und die Philosophie," in Χάριτες (1911).

74. Vv. 21–24; cf. LXI. 56–57. See p. 196.

75. Cf. also 27–29.

76. Choruses of youths and maidens were certainly known to Aeschylus. Cf. *fr.* 43 cited by Kroll. For choruses in Sappho's epithalamia we may compare Himerius, *Orat.* i. 21; see pp. 201–204.

77. *Frs.* 116 (and Himerius, *ibid.* i. 16), 127, 131.

78. E. Lobel (ΣΑΠΦΟΥΣ ΜΕΛΗ, 47) rightly expresses doubts concerning the authenticity of *fr.* 117 D, οἴαν τὰν ὑάκινθον, etc.

79. ἀμαμάξυδες: I do not find this reference in Diehl, but cf. Lobel, *op. cit.* 61 (*Incert. libri*, 57). Kroll cites also Eratosthenes' use of αὐροσχάς in the sense of τὸ κατὰ βότρυν κλῆμα. Cf. J. U. Powell, *Collectanea Alex.* (Oxford, 1925): 65, 68 (*Eratosth., frs.* 28, 37), and Reitzenstein, *Hermes*, XXXV (1900): 96.

80. Cf. Rothstein on Propert. i. 18. 19 and Menander, ii. 14. 12 (trees form unions with trees) and 15 (myths about the loves of trees).

81. Cf. R. Gimm, *De Vergilii stilo bucolico*, 123 (cited by Kroll).

82. Norden's view is essentially the same (*Einl. Alt.* I³: 4, 30).

83. Wilamowitz, *H. D.* II: 277 ff.; cf. Frank, *Catullus and Horace*, 53. Kroll repeats this view with a well justified "vielleicht."

NOTES FOR CHAPTER VIII

1. Ellis cites no significant parallels on fourteen of the short poems (about one-seventh of the total number): XXVIII, LIII, LXXVIII, LXXX, XCI, XCIII, XCIV, C, CIII, CIV, CVI, CXI, CXIII, CXV.

2. Cf. Catullus: habe . . . . quidquid hoc libelli.

3. *A. P.* IV. 1. At the end the poet generalizes: φίλοις μὲν ἐμοῖσι φέρω χάριν.

4. See especially Kroll.

5. Munro (4–5), although he exaggerates Martial's dependence.

6. *A. P.* VII. 189–216.

7. No less than nine of these poems deal with the ἄκρις, several others with the cicada.

8. Moschus, iv. 9; Callimachus, *Hymn* iii. 211; Terence, *Adel.* 903.

9. Kroll's notes contain all these parallels.

10. Cf. Martial's *Issa,* i. 109. For English parallels cf. Eleanor S. Duckett, *Catullus in English Poetry* (*Smith College Classical Studies*, No. 6 [Northampton, 1925]): 10–25.

11. F. Jacoby, *Rh. M.* LXIX (1914): 398 ff.; F. Leo, *Pl. F.*² 145.

12. Antiphanes, ii. 114, 235 K.

13. K. P. Schulze (*Röm. Elegiker,* p. 34, on VIII) quotes from Trevelyan's Life (II: 448): "The first lines of Miser Catulle; the lines to Cornificius [XXXVIII], written evidently from a sick bed; and part of the poem beginning 'Si qua recordanti' [LXXVI] affect me more than I can explain. They always move me to tears."

14. The paper was read before the Connecticut Academy and was published in their *Transactions,* XV (1909): 139–151—a publication not included in bibliographies of the Classics.

15. The poet's method is of the same *kind* however as that which he employs in LI (see pp. 111 ff.) and LXX (see p. 230 f).

16. Cf. III. 11–18, VII, XIII. 9–14, XXXVI, XCII. On XXXVI cf. H. Comfort, *Class. Phil.* XXIV (1929): 176–182.

17. The situation of the lover (as he wrongly conceives it) in Menander's Περικειρομένη is similar, but his mood and his treatment of the girl are very different.

18. In LXXVI the situation is similar so far as the girl's attitude is concerned, but the lover's attitude is widely different and the whole is based on reality.

19. Cf. P. Troll, *De elegiae Romanae origine* (Göttingen, 1911): 30–31.

20. Of course those who write a connected account of Catullus' love are prone to connect this poem with CVII which speaks of a reconciliation and so implies a quarrel.

21. Cf. also Meleager, *A. P.* V. 8. 5.

22. Poseidippos, *A. P.* V. 186 (same theme); cf. also Ovid, *A.* ii. 6. 43–44, Martial, x. 35. 19–21.

23. Cf. *A. P.* V. 24.

24. Kroll cites Plautus, *Cas.* 323; Ovid, *Met.* vii. 801; Petronius, 126. 18.

25. See p. 112 (on LI).

26. Cf. Horace, *Odes*, i. 20; iii. 29 (first part); Martial, iii. 12.

27. Frank, *Catullus*, 29, 83.

28. Paton's translation in *The Greek Anthology* (Loeb series).

29. Epicurus' birthday.

30. Cf. the stock joke of Plautus: if you have no invitation I'll dine with *you*, e.g., *Most.* 1004–1007.

31. So common that they became a nuisance; cf. XLIV and Lucilius, *A. P.* XI. 10.

32. XIII is in my opinion to be dated not later than 59 B.C. (see pp. 92 f., 262, n. 34). Those who prefer a date *ca.* 56–54 B.C. and identify the Socration of XLVII with Philodemus can hardly believe that Catullus modeled his poem on Philodemus, for they would have to assume that he imitated a poem addressed to a man whom he detested and composed by a poet at whom he sneered.

33. Cratinus, *fr.* 190 K.; Afranius, *fr.* 410 R., tanne arcula tua plena est aranearum?

34. Homer, *Od.* xviii. 192 ff.

35. Herondas, vi. 16; Aelian, *V. H.* vii. 6.

36. The probabilities favor *vostra* since in the MSS of Catullus the abbreviation *ura* (*vostra*) has much more often been mistaken for *nra* (*nostra*) than the reverse. O has here *ura*, not *vestra* (as Ellis indicates).

37. Pherecrates, *fr.* 58 K.; Callim. *A. P.* VI. 301; Wilamowitz thinks that this epigram stimulated Catullus (*H. D.* I: 176).

38. Petronius, 52. 7.

39. 58 K.

40. Lucilius and Alciphron were later than Catullus, but they were making use of a motive which was older. The Greek poets rarely borrowed from the Romans; they followed Greek traditions.

41. To save space I give only illustrations of the Greek parallels.

42. Kroll on LXXXV.

43. See p. 117 f.

44. Ellis himself is far more credulous about imitation of earlier Roman poets, see pp. 62 ff., 114 ff.

45. See pp. 230 f., 233 f.

46. Archilochus, *fr.* 88 D., Πάτερ Λυκάμβα, ποῖον ἐφράσω τόδε; etc; *fr.* 45 D., τίς ἄρα δαίμων καὶ τέου χολούμενος; both these fragments may have come from the same poem. Kroll, p. 74, and Hendrickson (*Class. Phil.* XX [1925]: 155–157) have made it probable that *fr.* 143 B (reconstructed from

Lucian), τέττιγα δ' εἴληφας πτεροῦ, also belongs to it. Furthermore Hendrickson (using Lucian) has pointed out other details in Catullus' poem which strengthen the impression that he had Archilochus in mind.

47. Kroll cites *A. P.* XII. 222 (Strato) and is inclined to believe that Catullus was thinking of similar epigrams. (The fragment of Archilochus is 107 D., Ἐρασμονίδη Χαρίλαε, etc.).

48. See pp. 35–40.

49. See p. 111 f.

INDEX